Rick Steves'

SNAPSHOT

Sevilla, Granada & Southern Spain

CONTENTS

INTRODUCTION

This Snapshot guide, excerpted from my guidebook *Rick Steves' Spain 2010*, introduces you to southern Spain's two top cities—Sevilla and Granada—and the surrounding Spanish heartland. When Americans think of Spain, they often picture this region, with its massive cathedrals, Moorish palaces, vibrant folk life, whitewashed villages, bright sunshine, and captivating rat-a-tat-tat of flamenco.

Sevilla is the soulful cultural heart of southern Spain, with an atmospheric old quarter and riveting flamenco shows. Granada, formerly the Moorish capital, is home to the magnificent Alhambra palace. Córdoba features Spain's top surviving Moorish mosque, the Mezquita. Make time to delve into Andalucía's sleepy, white-washed hill towns: Arcos de la Frontera, Ronda, and Grazalema. Spain's south coast, the Costa del Sol, is a palm-tree jungle of beach resorts and concrete, but has some appealing destinations—Nerja, Tarifa, and Gibraltar—beyond the traffic jams. And since it's so easy, consider an eye-opening side-trip to another continent by hopping the ferry to Tangier, the newly revitalized gateway to Morocco (and to Africa).

To help you have the best trip possible, I've included the following topics in this book:

• **Planning Your Time,** with advice on how to make the most of your limited time

• **Orientation,** including tourist information (abbreviated as TI), tips on public transportation, local tour options, and helpful hints

• **Sights** with ratings:

▲▲▲—Don't miss

▲▲—Try hard to see

▲—Worthwhile if you can make it

No rating—Worth knowing about

• **Sleeping** and **Eating,** with good-value recommendations in every price range

• **Connections,** with tips on trains, buses, and driving

Practicalities, near the end of this book, has information on money, phoning, hotel reservations, transportation, and other helpful hints, plus Spanish survival phrases.

To travel smartly, read this little book in its entirety before you go. It's my hope that this guide will make your trip more meaningful and rewarding. Traveling like a temporary local, you'll get the absolute most out of every mile, minute, and euro.

Buen viaje!

SEVILLA

Sevilla is the flamboyant city of Carmen and Don Juan, where bullfighting is still politically correct and little girls still dream of growing up to become flamenco dancers. While Granada has the great Alhambra and Córdoba has the remarkable Mezquita, Sevilla has a soul. (Soul—or *duende*—is fundamental to flamenco.) It's a wonderful-to-be-alive-in kind of place.

The gateway to the New World in the 16th century, Sevilla boomed when Spain did. The explorers Amerigo Vespucci and Ferdinand Magellan sailed from its great river harbor, discovering new routes and sources of gold, silver, cocoa, and tobacco. In the 17th century, Sevilla was Spain's largest and richest city. Local artists Diego Velázquez, Bartolomé Murillo, and Francisco de Zurbarán made it a cultural center. Sevilla's Golden Age—and its New World riches—ended when the harbor silted up and the Spanish empire crumbled.

In the 19th century, Sevilla was a big stop on the Romantic "Grand Tour" of Europe. To build on this tourism and promote trade among Spanish-speaking nations, Sevilla planned a grand exposition in 1929. Bad year. The expo crashed along with the stock market. In 1992, Sevilla got a second chance at a world's fair. This expo was a success, leaving the city with an impressive infrastructure: a new airport, train station, sleek bridges, and the super AVE bullet train (making Sevilla a 2.5-hour side-trip from Madrid). In 2007, the main boulevards—once thundering with noisy traffic and cutting the city mercilessly in two—were pedestrianized, giving Sevilla even more charm.

Today, Spain's fourth-largest city (pop. 700,000) is Andalucía's leading destination, buzzing with festivals, orange and jacaranda trees, sizzling summer heat, color, guitars, and castanets. James Michener wrote, "Sevilla doesn't *have* ambience, it *is* ambience." Sevilla has its share of impressive sights, but the real magic is the city itself, with its tangled Jewish Quarter, riveting flamenco shows, thriving bars, and teeming evening paseo.

Planning Your Time

If ever there was a big Spanish city to linger in, it's Sevilla. On a three-week trip, spend two nights and two days here. On even the

shortest Spanish trip, I'd zip here on the slick AVE train for a day trip from Madrid.

The major sights are few and simple for a city of this size; the cathedral and the Alcázar are worth about three hours, and a wander through the Santa Cruz district takes about an hour. You could spend half a day touring its other sights. Stroll along the bank of the Guadalquivir River and cross the Bridge of Triana (also known as the Isabel II Bridge) for a view of the cathedral and Golden Tower. An evening here is essential for the paseo and a flamenco show.

Bullfights take place on most Sundays in May and June, on Easter, and daily through the April Fair and in late September. Sevilla's Alcázar and Museo de Bellas Artes are closed on Monday, while the Museo Palacio de la Condesa de Lebrija is closed on Sunday. Tour groups clog the Alcázar and cathedral in the morning; go late in the day to avoid the lines.

Córdoba (see next chapter) is a convenient and worthwhile side-trip from Sevilla, or a handy stopover if you're taking the AVE to or from Madrid.

Orientation to Sevilla

For the tourist, this big city is small. Sevilla's major sights—including the lively Santa Cruz district and the Alcázar—surround the cathedral. The central north–south pedestrian boulevard, Avenida de la Constitución (with TIs, banks, and a post office), leads past the cathedral to Plaza Nueva (gateway to the shopping

district). Nearly everything is within easy walking distance. The bullring is a few blocks west of the cathedral, and Plaza de España is a few blocks south. Triana, the area on the west bank of the Guadalquivir River, is working-class and colorful, but lacks tourist sights. With most sights walkable, and taxis so friendly, easy, and reasonable (€4 for a short ride), I rarely bother with the bus.

Tourist Information

Sevilla has tourist offices wherever you need them—at the **airport** (Mon–Fri 9:00–21:00, Sat–Sun 11:00–15:00, tel. 954-449-128), **train station** (overlooking track 6, Mon–Fri 9:00–19:30, Sat–Sun 9:30–15:00, tel. 954-782-003), and three along Avenida de la Constitución. These are located on the river side of the **Alcázar** (Mon–Fri 9:00–19:30, Sat–Sun 9:30–15:00, Avenida de la Constitución 21, tel. 954-787-578); across from the **cathedral** (Mon–Sat 10:30–14:30 & 15:30–19:30, Sun 10:30–14:30, Plaza del Triunfo, tel. 954-501-001); and at **Plaza Nueva** (Mon–Fri 9:00–19:30, Sat–Sun 10:00–14:00, on Plaza San Francisco, tel. 954-595-288, free Internet access for 1 hour).

At any TI, ask for the city map, the English-language magazines *Welcome Olé* and *The Tourist*, and a current listing of sights with opening times. The free monthly events guide—*El Giraldillo*, written in Spanish basic enough to be understood by travelers—covers cultural events throughout Andalucía, with a focus on Sevilla. As some of the TIs are regional as well as for Sevilla, think of any information you might need for elsewhere in Andalucía (for example, if heading south, ask for the free *Route of the White Towns* brochure and a Jerez map). Helpful websites are www.turismosevilla.org and www.andalucia.org.

The **Sevilla Card** (sold at the ICONOS shop next to the Alcázar TI, daily 10:00–19:00, or at the train station's hotel room-finding booth on track 11) covers admission to most of Sevilla's sights (cathedral, Alcázar, Flamenco Dance Museum, Museo Palacio de la Condesa de Lebrija, Basílica de la Macarena, Bullfight Museum, Itálica), and gives discounts at some hotels and restaurants. There are two types of Sevilla Cards—the pricier one includes the hop-on, hop-off bus and the boat cruise; the other one doesn't. Serious sightseers might get their money's worth with one of the cheaper multi-day cards (€28 or €50/1 day, €32 or €60/2 days, €36 or €65/3 days, www.sevillacard.es). Seniors (over 65) get into the Alcázar free and into the cathedral almost free.

Arrival in Sevilla

By Train: Trains arrive at the sublime Santa Justa Station (with banks, ATMs, TI, and *consigna*/baggage storage—€3/day, below track 1). If you don't have a hotel room reserved, the room-finding

Greater Sevilla

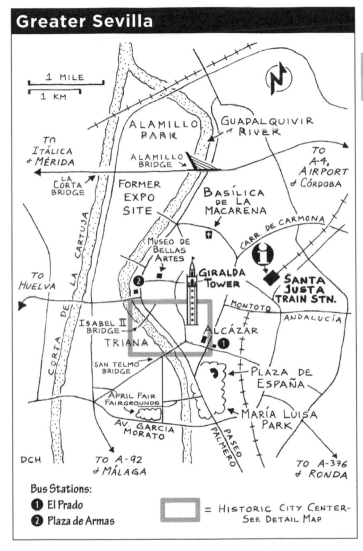

1 MILE

1 KM

TO ITÁLICA & MÉRIDA

ALAMILLO PARK

GUADALQUIVIR RIVER

ALAMILLO BRIDGE

LA CORTA BRIDGE

TO A-4, AIRPORT & CÓRDOBA

LA CARTUJA

FORMER EXPO SITE

BASÍLICA DE LA MACARENA

CARR. DE CARMONA

TO HUELVA

MUSEO DE BELLAS ARTES

❷

GIRALDA TOWER

ℹ

SANTA JUSTA TRAIN STN.

CORTA DE

ISABEL II BRIDGE

TRIANA

MONTOTO

ALCÁZAR

❶

ANDALUCÍA

SAN TELMO BRIDGE

APRIL FAIR FAIRGROUNDS

PLAZA DE ESPAÑA

MARÍA LUISA PARK

AV. GARCIA MORATO

PASEO PALMERO

DCH

TO A-92 & MÁLAGA

TO A-376 & RONDA

Bus Stations:
❶ El Prado
❷ Plaza de Armas

⬜ = HISTORIC CITY CENTER- SEE DETAIL MAP

booth above track 11 can help. You can also get maps and other tourist information here if the TI line is long (Mon–Sat 8:00–21:00, Sun 8:00–14:30). The plush little AVE Sala Club, designed for business travelers, welcomes those with a first-class AVE ticket and reservation (in front of track 1).

The town center is marked by the ornate Giralda Bell Tower, peeking above the apartment flats (visible from the front of the station—with your back to the tracks, using an imaginary clock for a compass, it's at 1 o'clock). To get into the center, it's a flat and boring 20-minute walk (longer if you get lost), a €5 taxi ride, or a short bus ride. Bus #C2 runs from 100 yards in front of the train station to Plaza de la Encarnación, but not to recommended hotels (€1.10, pay driver).

By Bus: Sevilla's two major bus stations both have information offices, cafeterias, and luggage storage. The **El Prado Station** covers most of Andalucía (daily 7:00–22:00, information tel. 954-417-111, no English spoken; luggage storage at back of station—€2/day, daily 9:00–21:00). To get downtown from the station, it's a 10-minute walk (use the color map in the front of this book). If your hotel is near Plaza Nueva, you could take the city's short tram from the station.

The **Plaza de Armas Station** (near the river, opposite the Expo '92 site) serves long-distance destinations such as Madrid, Barcelona, Lagos, and Lisbon. Luggage lockers are across from the ticket counters (€3/day). As you exit onto the main road (Calle Arjona), the bus stop is to the left, in front of the taxi stand (bus #C4 goes downtown, €1.10, pay driver, get off at Puerta de Jerez near main TI). Taxis to downtown cost around €5.

By Car: To drive into Sevilla, follow *centro ciudad* (city center) signs and stay along the river. For short-term parking on the street, the riverside Paseo de Cristóbal Colón has two-hour meters and hardworking thieves. Ignore the bogus traffic wardens who direct you to an illegal spot, take a tip, and disappear later when your car gets towed. For long-term parking, hotels charge as much as a normal garage. For simplicity, I'd just park at a central garage and catch a taxi to my hotel. Try the big one under the bus station at Plaza de Armas (€12/day), the Cristóbal Colón garage (by the bullring and river, €1.15/hr, €14/day), or the one at Avenida Roma/Puerta de Jerez (€14/24 hrs, cash only). For hotels in the Santa Cruz area, the handiest parking is the Cano y Cueto garage near the corner of Calle Santa María la Blanca and Menéndez Pelayo (€18/day, open 24/7, at edge of big park, unsigned and underground).

By Plane: The Especial Aeropuerto (EA) bus connects the airport with the train station and town center (€2.30, 2/hr, generally departs from airport at :15 and :45 past the hour, 30 min, buy ticket from driver). If going from downtown Sevilla to the airport, ask your hotelier or the TI where to catch it (the bus stop might change because of religious processions, construction, and other factors); in 2009, the stop was on Avenida del Cid by the Portugal Pavilion. You can also catch the bus at the Santa Justa train station. To taxi into town, go to one of the airport's taxi stands to ensure a fixed rate (€21–23, confirm price anyway); during Easter week the rate jumps to about €29, plus extra for luggage. For flight information, call 954-449-000.

Getting Around Sevilla

By Bus: On a hot day, buses in Sevilla can be a blessing. A single trip costs €1.10 (pay driver), or you can buy a Bonobus pass, which gives you 10 trips for €6 (shareable, sold at kiosks). The various #C buses make a circular loop that covers María Luisa Park and Basílica de la Macarena. The #C3 stops in Murillo Gardens, Triana (district on the west bank of the river), then Macarena. The #C4 goes the opposite direction without entering Triana. Spunky little #C5 is a minibus that winds through the old center of town, providing a fine and relaxing joyride (pick it up at Plaza Nueva). The #C5 can also be handy to get to the Museo de Bellas Artes.

By Taxi: Sevilla is a great taxi town. You can hail one anywhere (€3 drop, or €4 at night and on weekends, €21–23 to airport, extra for luggage and runs to/from the train and bus stations). While I'm quick to take advantage of a taxi, because of one-way streets and traffic congestion, you can often hoof it just as fast between central points.

Helpful Hints

Festivals: Sevilla's peak season is April and May, and it has two one-week festival periods when the city is packed: Holy Week and April Fair.

While **Holy Week** (Semana Santa) is big all over Spain, it's biggest in Sevilla. It's held the week between Palm Sunday and Easter Sunday (March 28–April 4 in 2010). Locals start preparing for the big event up to a year in advance. What would normally be a five-minute walk could take you an hour and a half if a procession crosses your path. But even these hassles seem irrelevant as you listen to the *saetas* (spontaneous devotional songs) and let the spirit of the festival take over.

Then, two weeks after Easter—after taking enough time off to catch its communal breath—Sevilla holds its **April Fair** (April 20–25 in 2010, described later in this chapter). This is a celebration of all things Andalusian, with plenty of eating, drinking, singing, and merrymaking (though most of the revelry takes place in private parties at a large fairground).

Book rooms well in advance for these festival times. Warning: Prices can go sky-high, food quality at touristy restaurants can plummet, and many hotels have four-night minimums.

Internet Access: Sevilla has plenty of places to get online. Near the recommended Santa Cruz hotels, head for **Internetia,** a thriving-with-students place that has a fine café and 30 terminals (€2.30/hr, Wi-Fi, disc-burning, daily 11:00–23:00, Avenida Menéndez Pelayo 43–45, tel. 954-534-003). Between the Alcázar and the river, try **Internet Workcenter** (daily

---

Cheap Tricks in Sevilla

- For an inexpensive lunch, many regular bar-cafeterias will make you a *bocadillo*. These are often simply ham and cheese or *tortilla española* (potato omelet) on a baguette, with no fixings. But at €3–4, they are perfect for a picnic in one of the many squares and parks. Plaza Doña Elvira is especially picturesque and shady.
- Instead of taking a guided tour, head to the Golden Tower and enjoy a walk along the Guadalquivir River. There's a bike path and plenty of sunbathers stretched out along the grassy sections. Spot the Giralda Bell Tower from a distance, look over at Triana, and watch rowers go down the river. You can also walk around a large sand-colored sculpture by the Basque artist Eduardo Chillida near the Isabel II Bridge.
- Need to get online? The Plaza Nueva TI on Plaza San Francisco offers free Internet access for up to one hour.

9:00–14:00 & 16:00–21:00, San Fernando 1, tel. 954-220-487). The **TI at Plaza Nueva** (on Plaza San Francisco) offers up to one hour of free Internet access from eight terminals, as well as free Wi-Fi (Internet available Mon–Fri 10:00–14:00 & 17:00–20:00, closed Sat–Sun).

Post Office: The post office is at Avenida de la Constitución 32, across from the cathedral (Mon–Fri 8:30–20:30, Sat 9:30–14:00, closed Sun).

Laundry: Lavandería Roma offers quick and economical drop-off service (€6/load wash and dry, Mon–Fri 9:30–14:00 & 17:30–20:30, Sat 9:00–15:00, closed Sun, 2 blocks inland from bullring at Castelar 2, tel. 954-210-535). Near the recommended Santa Cruz hotels, **La Segunda Vera Tintorería** has two machines for self-service (€10/load wash and dry, drop-off service also available, Mon–Fri 9:30–13:45 & 17:30–20:00, closed Sat–Sun, Avenida Menéndez Pelayo 11, tel. 954-534-219).

Train Tickets: The RENFE offices give out train schedules and sell train tickets. There's a RENFE Travel Center at the **train station** (daily 8:00–22:00, take a number and wait, tel. 902-240-202 for reservations and info) and one near **Plaza Nueva** in the center (Mon–Fri 9:30–14:00 & 17:30–20:00, Sat 10:00–13:30, closed Sun, Calle Zaragoza 29, tel. 954-211-455). Many travel agencies sell train tickets for the same price as the train station (look for a train sticker in agency windows). You can check schedules at www.renfe.es, but be warned that the English version of the site often freezes up during ticket purchases.

Sevilla

SEVILLA

Tours in Sevilla

Guided City Walks by Concepción—Concepción Delgado, an enthusiastic teacher and a joy to listen to, takes small groups on  English-language walks. Using me as her guinea pig, Concepción designed a fine two-hour **Sevilla Cultural Show & Tell.** This introduction to her hometown, sharing important insights the average visitor misses, is worthwhile, even on a one-day visit (€12/person, Sept–July Mon–Sat at 10:30; Aug Mon, Wed, and Fri at 10:30; starting from statue in Plaza Nueva).

For those wanting to really understand the city's two most important sights—which are tough to fully appreciate—Concepción also offers in-depth tours of the **cathedral** and the **Alcázar** (both tours last 1.25 hours, cost €6—not including entrance fees, and meet at 13:00 at the statue in Plaza del Triunfo; cathedral tours—Mon, Wed, and Fri; Alcázar tours—Tue, Thu, and Sat; no Alcázar tours in Aug).

While you can just show up for Concepción's tours, it's smart to confirm the departure times and reserve a spot (tel. 902-158-226, mobile 616-501-100, www.sevillawalkingtours.com, info @sevillawalkingtours.com). Concepción does no tours on Sundays or holidays.

Hop-on, Hop-off Bus Tours—Two competing city bus tours leave from the curb near the riverside Golden Tower. You'll see the buses parked with salespeople handing out fliers. Each does about an hour-long swing through the city with a recorded narration (€15, daily 10:00–21:00, green route has shorter option). The tours, which allow hopping on and off at four stops, are heavy on Expo '29 and Expo '92 neighborhoods—both zones of little interest in 2010. While the narration does its best, Sevilla is most interesting where buses can't go.

Horse and Buggy Tours—A carriage ride is a classic, popular way to survey the city and a relax-  ing way to enjoy María Luisa Park (€50 for a 45-min clip-clop, find a likable English-speaking driver for better narration). Look for rigs at Plaza América, Plaza del Triunfo, Golden Tower, Alfonso XIII Hotel, and Avenida Isabel la Católica.

Sevilla at a Glance

▲▲▲**Flamenco** Flamboyant, riveting music-and-dance per-formances, offered at clubs throughout town. **Hours:** Shows start as early as 19:00. See page 39.

▲▲**Cathedral and Giralda Bell Tower** The world's largest Gothic church, with Columbus' tomb, a treasury, and climb-able tower. **Hours:** July–Aug Mon–Sat 9:30–17:00, Sun 14:30–18:00; Sept–June Mon–Sat 11:00–18:00, Sun 14:30–19:00. See page 17.

▲▲**Alcázar** Palace built by the Moors in the 10th century, revamped in the 14th century, and still serving as royal digs. **Hours:** Peak season Tue–Sun 9:30–19:00, off-season Tue–Sun 9:30–17:00, closed Mon year-round. See page 25.

▲▲**Flamenco Dance Museum** High-tech museum explain-ing the history and art of Sevilla's favorite dance. **Hours:** Daily 9:00–19:00. See page 30.

▲▲**Basílica de la Macarena** Church and museum with the much-venerated Weeping Virgin statue and two significant floats from Sevilla's Holy Week celebrations. **Hours:** Daily 9:30–14:00 & 17:00–20:00. See page 34.

▲▲**Bullfight Museum** Guided tour of the bullring and its museum. **Hours:** Daily May–Oct 9:30–20:00, Nov–April 9:30–19:00, on fight days until 14:00. See page 36.

▲▲**Evening Paseo** Locals strolling in the cool of the evening, mainly along Avenida de la Constitución, Barrio Santa Cruz, the Calle Sierpes and Tetuán shopping pedestrian zone, and the Guadalquivir River. **Hours:** Spring through fall, until very late at night in summer. See page 39.

▲**Museo Palacio de la Condesa de Lebrija** A fascinating 18th-century aristocratic mansion. **Hours:** Mon–Fri 10:30–19:30, Sat 10:00–14:00, closed Sun. See page 31.

▲**Museo de Bellas Artes** Andalucía's top paintings, including works by Spanish masters Murillo and Zurbarán. **Hours:** Tue–Sat 9:00–20:30, Sun 9:00–14:30, closed Mon. See page 32.

▲**Bullfights** Some of Spain's best bullfighting, held at Sevilla's arena. **Hours:** Fights generally at 18:30 on most Sundays in May and June, on Easter, and daily through the April Fair and in late Sept. Rookies fight small bulls on Thursdays in July. See page 36.

SEVILLA

Boat Cruises—Boring one-hour panoramic tours leave every 30 minutes from the dock behind Torre de Oro. The low-energy recorded narration is hard to follow, but there's little to see anyway (overpriced at €15, tel. 954-561-692).

Andalusian Minibus Tours—Aussie Paul McGrath, who's lived in Sevilla for 11 years, takes small groups on all-day tours in his nine-seat minivan. You'll head to the villages south of Sevilla, which are difficult to reach without a car. Paul provides some commentary en route. This is an efficient, economic way to explore the great whitewashed towns along the "Route of the Pueblos Blancos." You'll leave in the morning and visit Olvera, Zahara, Grazalema, and Setenil de las Bodegas; the tour also includes a stop at the Moorish castle Aguzaderas, an olive-oil mill, and a swimming-stop option in the summer (€53, leaves daily from Torre de Oro at 9:00, returns about 19:30, call or email to reserve, mobile 657-889-875, www.theotherspain.galeon.com, the-other-spain @hotmail.com).

More Tours—**Visitours,** a typical big-bus tour company, does €85 all-day trips to Córdoba Tuesday, Thursday, and Saturday (tel. 954-460-985, mobile 686-413-413, www.visitours.es/in, visitours@terra .es). For other guides, contact the **Guides Association of Sevilla** (tel. 954-210-037, www.apitsevilla.com, visitas@apitsevilla.com).

Self-Guided Walk

Barrio Santa Cruz

Of Sevilla's once-thriving Jewish Quarter, only the tangled street plan and a wistful Old World ambience survive. This classy maze of lanes (too narrow for cars), small plazas, tile-covered patios,

and whitewashed houses with wrought-iron latticework draped in flowers is a great refuge from the summer heat and bustle of Sevilla. The narrow streets—some with buildings so close they're called "kissing lanes"—were actually designed to maximize shade. Even today, locals claim the Barrio Santa Cruz is three degrees cooler than the rest of the city.

Orange trees abound. Since they never lose their leaves, they provide constant shade. But forget about eating any of the oranges. They're bitter and used only to make vitamins, perfume, cat food, and that marmalade you can't avoid in British B&Bs.

The Barrio is made for wandering. Getting lost is easy, and I recommend doing just that. But to get started, here's a plaza-to-plaza walk that loops you through the *corazón* (heart) of the

Barrio Santa Cruz Self-Guided Walk

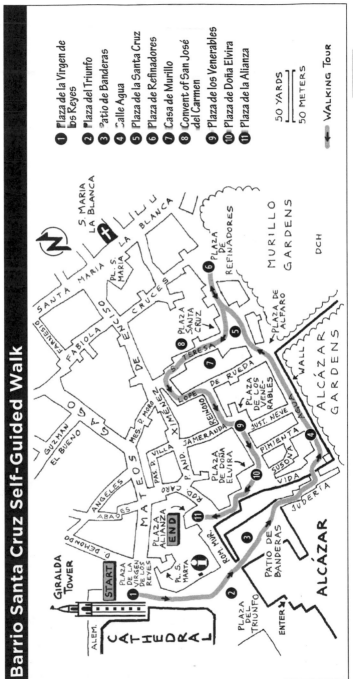

1. Plaza de la Virgen de los Reyes
2. Plaza del Triunfo
3. Patio de Banderas
4. Calle Agua
5. Plaza de la Santa Cruz
6. Plaza de Refinadores
7. Casa de Murillo
8. Convent of San José del Carmen
9. Plaza de los Venerables
10. Plaza de Doña Elvira
11. Plaza de la Alianza

50 YARDS
50 METERS

→ WALKING TOUR

neighborhood and back out again. Ideally, don't do the walk in the morning, when the Barrio's charm is trampled by tour groups. Early evening (around 18:00) is ideal. Start in front of the cathedral.

❶ Plaza de la Virgen de los Reyes: This square is dedicated to the Virgin of the Kings. See her tile on the wall. She's big here because she was brought by the Spanish king when he retook the town from the Moors in 1248. The fountain dates from 1929. From this peaceful square, look up the street leading away from the cathedral and notice the characteristic (government-protected) 19th-century architecture. The iron work is typical of Andalucía, and the pride of Sevilla. You'll see it and these traditional colors all over the town center.

• *Walk with the cathedral on your right (passing the guard who allows only real worshippers into the royal chapel).*

❷ Plaza del Triunfo: The "Plaza of Triumph" is named for the 1755 earthquake that destroyed Lisbon, but didn't rock Sevilla or its tower. Notice the statue, thanking the Virgin.

• *Pass through an opening in the Alcázar wall under the arch. You'll emerge into a courtyard called...*

❸ Patio de Banderas: Named for "flags," not Antonio, the Banderas Courtyard was once a kind of military parade ground for the royal guard. The barracks surrounding the square once housed the king's bodyguards. Today it offers a postcard view of the Giralda Bell Tower.

• *Exit the courtyard at the far corner, through the Judería arch. Walking alongside the Alcázar wall, take the first left, then right, through a small square and follow the narrow alleyway called...*

❹ Calle Agua: This street is named for the water pipes in the wall that flowed into the Alcázar (you can see them at the end of the lane—they follow the wall of the Alcázar gardens). On the left, peek through iron gates for the occasional glimpse of the flower-smothered patios of exclusive private residences. The patio at #2 is a delight—ringed with columns, filled with flowers, and colored with glazed tiles. The tiles are not only decorative; they keep buildings cooler in the summer heat. At the end of the street (look back to see the old plumbing) is an entrance into the pleasant Murillo Gardens (to the right), formerly the fruit-and-vegetable gardens for the Alcázar.

• *Don't enter the gardens now, but instead cross the square and continue 20 yards down a lane to...*

❺ Plaza de la Santa Cruz: Arguably the heart of the Barrio, this was once the site of a synagogue (there were three, now there are none), which Christians destroyed. They replaced the synagogue with a church, which the French (under Napoleon) then demolished. It's a bit of history that locals remember when they see

Sevilla's Jews

In the summer of 1391, smoldering anti-Jewish sentiment flared up in Sevilla. On June 6, the city's Jewish Quarter (Judería) was ransacked by Christian mobs. Four thousand Jews were killed, 5,000 Jewish families were driven from their homes, synagogues were stripped and transformed into churches, the Star of David came down, and the former Judería eventually became the neighborhood of the Holy Cross—Barrio Santa Cruz. Sevilla's uprising spread through Spain (and Europe), the first of many nasty pogroms during the next century.

Before the pogrom, Jews had lived in Sevilla for centuries as the city's respected merchants, doctors, and bankers. They flourished under the Muslim Moors. When Sevilla was "liberated" by King Ferdinand (1248), Jews were given protection by Spain's kings and allowed a measure of self-government, though they were confined to the Jewish neighborhood.

But by the 14th century, Jews were increasingly accused of everything from poisoning wells to ritually sacrificing Christian babies. Mobs killed suspected Jews, some of Sevilla's most respected Jewish citizens had their fortunes confiscated, and Jewish kids were mocked and bullied on the playground.

After 1391, Jews faced a choice: Be persecuted (even killed), relocate, or convert to Christianity. Those who converted—called *conversos,* New Christians, or *marranos* ("swine")—were always under suspicion of practicing their old faith in private, undermining true Christianity. Fanning the suspicion was the fact that Old Christians were threatened by this new social class of converted Jews who now had equal status.

To root out the perceived problem of underground Judaism, the "Catholic Monarchs" Ferdinand and Isabel established the Inquisition in Spain (1478). Under the direction of Grand Inquisitor Tomás de Torquemada, these religious courts arrested and interrogated *conversos* suspected of practicing Judaism. Using long solitary confinement and torture, they extracted confessions.

On February 6, 1481, Sevilla hosted Spain's first auto-da-fé ("act of faith"), a public confession and punishment for heresy. Six accused *conversos* were paraded barefoot into the cathedral, made to publicly confess their sins, then burned at the stake. Over the next three decades, thousands of *conversos* (some historians say hundreds, some say tens of thousands) were tried and killed in Spain.

In 1492, the same year the last Moors were driven from Spain, Ferdinand and Isabel decreed that all remaining Jews convert or be expelled (to Portugal and ultimately to Holland). Spain emerged as a nation unified under the banner of Christianity.

Bartolomé Murillo
(1617–1682)

The son of a barber of Seville, Bartolomé Murillo got his start selling paintings meant for export to the frontier churches of the Americas. In his 20s, he became famous after he painted a series of saints for Sevilla's Franciscan monastery. By about 1650, Murillo's sugary, simple, and accessible religious style was spreading through Spain and beyond.

Murillo painted street kids with cute smiles and grimy faces, and radiant young Marías with Ivory-soap complexions and rapturous poses (Immaculate Conceptions). His paintings view the world through a soft-focus lens, wrapping everything in warm colors and soft light, with a touch (too much, for some) of sentimentality.

Murillo became rich, popular, a family man, and the toast of Sevilla's high society. In 1664, his wife died, leaving him heartbroken, but his last 20 years were his most prolific. At age 65, Murillo died painting, falling off a scaffold. His tomb is lost somewhere under the bricks of Plaza de la Santa Cruz.

the red, white, and blue French flag marking the French consulate, now overlooking this peaceful square. The painter Murillo, who was buried in the now-gone church, lies somewhere below you. On the square you'll find the recommended Los Gallos flamenco bar and Bar El Tamboríl, which combusts nightly after midnight with impromptu flamenco.

• *Follow Calle Mezquita farther east to the nearby...*

❻ **Plaza de Refinadores:** Sevilla's most famous (if fictional) 17th-century citizen is honored here with a statue. Don Juan Tenorio—the original Don Juan—was a notorious sex addict and atheist who thumbed his nose at the stifling Church-driven morals of his day.

• *Backtrack to Plaza de la Santa Cruz and turn right (north) on Calle Santa Teresa. At #8 is...*

❼ **Casa de Murillo:** One of Sevilla's famous painters lived here, soaking in the ambience of street life and reproducing it in his paintings of cute beggar children (see sidebar).

• *Directly across from Casa de Murillo is the...*

❽ **Convent of San José del Carmen:** This is where St. Teresa stayed when she visited from her hometown of Ávila. The convent (closed to the public) keeps relics of the mystic nun, such as the manuscript of her treatise *Las Moradas* ("The Interior Castle," "where truth dwells").

Continue north on Calle Santa Teresa, then take the first left on Calle Lope de Rueda, then right on **Calle Reinoso.** This street—so narrow that the buildings almost touch—is one of the Barrio's "kissing lanes."

• *The street spills into...*

❾ Plaza de los Venerables: This square is another candidate for "heart of the Barrio." The streets branching off it ooze local ambience. The large harmonious Baroque-style Hospital de los Venerables (1675), once a priests' retirement home (the "venerables"), is now a museum (€4.75, includes audioguide). The highlight is the church and courtyard, featuring a round, sunken fountain. The museum also has a small Velázquez painting of Santa Rufina, one of two patron saints protecting Sevilla. The painting was acquired at a 2007 auction for more than €12 million.

• *Continuing west on Calle Gloria, you soon reach...*

❿ Plaza de Doña Elvira: This small square—with orange trees, tile benches, and a stone fountain—sums up our Barrio walk. Shops sell work by local artisans, such as ceramics, embroidery, and fans.

• *Cross the plaza and head north along Calle Rodrigo Caro into...*

⓫ Plaza de la Alianza: Ever consider a career change? Gain inspiration at the John Fulton Studio, a former art gallery featuring the work of the American who pursued two dreams. Though born in Philadelphia, Fulton got hooked on bullfighting. He trained in the tacky bullrings of Mexico, then in 1956 he moved to Sevilla, the world capital of the sport. His career as matador was not topnotch, and the Spaniards were slow to warm to the Yankee, but his courage and persistence earned their grudging respect. After retirement, he put down the cape and picked up a brush, making the colorful paintings in this studio.

• *From Plaza de la Alianza, you can return to the cathedral by turning left (west) on Calle Romero Murube (along the wall). Or head northeast on Callejón de Rodrigo Caro, which intersects with Calle Mateos Gago, a street lined with atmospheric tapas bars.*

Sights in Sevilla

▲▲Cathedral and Giralda Bell Tower

Sevilla's cathedral is the third-largest church in Europe (after St. Peter's at the Vatican and St. Paul's in London), and the largest Gothic church anywhere. When they ripped down a mosque of brick on this site in 1401, the Reconquista Christians bragged, "We'll build a cathedral so huge that anyone who sees it will take us for madmen." They built for 120 years. Even today, the descendants

of those madmen proudly display an enlarged photocopy of their *Guinness Book of Records* letter certifying, "The cathedral with the largest area is: Santa María de la Sede in Sevilla, 126 meters long, 82 meters wide, and 30 meters high."

Cost and Hours: €8; July–Aug Mon–Sat 9:30–17:00, Sun 14:30–18:00; Sept–June Mon–Sat 11:00–18:00, Sun 14:30–19:00; last entry one hour before closing, WC and drinking fountain inside near entrance and in courtyard near exit, tel. 954-214-971.

Tours: My self-guided tour (next) covers the basics. The €3 audioguide explains each side chapel for anyone interested in all the old paintings and dry details. For €6, you can enjoy Concepción Delgado's tour instead.

◒ Self-Guided Tour: Enter the cathedral at the south end (closest to the Alcázar, with a full-size replica of the Giralda's weathervane statue in the patio).

• *First, head to the...*

Art Pavilion: Just past the turnstile, you step into a pavilion of paintings that once hung in the church, including works by Sevilla's two 17th-century masters—Bartolomé Murillo *(St. Ferdinand)* and Francisco de Zurbarán *(St. John the Baptist in the Desert)*. Also find a painting showing the two patron saints of Sevilla—Santa Justa and Santa Rufina. They are easy to identify by their pots and palm branches, and the bell tower symbolizing the town they protect. As you tour the cathedral, keep track of how many depictions of this dynamic and saintly duo you spot. They're everywhere.

• *Walking past a rack of church maps and a WC, enter the actual church.*

Restoration Braces: The first things you'll see are the restoration braces supporting huge pillars. These are intended to help keep the building from collapsing as people search for an answer to the problem of the pillars' cracking. (But I'd move right along.)

• *In the center of the church, sit down in front of the...*

High Altar: Look through the wrought-iron Renaissance grille at what's called the largest altarpiece *(retablo mayor)* ever made—65 feet tall, with 44 scenes from the life of Jesus carved out of walnut and chestnut, blanketed by a staggering amount of gold leaf (and dust). The work took three generations to complete (1481–1564). The story is told left to right, bottom (birth of Jesus) to top (Pentecost), with the Crucifixion at the dizzying summit.

Sevilla's Cathedral

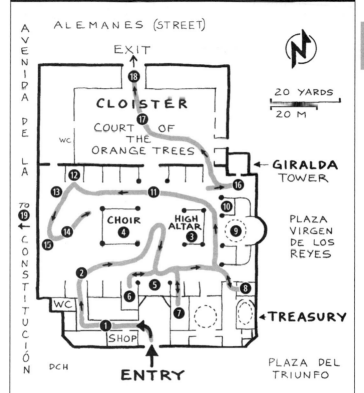

SEVILLA

1. Art Pavilion
2. Pillar Restoration Braces
3. High Altar
4. Choir
5. Tomb of Columbus
6. Antigua Chapel
7. Sacristy
8. Treasury
9. Royal Chapel
10. Chapel of St. Peter
11. View of Plateresque Ceiling
12. Chapel of St. Anthony
13. Pennant of Fernando III
14. Back of the Nave
15. MURILLO – Guardian Angel
16. Giralda Tower Climb Entrance
17. Court of the Orange Trees
18. Moorish-Style Doorway
19. To Nun-Baked Goodies

• *Turn around and check out the...*

Choir: Facing the high altar, the choir features an organ of 7,000 pipes (played at the 10:00 Mass Mon–Fri, not in July–Aug, free for worshippers). A choir area like this one (an enclosure within the cathedral for more intimate services) is common in Spain and England, but rare in churches elsewhere. The big, spinnable book holder in the middle of the room held giant hymnals—large enough for all to chant from in a pre-Xerox age when there weren't enough books for everyone.

• *Now turn 90 degrees to the left and march to find the...*

Tomb of Columbus: In front of the cathedral's entrance for pilgrims are four kings who carry the tomb of Christopher Columbus. His pallbearers represent the regions of Castile, Aragon, León, and Navarre (identify them by their team shirts). Columbus even traveled a lot posthumously. He was buried first in Spain, then in Santo Domingo in the Dominican Republic, then Cuba, and finally—when Cuba gained independence from Spain, around 1900—he sailed home again to Sevilla. Are the remains actually his? Sevillans like to think so. (Columbus died in 1506. Five hundred years later, to help celebrate the anniversary of his death, DNA samples gave Sevillans the evidence they needed to substantiate their claim.) High above on the left is a mural of St. Christopher—patron saint of travelers—from 1584. The clock above has been ticking since 1788.

• *Head to the next chapel on the right to find the...*

Antigua Chapel: Within this chapel is the gilded fresco of the Virgin Antigua, the oldest art in the church. It was actually painted onto a horseshoe-shaped prayer niche of the former mosque on this site. After Sevilla was reconquered in 1248, the mosque served as a church for about 120 years—until it was torn down to make room for this huge cathedral. Builders, captivated by the beauty of the Virgin holding the rose and the Christ Child holding the bird (and knowing that she was considered the protector of sailors in this port city), decided to save the fresco.

• *Exiting the chapel, we'll tour the cathedral counterclockwise. As you explore, note that its many chapels are described in English, and many of the windows have their dates worked into the design. Just on the other side of Columbus, step into the...*

Sacristy: This space is used each morning before Mass. The Goya painting above the altar features Justa and Rufina—the two patron saints of Sevilla, who were martyred in ancient Roman times. In addition to the town bell tower, they're always shown with their trademark items. I say they're each holding a bowl of *gazpacho* (particularly refreshing on hot summer days) and sprigs of rosemary from local Gypsies (an annoyance even back then). Art historians claim that since they were pottery-makers, they are shown with earthenware, and the sprigs are palm leaves—symbolic of their martyrdom. Whatever.

• *A few rooms over is the...*

Treasury: The *tesoro* fills several rooms in the corner of the church. Start by marveling at the ornate, 16th-century Plateresque dome of the main room, a grand souvenir from Sevilla's Golden Age. The intricate masonry resembles lacy silverwork (it's named for *plata*—silver). God is way up in the cupola. The three layers of figures below him show the heavenly host; relatives in purgatory—hands folded—looking to heaven and hoping you do them well; and the wretched in hell, including a topless sinner engulfed in flames and teased cruelly by pitchfork-wielding monsters. Locals use the 110-pound silver monstrance, which dominates this room, to parade the holy host (communion bread) through town during Corpus Christi festivities.

Wander deeper into the treasury to find a unique oval dome. It's in the 16th-century chapter room *(sala capitular),* where monthly meetings take place with the bishop (he gets the throne, while the others share the bench). The paintings here are by Murillo: a fine *Immaculate Conception* (1668, above the bishop's throne) and portraits of saints important to Sevillans.

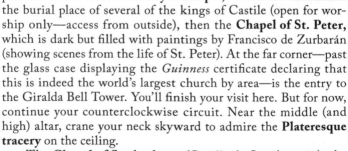

The wood-paneled "room of ornaments" shows off gold and silver reliquaries, which hold hundreds of holy body parts, as well as Spain's most valuable crown. The Corona de la Virgen de los Reyes sparkles with 11,000 precious stones and the world's largest pearl—used as the torso of an angel. Opposite the crown is a reliquary featuring "a piece of the true cross."

• *Leave the treasury and cross through the church to see...*

More Church Sights: First you'll pass the closed-to-tourists **Royal Chapel,** the burial place of several of the kings of Castile (open for worship only—access from outside), then the **Chapel of St. Peter,** which is dark but filled with paintings by Francisco de Zurbarán (showing scenes from the life of St. Peter). At the far corner—past the glass case displaying the *Guinness* certificate declaring that this is indeed the world's largest church by area—is the entry to the Giralda Bell Tower. You'll finish your visit here. But for now, continue your counterclockwise circuit. Near the middle (and high) altar, crane your neck skyward to admire the **Plateresque tracery** on the ceiling.

The **Chapel of St. Anthony** (Capilla de San Antonio), the last chapel on the right, is used for baptisms. The Renaissance

Immaculate Conception

Throughout Sevilla and Spain, you'll see paintings titled *The Immaculate Conception,* all looking quite similar. Young, lovely, and beaming radiantly, these virgins look pure, untainted... you might even say "immaculate." According to Catholic doctrine, Mary, the future mother of Jesus, entered the world free from the original sin that other mortals share. When she died, her purity allowed her to be taken up directly to heaven (the Assumption).

The doctrine of Immaculate Conception can be confusing, even to Catholics. It does not mean that the Virgin Mary herself was born of a virgin. Rather, Mary's mother and father conceived her in the natural way. But at the moment Mary's soul animated her flesh, God granted her a special exemption from original sin. The doctrine of Immaculate Conception had been popular since medieval times, though it was not codified until 1854. It was Sevilla's own Bartolomé Murillo (1617–1682) who painted the model of this goddess-like Mary, copied by so many lesser artists. In Counter-Reformation times (when Murillo lived), paintings of a fresh-faced, ecstatic Mary made abstract doctrines like the Immaculate Conception and the Assumption tangible and accessible to all.

An easy way to recognize an image of the Immaculate Conception is to look for the following clues: a radiant crown, a crescent moon at Mary's feet, and often a pose showing Mary stepping on cherubs' heads. Paintings by Murillo frequently portray Mary in a blue robe with long, wavy hair—young and innocent.

baptismal font has delightful carved angels dancing along its base. In Murillo's painting, *Vision of St. Anthony* (1656), the saint kneels in wonder as a baby Jesus comes down surrounded by a choir of angels. Anthony is one of Iberia's most popular saints. As he is the patron saint of lost things, people come here to pray for Anthony's help in finding jobs, car keys, and life partners. Above that is the *Baptism of Christ,* also by Murillo. You don't need to be an art historian  to know that the stained glass dates from 1685. And by now, you must know who the women are...

Nearby, a glass case displays the **pennant of Fernando III,** which was raised over the minaret of the mosque on November 23, 1248, as Christian forces finally expelled the Moors from Sevilla. For centuries, it was paraded through the city on special days.

Continuing on, stand at the **back of the nave** (behind the choir) and appreciate the ornate immensity of the church. Can you see the angels trumpeting on their Cuban mahogany? Any birds?

Turn around. The massive candlestick holder dates from 1560. To the left is a niche with **Murillo's *Guardian Angel*** pointing to the light and showing an astonished child the way.

• *Backtrack the length of the church toward the Giralda Bell Tower, and notice the bulk of the choir's Baroque pipe organ. The exit sign leads to the Court of the Orange Trees and the exit. But first, some exercise.*

Giralda Tower Climb: Your church admission includes entry to the bell tower. Notice the beautiful Moorish simplicity as you climb to its top, 330 feet up, for a grand city view. The spiraling ramp was designed to accommodate riders on horseback, who galloped up five times a day to give the Muslim call to prayer.

• *Go back down the stairs and visit the...*

Court of the Orange Trees: Today's cloister was once the mosque's Court of the Orange Trees (Patio de los Naranjos).

Twelfth-century Muslims stopped at the fountain in the middle to wash their hands, face, and feet before praying. The ankle-breaking lanes between the bricks were once irrigation streams—a reminder that the Moors introduced irrigation to Iberia. The mosque was made of bricks; the church is built of stone. The only remnants of the mosque today are the Court of the Orange Trees, the Giralda Bell Tower, and the site itself.

• *You'll exit the cathedral through the Court of the Orange Trees (if you need to use the WCs, they're at the far end of the courtyard, downstairs). As you leave, notice the arch over the...*

Moorish-Style Doorway: As with much of the Moorish-looking art in town, it's actually Christian—the two coats of arms are a giveaway. The relief above the door (looking in from outside) shows the Bible story of Jesus ridding the temple of the merchants...a reminder to contemporary merchants that there will be no retail activity in the church. The plaque on the right is one of many scattered throughout town showing a place mentioned in the books of Miguel de Cervantes, the great 16th-century Spanish writer. (In this case, the topic was pickpockets.) The huge green doors predate the church. They are a bit of the surviving pre-1248 mosque—wood covered with bronze. Study the fine workmanship.

Giralda Tower Exterior: Step across the street from the exit gate and look at the bell tower. Formerly a Moorish minaret from

Christopher Columbus
(1451–1506)

This Italian wool-weaver ran off to sea, was shipwrecked in Portugal, married a captain's daughter, learned Portuguese and Spanish, and convinced Spain's monarchs to finance his bold scheme to trade with the East by sailing west. On August 3, 1492, Columbus set sail from Palos (near Huelva, 60 miles west of Sevilla) with three ships and 90 men, hoping to land in Asia, which Columbus estimated was 3,000 miles away. Three thousand miles later—with the superstitious crew ready to mutiny, having seen evil omens like a falling meteor and a jittery compass—Columbus landed on an island in the Bahamas (October 12, 1492), convinced he'd reached Asia. They traded with the "Indians" and returned home to Palos harbor, where they were received as heroes.

Columbus made three more voyages to the New World and became rich with gold. He gained a bad reputation among the colonists, was arrested, and returned to Spain in chains. Though pardoned, Columbus fell out of favor with the court. On May 20, 1506, he died in Valladolid. His son said he was felled by "gout and by grief at seeing himself fallen from his high estate," but historians speculate that diabetes or syphilis may have contributed. Columbus died thinking he'd visited Asia, unaware he'd opened up Europe to a New World.

which Muslims were called to prayer, it became the cathedral's bell tower after the Reconquista. A 4,500-pound bronze statue

symbolizing the Triumph of Faith (specifically, the Christian faith over the Muslim one) caps the tower and serves as a weather vane (*giraldillo* in Spanish). In 1356, the original top of the tower fell. You're looking at a 16th-century Christian-built top with a ribbon of letters proclaiming, "The strongest tower is the name of God" (you can see *Fortisima*—"strongest"—from this vantage point).

Now circle around for a close look at the corner of the tower at ground level. Needing more strength than their bricks could provide for the lowest section of the tower, the Moors used Roman-cut stones. You can actually read the Latin chiseled onto one of the stones 2,000 years ago. The tower offers a brief recap of the city's history—sitting on a Roman foundation, a long Moorish period capped by our Christian age. Today, by law, no building can be higher than the statue atop the tower.

• *If you've worked up an appetite, finish your cathedral tour with some...*

Nun-Baked Goodies: Stop by the El Torno Pasteleria de Conventos, a co-op where the various orders of cloistered nuns send their handicrafts (such as baby's baptismal dresses) and baked goods to be sold. "El Torno" is the lazy Susan that the cloistered nuns spin to sell their cakes and cookies without being seen. You'll have to go to a convent to see the *torno*, but this humble little hole-in-the-wall shop is still worth a peek (Sept–July Mon–Fri 10:00–13:30 & 17:00–19:30, Sat–Sun 10:30–14:00, closed Aug, across Avenida de la Constitución, immediately in front of the cathedral's biggest door, follow *dulces de convento* sign down a little covered lane to Plaza Cabildo 21, tel. 954-219-190).

Near the Cathedral

Avenida de la Constitución—Old Sevilla is bisected by its grand boulevard. It was named to celebrate the 1978 democratic constitution the Spanish people adopted as they moved quickly after the 1975 death of Franco to establish their freedom. Long a commercial street, it was made into a pedestrian boulevard in 2007. Overnight, the city's paseo route took on a new dimension. And suddenly cafés and shops here had an appeal. (Two Starbucks moved in, placed strategically like bookends on the boulevard, but they're having a tough time winning the loyalty of locals who like small coffees for €1 rather than mammoth ones for €4.) The tram line (which is infamous for being short—only three-quarters of a mile long) is controversial, as it violates what might have been a more purely people zone.

Alcázar and Nearby

▲▲**Alcázar**—Originally a 10th-century palace built for the governors of the local Moorish state, this building still functions as

a royal palace...the oldest in use in Europe. What you see today is an extensive 14th-century rebuild, done by Moorish (Mudejar) workmen for the Christian king, Pedro I. Pedro was nicknamed either "the Cruel" or "the Just," depending on which end of his sword you were on.

Cost and Hours: €7.50; peak season Tue–Sun 9:30–19:00, off-season Tue–Sun 9:30–17:00, closed Mon year-round; tel. 954-502-323. Tour groups clog the palace and rob it of any mystery in the morning (especially on Tue); come as late as possible.

Tours: The fast-moving, easy-to-use €3

audioguide gives you an hour of information as you wander—if you want that much (drop it off at the exit). Again, rather then renting the audioguide, you could follow my self-guided tour (next), or consider Concepción Delgado's €6 Alcázar tour.

❍ Self-Guided Tour: The Alcázar is a thought-provoking glimpse of a graceful Al-Andalus (Moorish) world that might have survived its Castilian conquerors...but didn't. The floor plan is intentionally confusing, part of the style designed to make experiencing the place more exciting and surprising. While Granada's Alhambra was built by Moors for Moorish rulers, what you see here is essentially a Christian ruler's palace, built in the Moorish style.

Just past the turnstiles, walk through the **Patio of the Lions** and stop under the arch of the wall to orient yourself. Facing the **Patio de la Montería**, you see the palace's three wings. The wing on the right is the 16th-century Admiral's Apartments; straight ahead is King Pedro the Cruel's Palace; and on the left is the 13th-century Gothic wing. You'll tour them in that order (entering the Gothic wing from within Pedro's palace).

Before starting, notice the public WCs in the far-left corner, and a staircase in the far-right corner leading up to the lived-in **Royal Apartments**. (These are available by tour only. They're similar to what you'll see downstairs, but with furniture. If interested, go there now to book a spot—€4 for a 25-min escorted walk through 15 rooms with an audioguide, 15 people per tour, lockers provided for your visit.)

• *Start by heading to the...*

Admiral's Apartments: When Queen Isabel debriefed Columbus here after his New World discoveries, she realized this could be big business. In 1503, she created this wing to administer Spain's New World ventures. Step inside.

Straight ahead, through the main hall, you'll find the Admiral's Lounge with a chapel featuring a **painting of Santa María de los Buenos Aires Chapel** (St. Mary of the Fair Winds—or, as many Spanish boys would say, "of the Good Farts"). The Virgin of the Fair Winds was the patron saint of navigators and a favorite of Columbus. Many historians believe that the fine Virgin of the Navigators altarpiece (painted by Alejo Fernández in the 1530s) has the only portrait of Ferdinand (on left, with gold cape) with Columbus. Columbus is the blond guy on the right. Columbus' son said of his dad: "In his youth his hair was blond, but when he reached 30, it all turned white." As it's likely the earliest known

Alcázar

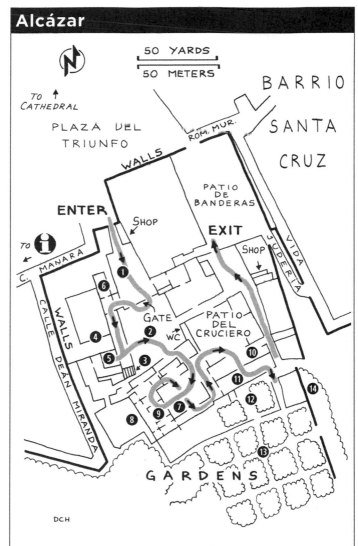

TO CATHEDRAL

PLAZA DEL TRIUNFO

BARRIO

SANTA

CRUZ

WALLS

ROM. MUR.

PATIO DE BANDERAS

ENTER

SHOP

EXIT

SHOP

TO ℹ

C. MANARA

WALLS

CALLE DEAN MIRANDA

GATE

WC

PATIO DEL CRUCIERO

J. JUDERIA

VIDA

GARDENS

DCH

1 Patio of the Lions
2 Patio de la Montería
3 Stairs to Royal Apartments
4 Admiral's Apartments
5 Painting of Santa María de los Buenos Aires Chapel
6 Ornate Fans
7 Court of the Maidens

8 King Pedro the Cruel's Palace
9 Dolls' Court
10 Gothic Wing
11 Big Tapestries
12 Moorish Garden
13 Christian Garden
14 Elevated Walkway

portrait of Columbus, it also might be the most accurate. Notice how the Virgin's cape seems to protect everyone under it—even the Native Americans in the dark background (the first time "Indians" were painted in Europe). Left of the painting is a model of Columbus' *Santa María*, his flagship and the only one of his three ships not to survive the 1492 voyage. Columbus complained that the *Santa María*—a big cargo ship, different from the sleek *Niña* and *Pinta* caravels—was too slow. On Christmas Day, it ran aground and tore a hole in its hull. The ship was dismantled to build the first permanent structure in America, a fort for 39 colonists. (After Columbus left, the natives burned the fort and killed the colonists.) Opposite the altarpiece (in the center of the back wall) is the family coat of arms of Columbus' descendants, who now live in Spain and Puerto Rico. Using Columbus' Spanish name, it reads: "To Castile and to León, Colón gave a new world."

Before leaving, return to the still-used reception room and pop into the room beyond the grand piano for a look at **ornate fans** (mostly foreign, described in English) and a long painting showing 17th-century Sevilla during Holy Week. Follow the procession, which is much like today's procession of traditional floats, carried by teams of 24 to 48 men and followed by a parade of KKK-looking penitents (who have worn these traditional costumes for centuries—long before such hoods became associated with racism in the American South).

• *Return to the main courtyard, enter the middle wing, and walk to the left through the vestibule until you hit the big courtyard called the* **Court of the Maidens** *(Patio de las Doncellas).*

King Pedro the Cruel's Palace: This is the 14th-century nucleus of the complex—the real Alcázar. Centered around the elegantly proportioned Court of the Maidens, the palace is decorated in 14th-century Moorish style below and a 16th-century Renaissance style above.

As you explore this wing, circulate counterclockwise through rooms branching off of this central courtyard and imagine day-to-day life in the palace (with VIP guests tripping on the tiny but jolting steps). King Pedro (1334–1369) cruelly abandoned his wife and moved into the Alcázar with his mistress. He hired Muslim workers from Granada to re-create the romance of that city's Alhambra in Sevilla's stark Alcázar. The designers created a microclimate engineered for coolness: water, plants, pottery, thick walls, and darkness. Even with the inevitable hodgepodge of style that comes with 600 years of renovation, this is considered Spain's best example of the Mudejar style. Notice the sumptuous ceilings; you'll see peacocks, castles, and kings that you wouldn't find in religious Muslim decor, which avoids images. The stylized Arabic script survives, creating a visual chant of verses from the Quran seen in Moorish buildings (including the Alhambra). The artisans added propaganda phrases such as, "Dedicated to the magnificent Sultan Pedro—thanks to God!"

The second courtyard, the smaller and more delicate **Dolls' Court** (Patio de las Muñecas), was for the king's private and family life. Originally, the center of the courtyard had a pool, cooling the residents and reflecting the decorative patterns once brightly painted on the walls.

• *Leave this wing from the big courtyard. Head to the staircase opposite from where you entered, and climb up into the...*

Gothic Wing: This wing of the palace shows fine tapestries from Brussels (1554). Find the second hall—with the **biggest tapestries**. These celebrate Emperor Charles V's 1535 victory in Tunis over the Turks (described both in Spanish along the top and in Latin along the bottom). The map tapestry comes with an unusual perspective—with Africa at the top (it's supposed to be from a Barcelona aerial perspective). Find the big fortified city in the middle (Barcelona, just above eye level), Santiago de Compostela, Lisboa (Lisbon), Gibraltar, the west edge of Italy, Rome, Sicily, and the Mediterranean islands. Don't try to navigate by this early map. Montserrat, which is just a few miles outside of Barcelona, is shown all the way over by Lisbon. The artist paints himself holding the legend—with a scale in both leagues and miles. This is an 18th-century copy of the original.

• *Head outside to...*

The Gardens: This space is full of tropical flowers, wild cats, cool fountains, and hot tourists. The intimate geometric zone near-

est the palace is the Moorish garden. The far-flung garden beyond that was the backyard of the Christian ruler. The **elevated walkway** along the left side of the gardens (access at both ends) provides fine views. You can explore the gardens and return via this walkway, or vice versa.

Archivo de Indias—The Lonja Palace (across the street from Alcázar) was designed by the same person who designed El Escorial. Originally a market, it's the top building from Sevilla's 16th-century glory days. Today, it houses the archive of documents from the discovery and conquest of the New World. This could be fascinating, but little of importance is on display (old maps of Havana). The displays are in Spanish, but you can pick up English brochures describing both permanent and temporary exhibits (free,

Mon–Sat 9:00–16:00, Sun 10:00–14:00, tel. 954-500-528).

Between the River and the Cathedral

Hospital de la Caridad—This Charity Hospital was founded by a nobleman in the 17th century. Peek into the fine courtyard. On the left, the chapel has some gruesome art (above both doors) illustrating that death is the great equalizer, and an altar so sweet only a Spaniard could enjoy it. The Dutch tiles depicting scenes of the Old and New Testament are a reminder of the time when the Netherlands was under Spanish rule in the mid-16th century (€5, slightly interesting audioguide for €2, erratic hours, but typically Mon–Sat 9:00–13:30 & 15:30–19:30, Sun 9:00–13:00, last entry 30 min before closing, tel. 954-223-232).

Golden Tower (Torre del Oro) and Naval Museum—Sevilla's historic riverside Golden Tower was the starting point and ending point for all shipping to the New World. It's named for the golden tiles that once covered it—not for all the New World booty that landed here. Since the Moors built it in the 13th century, it has been part of the city's fortifications, with a heavy chain draped across the river to protect the harbor. Today it houses a dreary little naval museum. Looking past the dried fish and charts of knots, find the mural showing the world-spanning journeys of Vasco da Gama, the model of Columbus' *Santa María* (the first ship to land in the New World), and an interesting mural of Sevilla in 1740. Enjoy the view from the balconies upstairs. The Guadalquivir River is now just a trickle of its former self, after canals built in the 1920s siphoned off most of its water to feed ports downstream (€2, includes audioguide, Sept–July Tue–Fri 10:00–14:00, Sat–Sun 11:00–14:00, closed Mon and Aug, tel. 954-222-419).

North of the Cathedral, near Plaza Nueva

▲▲**Flamenco Dance Museum (Museo del Baile Flamenco)**—If you want to understand more about the dance that embodies the spirit of southern Spain, this museum—while overpriced at €10—does the trick. The grande dame of flamenco, Cristina Hoyos, has collected a few artifacts and costumes and put together a series of videos explaining the art of flamenco. One particularly interesting film illustrates the key elements of the dance form: pain, joy, elegance, seduction, soul, and—I believe—love of ham (€10, daily 9:00–19:00, Calle Manuel Rojas Marcos 3, about three blocks east of Plaza Nueva, tel. 954-340-311, www.museo flamenco.com). Watch a dance class when visiting the museum, or participate in a one-hour lesson and take a little *olé* home with you (€60/person max, prices go down with more people, shoes provided). There are also dance shows on Friday and Saturday at 19:30 (€25, €30 combo-ticket includes museum and show, 10 percent discount off museum, show, or combo-ticket with this book in 2010).

▲**Museo Palacio de la Condesa de Lebrija**—This aristocratic mansion takes you back into the 18th century like no other place in town. The Countess of Lebrija was a passionate collector of antiquities. Her home's ground floor is paved with Roman mosaics (that you actually walk on) and lined with musty old cases of Phoenician, Greek, Roman, and Moorish artifacts—mostly pottery. To see a plush world from a time when the nobility had a private priest and their own chapel, take a quickie tour of the upstairs, which shows the palace as the countess left it when she died in 1938 (€4 for unescorted visit of ground floor, €8 includes tour of "lived-in" upstairs offered every 45 min, Mon–Fri 10:30–19:30, Sat 10:00–14:00, closed Sun, free and obligatory bag check, Calle Cuna 8, tel. 954-227-802).

South of the Cathedral, near Plaza de España

University—Today's university was yesterday's *fábrica de tabacos* (tobacco factory), which employed 10,000 young female *cigareras*—including the saucy femme fatale of Bizet's opera *Carmen*. In the 18th century, it was the second-largest building in Spain, after El Escorial. Wander through its halls as you walk to Plaza de España. The university's bustling café is a good place for cheap tapas, beer, wine, and conversation (Mon–Fri 8:00–21:00, Sat 9:00–13:00, closed Sun).

Plaza de España—This square, the surrounding buildings, and the nearby María Luisa Park are the remains of the 1929 international fair, where for a year the Spanish-speaking countries of the world enjoyed a mutual-admiration fiesta. When they finish the restoration work here (it's taking years), this delightful area—the epitome of world's fair-style architecture—will once again be great for  people-watching (especially during the 19:00–20:00 peak paseo hour). The park's highlight is the former Spanish Pavilion. Its tiles (a trademark of Sevilla) show historic scenes and maps from every province of Spain (arranged in alphabetical order, from Álava to Zaragoza). Climb to one of the balconies for a fine view. Beware: This is a classic haunt of thieves and con artists. Believe no one here. Thieves, posing as lost tourists, will come at you with a map unfolded to hide their speedy, greedy fingers.

Away from the Center
▲Museo de Bellas Artes

Sevilla's passion for religious art is preserved and displayed in its Museum of Fine Art. While most Americans go for El Greco, Goya, and Velázquez (not a forte of this collection), this museum gives a fine look at the other, less-appreciated Spanish masters: Zurbarán and Murillo. Rather than exhausting, the museum is pleasantly enjoyable.

Cost, Hours, Location: €1.50, Tue–Sat 9:00–20:30, Sun 9:00–14:30, closed Mon, last entry 15 min before closing, tel. 954-220-790. The museum is at Plaza Museo 9; it's a 15-minute walk from the cathedral, or a short ride on bus #C5 from Plaza Nueva. If coming from La Macarena (described next), take bus #C4 to the Torneo stop and walk inland four blocks. Pick up the English-language floor plan, which explains the theme of each room.

Background: Several of Spain's top artists—Zurbarán, Murillo, and Velázquez—lived in Sevilla. This was Spain's wealthy commercial capital, like New York City, while Madrid was a newly built center of government, like Washington, D.C. In the early 1800s, Spain's liberal government was disbanding convents and monasteries, and secular fanatics were looting churches. Thankfully, the region's religious art was rescued and hung safely here in this convent-turned-museum.

Spain's economic Golden Age (the 1500s) blossomed into the Golden Age of Spanish painting (the 1600s). Artists such as Zurbarán combined realism with mysticism. He painted balding saints and monks with wrinkled faces and sunburned hands. The style suited Spain's spiritual climate, as the Catholic Church used this art in its Counter-Reformation battle against the Protestant rebellion.

⊙ Self-Guided Tour: The core of the collection is in Rooms 3 through 10. Most of the major works are displayed in Room 5, the convent's former chapel. It's difficult not to say "Wow!" when entering. Tour the collection starting upstairs in Room 10 (head into the cloister and climb the grand staircase). Then, after exploring the first floor according to your interests, finish in Room 5.

Francisco de Zurbarán (thoor-bar-AHN, 1598–1664) paints saints and monks, and the miraculous things they experience, presented with unblinking, crystal-clear, brightly lit, highly detailed realism. Monks and nuns could meditate upon Zurbarán's meticulous paintings (Room 10 and the room leading to 10) for hours, finding God in the details.

Zurbarán shines a harsh spotlight on his subject, creating strong shadows. Like the secluded monks themselves, Zurbarán's people stand starkly isolated against a dark single-color background. He was the ideal painter of the austere religion of 17th-century Spain.

In Zurbarán's *St. Hugo Visiting the Carthusian Monks at Supper* (Room 10), white-robed

monks gather together for their simple meal in the communal dining hall. Above them hangs a painting of Mary, Baby Jesus, and John the Baptist. Zurbarán created paintings for monks' dining halls like this. His audience: celibate men and women who lived in isolation, as in this former convent, devoting their time to quiet meditation, prayer, and Bible study.

In *The Virgin of the Caves* (also in Room 10, just to the right), study the piety and faith in the monks' rustic faces. Zurbarán shows a protective Mary with her hands on the heads of the two top monks of that order. Note the loving detail on the cape embroidery, the brooch, and the flowers at her feet. But also note the angel babies holding the cape, with their painfully double-jointed arms. Zurbarán was no Leonardo.

The *Apotheosis of St. Thomas Aquinas* (ground level, Room 5) is considered Zurbarán's most important work. It was done at the height of his career, when stark realism was all the rage. Here again Zurbarán presents the miraculous moment (when the saint gets his spiritual awakening) in a believable, down-to-earth way.

Bartolomé Murillo (mur-EE-oh, 1617–1682) was another hometown boy. In Room 5, his *Madonna and Child* (*La Servilleta*,

1665; at the end of the room in the center, where the church's altar would have been) shows the warmth and appeal of his work. By about 1650, Murillo's easy-to-appreciate style had replaced Zurbarán's harsh realism.

The Immaculate Conception (several versions in the museum, ground floor, Room 5) was Murillo's favorite subject. To many Spaniards, Mary is their main connection to heaven. They pray directly to her, asking her to intercede for them with God. Murillo's Marys are always receptive and ready to help.

▲▲Basílica de la Macarena

Sevilla's Holy Week (Semana Santa) celebrations are Spain's grandest. During the week leading up to Easter, the city is packed

with pilgrims witnessing 50 processions carrying about 100 religious floats. Get a feel for this event by visiting Basílica de la Macarena (built in 1947) to see the two most impressive floats and the darling of Holy Week, the Weeping Virgin (Virgen de la Macarena, a.k.a. La Esperanza). The church's museum has been closed for restoration, but should reopen in 2010—before making the trip, confirm at the TI that it's open and that you can see the *paso* (Mary's silver float, carried in the Holy Week procession).

Cost, Hours, Location: Church free, museum-€3.50, buy ticket at shop by entrance, daily 9:30–14:00 & 17:00–20:00, taxi to Puerta Macarena or bus #C3 or #C4 from Puerta de Jerez or Menéndez Pelayo, tel. 954-901-800.

❍ Self-Guided Tour: Grab a pew and study Mary, complete with crystal teardrops. She's like a 17th-century doll with human hair and articulated arms, and even dressed with underclothes. Her beautiful expression—halfway between smiling and crying—is moving, in a Baroque way. Her weeping can be contagious—look around you. Filling a side chapel (on the left) is the Christ of the Sentence (from 1654), showing Jesus the day he was condemned.

The two most important floats of the Holy Week parades—the floats that Jesus and Mary ride every Good Friday—are parked behind the altar (through the door left of the altar, museum ticket required).

The three-ton float that carries Jesus is slathered in gold leaf and shows a commotion of figures acting out the sentencing of Christ (whose statue—the one you saw in the church—is placed in the front of this crowd). Pontius Pilate is about to wash his hands. Pilate's wife cries as a man reads the death sentence. During the Holy Week procession, pious Sevillan women wail in the streets while relays of 48 men carry this float on the backs of their necks—only their feet showing under the drapes—as they shuffle through the streets from midnight until 14:00 in the afternoon every Good Friday. (The photo on the wall behind Pilate shows the float—with the bound Christ of the Sentence in place—pulling out of the church on Good Friday in 1986.) Shuffle upstairs for another perspective.

La Esperanza follows the Sentencing of Christ in the procession. Mary's smaller, 1.5-ton float, in the next room, seems all silver and candles—"strong enough to support the roof, but tender enough to quiver in the soft night breeze." Mary has a wardrobe of three huge mantles (each displayed here), worn in successive years. They are about 100 years old. Her six-pound gold crown/halo (in a glass case in the wall) is from 1913. This float has a mesmerizing effect on the local crowds. They line up for hours, clapping, weeping, and throwing roses as it slowly works its way through the city. My Sevillan friend explained, "She knows all the problems of Sevilla and its people. We've been confiding in her for centuries. To us, she is hope. That's her name—Esperanza."

Before leaving, find the case of matador garb (also upstairs) given to the church by bullfighters over the years. They are a token of thanks for the protection they feel they received from La Macarena. Considered the protector of bullfighters, she's big in bullring chapels. In 1912, the bullfighter José Ortega, hoping for protection, gave her the five emerald brooches she wears. It worked for eight years...until he was gored to death in the ring. (This was such a big deal that La Macarena was dressed in black—the only time that has happened.)

Outside, notice the best surviving bit of Sevilla's old walls. Originally Roman, what remains today is 12th-century Moorish, a reminder that off and on for centuries Sevilla was the capital of the Islamic kingdom in Iberia.

And yes, it's from this city that a local dance band (Los del Río) changed the world by giving us "The Macarena."

Near Sevilla

Itálica—One of Spain's most impressive Roman ruins is found outside the sleepy town of Santiponce, about six miles northwest of Sevilla. Founded in 206 B.C. for wounded soldiers recuperating from the Second Punic War, Itálica became a thriving town of great agricultural and military importance. It was the birthplace of famous Roman emperors Trajan and Hadrian. Today its best-preserved ruin is its amphitheater—one of the largest in the Roman Empire—with a capacity for 30,000 spectators. Other highlights include beautiful floor mosaics, such as the one in Casa de los Pájaros (House of the Birds) that shows more than 30 species of birds. To avoid the midday heat, plan your visit to arrive early or late, and definitely bring water (€1.50; April–Sept Tue–Sat 8:30–21:00, Sun 9:00–15:00; Oct–March Tue–Sat 9:00–18:00, Sun 10:00–16:00; closed Mon year-round; tel. 955-622-266).

Getting There: You can get to Itálica on bus #M172 (30-min trip, frequent departures from Sevilla's Plaza de Armas Station). If you're driving, head west out of Sevilla in the direction of Huelva; after you cross the second branch of the river, turn north

SEVILLA

on N-630, and after a few miles, get off at Santiponce. Drive past pottery warehouses and through the town to the ruins at the far (west) end.

Experiences in Sevilla

Bullfighting

▲**Bullfights**—Some of Spain's best bullfighting is done in Sevilla's 14,000-seat bullring, Plaza de Toros. Fights are held (generally at 18:30) on most Sundays in May and June; on Easter; and daily during the April Fair (April 20–25 in 2010) and at the end of September (during the Feria de San Miguel). These serious fights, with adult matadors, are called *corrida de toros* and often sell out in advance. On many Thursday evenings in July, there are *novil-*

lada fights, with teenage novices doing the killing and smaller bulls doing the dying. *Corrida de toros* seats range from €25 for high seats looking into the sun to €150 for the first three rows in the shade under the royal box; *novillada* seats are half that—and easy to buy at the arena a few minutes before show time (ignore scalpers outside; get information at a TI, your hotel, by phone, or online; tel 954-210-315, www.lamaestranza.es).

▲▲**Bullfight Museum**—Follow a bilingual (Spanish and English) 25-minute guided tour through the bullring's strangely quiet and empty arena, its museum, and the chapel where the matador prays before the fight. (Thanks to readily available blood transfusions, there have been no deaths in nearly three decades.) The two most revered figures of Sevilla, the Virgin of Macarena and the Christ of Gran Poder (All Power), are represented in the chapel. In the museum, you'll see great classic scenes and the heads of a few bulls—awarded the bovine equivalent of an Oscar for a particularly good fight. The city was so appalled when the famous matador Manolete was killed in 1947 that even the mother of the bull that gored him was destroyed. Matadors—dressed to kill—are heartthrobs in their "suits of light." Many girls have their bedrooms wallpapered with posters of cute bullfighters. (€6, entrance with escorted tour only—no free time inside, 3/hr, daily May–Oct 9:30–20:00, Nov–April 9:30–19:00, until 14:00 on fight days, when chapel and horse room are closed.) While they take groups of up to 50, it's still wise to call or drop by to reserve a spot in the busy season (tel. 954-210-315).

The April Fair

For seven days each April (April 20–25 in 2010), much of Sevilla is packed into its vast fairgrounds for a grand party. The fair, seem-ing to bring all that's Andalusian together, feels friendly, sponta-neous, and very real. The local passion for horses, flamenco, and sherry is clear—riders are ramrod straight, colorfully clad girls ride sidesaddle, and everyone's drink-ing sherry spritzers. Women sport outlandish dresses that would look clownish all alone but are somehow brilliant here en masse. Horses clog the streets in an endless parade until about 20:00, when they clear out and the streets fill with exuberant locals. The party goes for literally 24 hours a day for the entire week.

Countless private party tents, or *casetas,* line the lanes. Each tent is the private party zone of a family, club, or association. You need to know someone in the group—or make friends quickly—to get in. Because of the exclusivity, it has a real family-affair feeling. In each *caseta,* everyone knows everyone. It seems like a thousand wedding parties being celebrated at the same time.

Any tourist can have a fun and memorable evening by sim-ply crashing the party. The city's entire fleet of taxis (who'll try to charge double) and buses seems dedicated to shuttling people from downtown to the fairgrounds. With the traffic jams, you may be better off hiking: From the Golden Tower, cross the San Telmo Bridge to Plaza de Cuba and hike down Calle Asunción. You'll see the towering gate to the fairgrounds in the distance. Just follow the crowds (there's no admission charge). Arrive before 20:00 to see the horses, but stay later, as the ambience improves after they giddy-up on out. Some of the larger tents are sponsored by the city and open to the public, but the best action is in the streets, where party-goers from the livelier *casetas* spill out. Although private tents have bouncers, everyone is so happy that it's not tough to strike up an impromptu friendship, become a "special guest," and be invited in. The drink flows freely, and the food is fun and cheap.

Shopping in Sevilla

For the best local shopping experience, follow my shopping stroll (see next). The popular pedestrian streets Sierpes, Tetuán, and Velázquez—along with the surrounding lanes near Plaza Nueva—are packed with people and shops. Small shops close between 13:30 and 16:00 or 17:00 on weekdays, as well as on Saturday afternoons and all day Sunday. But big ones such as El Corte Inglés stay open (and air-conditioned) right through the siesta. El Corte Inglés also has a supermarket downstairs and a good but expensive restaurant (Mon–Sat 10:00–22:00, closed Sun). Popular souvenir items include ladies' fans, ceramics, and items related to flamenco (castanets, guitars, costumes) and bullfighting posters).

Collectors' markets hop on Sunday: stamps and coins at Plaza del Cabildo (near the cathedral) and art on Plaza del Museo (by the Museo de Bellas Artes).

Mercado del Arenal, the covered fish-and-produce market, is perfect for hungry photographers (Mon–Sat 9:00–14:30, closed Sun, least lively on Mon, on Calle Pastor y Landero at Calle Arenal, just beyond bullring). For suggestions on dining here (including a small café-bar for breakfast and a fish restaurant inside), see "Eating."

▲▲Shopping Paseo Tour

While many tourists never get beyond the cathedral and the Santa Cruz neighborhood, it's important to wander west into the lively pedestrian shopping center of town. These streets—Calle Tetuán (which becomes Velázquez), Calle Sierpes, and Calle Cuna—also happen to be part of the oldest section of Sevilla. A walk here is a chance to join one of Spain's liveliest paseos—that bustling celebration of life that takes place before dinner each evening, when everyone is out strolling. Locals stroll to show off their fancy shoes and make the scene. This walk (if done between 18:00 and 20:00) gives you a look at the paseo scene and the town's most popular shops. You'll pass windows displaying the best in both traditional and trendy fashion. The walk ends at a plush mansion of a local countess (open to the public).

Start on the pedestrianized **Plaza Nueva,** a 19th-century square facing the ornate city hall, which features a statue of Ferdinand III, a local favorite because he freed Sevilla from the Moors in 1248. From here, wander the length of **Calle Tetuán** (notice the latest in outrageous shoes). Calle Tetuán becomes **Velázquez,** and ends at La Campana (a big intersection and popular meeting point, with the super department store, El Corte Inglés, just beyond). At La Campana, tempt yourself with sweets at the venerable Confitería La Campana.

Next, take two rights to get to **Calle Sierpes,** great for shopping and strolling. Calle Sierpes is the main street of the Holy Week processions—imagine it packed with celebrants and its balconies bulging with spectators. At the corner of Sierpes and Jovellanos/Sagasta, you're near several fine shops featuring Andalusian accessories. Drop in to see how serious local women are about their fans, combs, shawls, and *mantillas* (ornate head scarves). Andalusian women have various fans to match different dresses. The *mantilla* comes in black (worn only on Good Friday and by the mother of the groom at weddings) and white (worn at bullfights during the April Fair).

From here, turn left down **Calle Sagasta**. Notice that the street has two names—the modern version and a medieval one: Antigua Calle de Gallegos ("Ancient Street of the Galicians"). With the Christian victory in 1248, the Muslims were given one month to evacuate. To consolidate Christian control, settlers from the north were planted here. This street was home to the Galicians.

Finally, at the charming Plaza del Salvador, backtrack left along **Calle Cuna,** famous for its exuberant flamenco dresses and classic wedding dresses. (Flamenco miniskirts have been popular in recent years, but now hemlines are falling again.) If all this shopping makes you feel like a countess, Calle Cuna leads to the Museo Palacio de la Condesa de Lebrija.

Nightlife in Sevilla

▲▲**Evening Paseo**—Sevilla is meant for strolling. The paseo thrives every non-winter evening in these areas: along either side

of the river between the San Telmo and Isabel II bridges (Paseo de Cristóbal Colón and Triana district; see "Eating"), up Avenida de la Constitución, around Plaza Nueva, at Plaza de España, and throughout the Barrio Santa Cruz. On hot summer nights, even families with toddlers are out and about past midnight. Spend some time rafting through this sea of humanity. Savor the view of floodlit Sevilla by night from the far side of the river—perhaps over dinner.

▲▲▲**Flamenco**—This music-and-dance art form has its roots in the Roma (Gypsy) and Moorish cultures. Even at a packaged "flamenco evening," sparks fly. The men do most of the flamboyant machine-gun footwork. The women concentrate on graceful turns

4 Reyes Catholicos

and a smooth, shuffling step. Watch the musicians. Flamenco guitarists, with their lightning-fast finger-roll strums, are among the best in the world. The intricate rhythms are set by castanets or the hand-clapping (called *palmas*) of those who aren't dancing at the moment. In the raspy-voiced wails of the singers, you'll hear echoes of the Muslim call to prayer.

Like jazz, flamenco thrives on improvisation. Also like jazz, good flamenco is more than just technical proficiency. A singer or dancer with "soul" is said to have *duende*. Flamenco is a happening, with bystanders clapping along and egging on the dancers with whoops and shouts. Get into it. For a tourist-oriented flamenco show, your hotel can get you night-club show tickets (happily, since they snare a hefty commission for each sale). But it's easy to book a place on your own.

Casa de la Memoria de Al-Andalus ("House of the Memory of Al-Andalus"), run by Andalusian-culture devotees Sebastián and Rosana, offers more of an intimate concert with a smaller cast and more classic solos. Other, touristy flamenco shows give you all the clichés, and they can feel crass; here, you'll enjoy an elegant and classy musical experience. In an alcohol-free atmosphere, 90 tourists sit on three rows of folding chairs circling a small stage for shows featuring flamenco and other Andalusian music performed by young professional local musicians. It's all acoustic, and the nightly musical mix varies according to the personalities of the performers. It's also a perfect place to practice your Spanish fan *(abanico)* skills on warm nights. Concerts are nightly all year at 21:00. With demand, shows are added at 22:30 in summer, or 19:30 during the rest of the year (€15, one-hour shows, reservations smart, box office open 10:00–14:00 and 18:00–22:00, same-day tickets generally available but better to buy tickets a day or more beforehand, arrive early for front-row seats, in Barrio Santa Cruz, adjacent to Hotel Alcántara at Ximénez de Enciso 28, tel. 954-560-670, memoria@terra.es).

Los Gallos presents nightly two-hour shows at 20:00 and 22:30 (€30 ticket includes a drink, €3/person discount with this book in 2010—but limited to two admissions, arrive 30 min early for best seats, noisy bar but no food served, Plaza de la Santa Cruz 11, tel. 954-216-981, managers José and Nuria promise goose bumps).

El Arenal has arguably more professional performers and a classier setting for its show—but dinner customers get the preferred seating, and waiters are working throughout the performance (€36 ticket includes a drink, €70 includes dinner, shows at 20:00 and 22:00, near bullring at Calle Rodó 7, tel. 954-216-492).

El Patio Sevillano is more of a variety show (€37 ticket includes a drink, 15 percent discount with Sevilla Card, shows at 19:00 and 21:30, next to bullring at Paseo de Cristóbal Colón, tel. 954-214-120).

The packaged shows described above can be a bit sterile, and an audience of tourists doesn't help. But I find both Los Gallos and El Arenal entertaining and riveting. While El Arenal may have a slight edge on talent, Los Gallos has a cozier setting, with cushy rather than hard chairs—and it's a bit cheaper.

Impromptu flamenco still erupts spontaneously in bars throughout the old town after midnight. Just follow your ears as you wander down Calle Betis, leading off Plaza de Cuba across the bridge. The **Lo Nuestro** and **Rejoneo** bars are local favorites (at Calle Betis 31A and 31B). Or find these:

Bar El Tamboríl is a funky local bar dedicated to the Virgin Mary—buried in the touristy Santa Cruz neighborhood, yet somehow still overlooked. It comes to life each midnight with a sung prayer. This kicks off the impromptu flamenco music (tourists welcome, no cover—just buy a drink, €4 wine, €7 cocktails, 50 yards in front of the Los Gallos flamenco show at Plaza de Santa Cruz, mobile 652-188-244).

La Carbonería Bar is the sangria equivalent of a beer garden. If the Beach Boys sang flamenco, they'd hang out here. It's a sprawling place with a variety of rooms leading to a big open tented area filled with young locals, casual guitar strummers, and nearly nightly flamenco music after midnight (no dancing). Located just a few blocks from most of my recommended hotels, this is worth finding if you're not quite ready to end the day (no cover, €2 sangria, daily 20:00–3:00 in the morning; near Plaza Santa María—find Hotel Fernando III, the side alley Céspedes dead-ends at Levies, head left to Levies 18, unsigned door).

Sleeping in Sevilla

All of my listings are centrally located, mostly within a five-minute walk of the cathedral. The first are near the charming but touristy Santa Cruz neighborhood. The last group is just as central but closer to the river, across the boulevard in a more workaday, less touristy zone.

Room rates as much as double during the two Sevilla fiestas (Holy Week—March 28–April 4 in 2010; and the weeklong

Sleep Code

(€1 = about $1.40, country code: 34)
S = Single, **D** = Double/Twin, **T** = Triple, **Q** = Quad, **b** = bathroom,
s = shower only. Unless otherwise noted, credit cards are accepted, hoteliers speak enough English, tax is usually included, and breakfast generally costs extra.

To help you easily sort through these listings, I've divided the rooms into three categories, based on the price for a standard double room with bath during high season:

$$$ **Higher Priced**—Most rooms €100 or more.
 $$ **Moderately Priced**—Most rooms between €60-100.
  $ **Lower Priced**—Most rooms €60 or less.

April Fair, held two weeks after Easter—April 20–25 in 2010). In general, the busiest and most expensive months are April, May, September, and October. Hotels put rooms on the discounted push list in July and August—when people with any sense avoid this furnace—and from November through February. Prices generally include the 7 percent IVA tax. A price range indicates low- to high-season prices (but I have not listed festival prices). Ground-floor rooms come with more noise. Ask for upper floors *(piso alto)*. Always telephone to reconfirm what you think is a reservation.

If you do visit in July or August, the best values are central business-class places. They offer summer discounts and provide a necessary cool, air-conditioned refuge. But be warned that Spain's air-conditioning often isn't the icebox you're used to, especially in Sevilla. The best setup is an individual remote-controlled air-conditioner. If a hotel has central air-conditioning, owners often turn it off during the day—and even when it's on, they control the temperature.

Santa Cruz Neighborhood

These places are off Calle Santa María la Blanca and Plaza Santa María. The most convenient parking lot is the underground Cano y Cueto garage near the corner of Calle Santa María la Blanca and Menéndez Pelayo (€18/day, open 24/7, at edge of big park, unsigned). A fine Internet café and self-service launderette are a couple of blocks away up Menéndez Pelayo (see "Helpful Hints").

$$$ Hotel Las Casas de la Judería has quiet, elegant rooms and suites tastefully decorated with hardwood floors and a Spanish flair. The rooms, which surround a series of peaceful courtyards,

Santa Cruz Hotels, Restaurants, and Flamenco

1. Hotel Las Casas de la Judería
2. Hotel Amadeus, La Música de Sevilla, Pensión Córdoba & Hostal Buen Dormir
3. Hotel Alcántara & Casa de la Memoria de Al-Andalus (Flamenco, Music)
4. YH Giralda
5. Pensión San Benito
6. Cervecería Giralda
7. Bodega Santa Cruz
8. Las Teresas Bar
9. Corral del Agua Restaurante
10. Restaurante Modesto (2)
11. Freiduría Puerta de la Carne
12. Bar Restaurante El 3 de Oro
13. Restaurante San Marco
14. Café Bar Carmela
15. Los Gallos Flamenco
16. Bar El Tamboril
17. To La Carbonería Bar
18. To Internet Café & Launderette

are a romantic splurge (Sb-€112, Db-€140–200, extra bed-€45; low-season prices—July, Aug, and late-Nov–Feb—are discounted a further 10 percent to those with this book who ask in 2010, but check their website for even better rates; expensive but great buffet breakfast-€19, air-con, elevator, valet parking-€19/day, Plaza Santa María 5, tel. 954-415-150, fax 954-422-170, www.casasypalacios.com, juderia@casasypalacios.com).

$$ Hotel Amadeus is a little gem that music-lovers will appreciate (it even has a couple of soundproof rooms with pianos—something I've never seen anywhere else in Europe). It's lovingly decorated with a music motif around a little courtyard and a modern glass elevator that takes you to a roof terrace. While small, this 14-room place is classy and comfortable, with welcoming public spaces and a very charming staff. The €8.50 breakfast comes on a trolley—enjoy it in your room, in the lounge, or in the delightful roof garden (Sb-€88, Db-€98, big Db-€115, 2 suites-€125 and €155, cheaper July–Aug, air-con, elevator, free Internet access, laundry-€15, Calle Farnesio 6, tel. 954-501-443, fax 954-500-019, www.hotelamadeussevilla.com, reservas@hotelamadeussevilla.com, wonderfully run by María Luisa and her staff—Zaida and Cristina). Their next-door annex is every bit as charming and a similarly good value: **$$$ La Música de Sevilla** offers six additional, beautifully appointed rooms; three rooms face the interior patio, and three are streetside with small balconies (patio Db-€115, exterior Db-€136, air-con, reserve and check in at Hotel Amadeus).

$$ Hotel Alcántara offers more no-nonsense comfort than character. Well-located but strangely out of place in the midst of the Santa Cruz jumble, it rents 21 slick rooms at a good price (Sb-€68, small Db-€79, bigger Db twin-€89, fancy Db-€112, 10 percent discount or a free breakfast—your choice—if you pay in cash and show this book in 2010, breakfast-€5, air-con, elevator, free Wi-Fi, rentable laptop, Ximénez de Enciso 28, tel. 954-500-595, fax 954-500-604, www.hotelalcantara.net, info@hotelalcantara.net). The hotel is adjacent to Casa de la Memoria de Al-Andalus, which offers concerts (described earlier under "Flamenco").

$$ YH Giralda, once an 18th-century abbots' house, is now a charming 14-room hotel tucked away on a little street right off Mateo Gagos, just a couple of blocks from the cathedral. The exterior rooms have windows onto a pedestrian street, and a few of the interior rooms have small windows that look into the inner courtyard (Sb-€54–80, Db-€62–90, Tb-€109–123, more on weekends, no breakfast, air-con, Calle Abades 30, tel. 954-228-324, fax 954-227-019, www.yh-hoteles.com, yhgiralda@yh-hoteles.com).

Auditoro Álvarez Quintero

Flamenco Show → view #48

Hotel Becquer

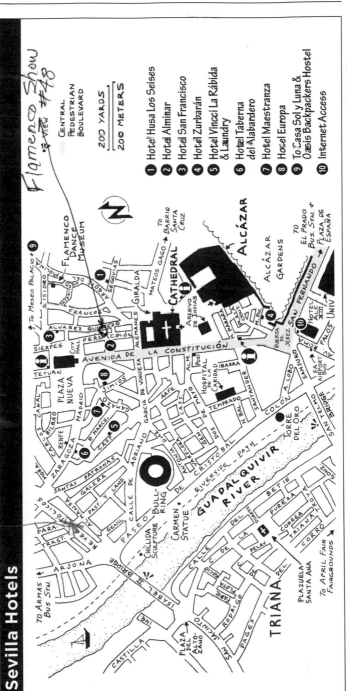

Sevilla Hotels

1 Hotel Husa Los Seises
2 Hotal Alminar
3 Hotel San Francisco
4 Hotel Zurbarán
5 Hotel Vincci La Rábida & Laundry
6 Hotel Taberna del Alabardero
7 Hotel Maestranza
8 Hocel Europa
9 To Casa Sol y Luna & Oasis Backpackers Hostel
10 Internet Access

200 YARDS
200 METERS

$ Pensión Córdoba, a homier and cheaper option, has 12 tidy, quiet rooms, solid modern furniture, and a showpiece tiled courtyard (S-€30, Sb-€40, D-€50, Db-€60, no breakfast, cash only, central air-con—on from evening to morning, on a tiny lane off Calle Santa María la Blanca at Farnesio 12, tel. 954-227-498, www.pensioncordoba.com, Ana and María).

$ Hostal Buen Dormir ("Good Sleep") is a quirky little family-run place with turtles and children in the blue-tinted courtyard. They rent 17 cheap, clean, basic rooms on a very quiet traffic-free lane. If there's a problem with your room, go to reception. Rene says if you don't tell him, he can't fix it (S-€20, D-€30, Ds-€35, Db-€40, Ts-€50, Tb-€55, air-con in all rooms except singles, Farnesio 8, tel. 954-217-492, Miriam and Rene).

$ Pensión San Benito, with eight humble rooms, faces a traditional Sevilla courtyard buried at the end of a dead-end lane just off Plaza Santa María. The rooms are dark, with windows that open onto an inner courtyard. The hardworking owners don't speak English, but offer some of the most conveniently located cheap rooms in town (S-€20, D-€36, Db-€42, Tb-€60, no breakfast, no air-con, parking-€12, on a tiny lane next to Cano y Cueto at Calle Canarios 4, tel. 954-415-255, www.hostalsanbenito.com, burlon11@hotmail.com, the woman of the house—Charo—has that coo-chee-coo Charo attitude). They also rent two fully equipped apartments next door (about €35/person).

Near the Cathedral

$$$ Hotel Husa Los Seises is a modern 42-room business-class place spliced tastefully into the tangled old town. It offers a fresh and spacious reprieve for anyone ready for a mix of old and contemporary luxury. You'll eat breakfast amid Roman ruins. Its rooftop garden includes a pool and a great cathedral view (Db-€170–215, Tb for €30 more, lower prices in July–Aug and Dec–Feb, breakfast-€16, air-con, elevator, valet parking-€20/day, 2 blocks northwest of cathedral at Segovias 6, tel. 954-229-495, fax 954-224-334, www.hotellosseises.com, info@hotellosseises.com).

$$$ Hotel Alminar, opened in 2005, is a plush and elegant little place that rents 12 fresh, slick, minimalist rooms (Db-€95–125, superior Db-€115–155, extra bed-€25, breakfast-€6, air-con, just 100 yards from the cathedral at Álvarez Quintero 52, tel. 954-293-913, fax 954-212-197, www.hotelalminar.com, reservas@hotelalminar.com).

$$ Hotel San Francisco may have a classy facade, but inside it's sparse, clean, and quiet. It offers 17 rooms with metal doors and a central location (Sb-€40–55, Db-€50–68, Tb-€62–80, no breakfast, air-con, elevator, small rooftop terrace, located on quiet pedestrian street at Álvarez Quintero 38, tel. 954-501-541, www .sanfranciscoh.com, info@sanfranciscoh.com, Carlos).

$$ **Hotel Zurbarán** needs a fresh coat of blue paint, but its nine rooms are a decent deal, and the courtyard is pleasantly decorated with hanging plants and wicker furniture (Db-€55–90, Tb €60–90, book direct for these rates, air-con, Mariana de Pineda 10, tel. 954-210-646, hostalzubaran@grupo-piramide.com).

West of Avenida de la Constitución

$$$ **Hotel Vincci La Rábida,** part of a big, impersonal hotel chain, offers four-star comfort with its 90 rooms, huge and inviting courtyard lounge, and powerful air-conditioning. Its pricing is dictated by a magical computer that has perfect price discrimination down to a science (see website for prices; on average it's Db-€132, spiking to €200 when possible and dipping to €80 during slow times, when that air-con is most welcome; Castelar 24, tel. 954-501-280, fax 954-216-600, www.vinccihoteles.com, larabida @vinccihoteles.com).

$$$ **Hotel Taberna del Alabardero** is a unique hotel with only seven rooms occupying the top floor of a poet's mansion (above a classy restaurant, Taberna del Alabardero, listed in "Eating"). It's nicely located and a great value. The ambience is perfectly 1900 (Db-€130–160, Db suite-€150–190, 10 percent discount with this book in 2010, includes breakfast, air-con, elevator, closed in Aug, Zaragoza 20, tel. 954-502-721, fax 954-563-666, www.taberna delalabardero.es, hotel.alabardero@esh.es).

$$ **Hotel Maestranza,** sparkling with loving care and charm, has 18 small, clean, simple rooms well-located on a street just off Plaza Nueva. To escape the noise from the tapas bars below, ask for an interior room, especially on weekends (Sb-€53, Db-€87, extra bed-€20, 5 percent cash discount, check website for seasonal rates, family suite, no breakfast, air-con, elevator, free Wi-Fi, Gamazo 12, tel. 954-561-070, fax 954-214-404, www.hotelmaestranza.es, sevilla@hotelmaestranza.es, Antonio).

$$ **Hotel Europa** is a somber and sturdy place renting 23 rooms around an elegant wicker-furniture courtyard in what was a traditional old mansion (Db-€50–90, 40 percent more for Tb, 10 percent discount if you show this book and pay cash in 2010, no breakfast, air-con, elevator, parking-€16/day, 200 yards from cathedral and Plaza Nueva on a tranquil street, Calle Jimios 5, tel. 954-500-443, fax 954-210-016, www.hoteleuropasevilla.com, info@hoteleuropasevilla.com, Claudio).

North of Plaza Nueva, Between Plaza de la Encarnación and Plaza de la Alfalfa

$ Casa Sol y Luna is quaint, with a cordial staff. Run by an Englishman named Geno and his Spanish wife, Esther, it's inexpensive, but a bit farther (10-min walk) from the cathedral (S-€22, D-€38, Db-€45, cash only, Calle Pérez Galdós 1A, tel. 954-210-682, www.casasolyluna1.com, info@casasolyluna1.com).

$ Oasis Backpackers Hostel is the best new spot for cheap beds and a fine place to hang out and connect with young backpackers. Each room, with four double bunks, comes with a modern bathroom and individual lockers. The rooftop terrace—with lounge chairs, a small pool, and adjacent kitchen—is well-used (64 bunk beds in 8 rooms, €15–20/bed, includes breakfast, free Internet access, just off Plaza de la Encarnación behind the church at #29 1/2 on the tiny and quiet lane, tel. 954-293-777, www.hostelsoasis .com). They also have popular branches in Lisbon and Granada.

Eating in Sevilla

Local soups, such as *salmorejo* (Córdoba-style super-thick *gazpacho*) and *ajo blanco* (almond-based with garlic), are tasty. A popular Andalusian meal is fried fish, particularly marinated *adobo*. I like *taquitos de merluza* (hake fish), but for a mix of fish, ask for *frito variado*.

Restaurants generally serve lunch from 13:00 to 16:00 and dinner from 20:00 until very late (Spaniards don't start dinner until about 21:00). If you're hungry for dinner before the locals are, do the tapas tango. Wash down your tapas with *fino* (chilled dry sherry) or the more refreshing *tinto de verano* ("summer red wine"), an Andalusian red wine with soda, like a mild sangria. A good, light white wine is *barbadillo*. And for a heavy red, always go for the Rioja.

Eating in Triana, Across the River

The colorful Triana district—on the west bank of the river, between the San Telmo and Isabel II bridges—is filled with rustic and fun eateries. The riverside and traffic-free Calle Betis is lined with a variety of places to eat, from fine riverside restaurants to sloppy fish joints. It also comes with good picnic and take-out opportunities for romantic urchins.

Tapas in a Triana Neighborhood Joint

Bars along the river and the parallel street one block inland are good for tapas. Before sitting down, walk to the Santa Ana church (midway between the bridges, two blocks off the river), where

Sevilla Restaurants and Flamenco

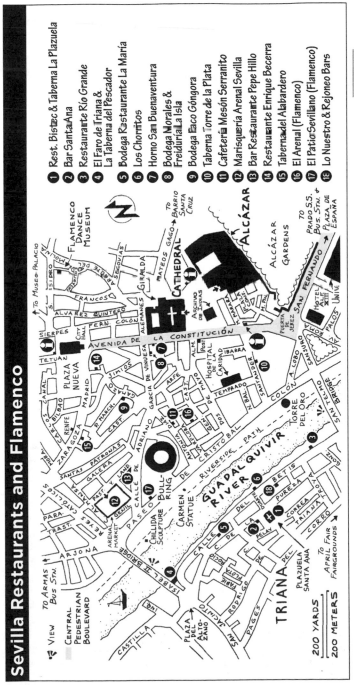

1. Rest. Bistec & Taberna La Plazuela
2. Bar Santa Ana
3. Restaurante Río Grande
4. El Faro de Triana & La Taberna del Pescador
5. Bodega Restaurante La María
6. Los Chorritos
7. Horno San Buenaventura
8. Bodega Morales & Freiduría La Isla
9. Bodega Paco Góngora
10. Taberna Torre de la Plata
11. Cafetería Mesón Serranito
12. Marisquería Arenal Sevilla
13. Bar Restaurante Pepe Hillo
14. Restaurante Enrique Becerra
15. Taberna del Alabardero
16. El Arenal (Flamenco)
17. El Patio Sevillano (Flamenco)
18. Lo Nuestro & Rejoneo Bars

tables spill into the square (Plazuela de Santa Ana) in the shadow of the floodlit church spire. It feels like the whole neighborhood is out celebrating.

Restaurante Bistec, with most of the square's tables, does grilled fish with gusto. They're enthusiastic about their cod cakes and calamari. Consider their indoor seating and the fun at the bar before sitting out on the square (€7 half-*raciones,* €13 full *raciones,* Thu–Tue 11:30–16:00 & 20:00–24:00, closed Wed, also closed Sun afternoons in winter, Plazuela de Santa Ana, tel. 954-274-759).

Taberna La Plazuela is self-service, doing simpler fare with enticing €12 *tostones* (giant fancy Andalusian bruschetta, good for 3–4 people) and €2 *montaditos* (little sandwiches). Get what you want and grab a table on the leafy square. Ignore the printed menu and read the daily specials board (same hours and owners as Restaurante Bistec, earlier).

Bar Santa Ana, just a block away on the side of the church, is a rustic neighborhood sports-and-bull bar with great seating on the street. Peruse the interior, draped in bullfighting and Weeping Virgin memorabilia. It's always busy with the neighborhood gang enjoying fun tapas like *delicia de solomillo* (tenderloin) and the bar's willingness to serve even cheap tapas at the outdoor tables (long hours, typically closed one day per week—closed Sun during April Fair, facing the side of the church at Pureza 82, tel. 954-272-102).

Riverside Dinners in Triana

Restaurante Río Grande is your stuffy, candlelit-fancy option— *the* place for a restaurant dinner with properly attired waiters and a full menu rather than tapas. Dining on the terrace is less expensive and more casual (€35 dinners, daily 13:00–16:00 & 20:00–24:00, air-con, paella and rice dishes are the house specialty, next to the San Telmo Bridge, tel. 954-273-956).

El Faro de Triana is actually the old yellow bridge tower overlooking the Isabel II Bridge. While professional, it's less formal and quirkier than Río Grande. They offer inexpensive tapas, €15 à la carte dishes, and grand views over the river from the top floor (the views are better than the food). Choose from four dining zones: rooftop, outdoor terrace just below the rooftop (perhaps the best), riverside metal tables on the sidewalk, and the bar. There's no cover charge, but they don't serve tapas on the roof or riverside (open daily, bar—8:00–24:00, restaurant—13:00–17:00 & 20:15–24:00, tel. 954-336-192).

La Taberna del Pescador, with tablecloths on its riverside tables, is fancier and more expensive (€12 and up *raciones* on the river, Wed–Mon 12:00–16:00 & 20:00–24:00, closed Tue, 50 yards from Puente de Isabel II on Calle Betis, tel. 954-330-069).

Bodega Restaurante La María also offers fine tablecloth-type restaurant seating on the riverside, but with a formal menu rather than tapas (€18 fish and meat plates, Wed–Mon 13:00–16:00 & 20:00–24:00, closed Tue, Calle Betis 12, tel. 954-338-461).

Los Chorritos is a carefree and sloppy riverside eatery—my choice for hearty seafood, great prices, and a fun atmosphere. They are enthusiastic about what the menu calls "roast" sardines—grilled rather than fried. Their banner reads, roughly, "Sardines rule. They don't bite. Can't eat just one. Go for it" (€6 half *raciones*, €10 *raciones*, closed Mon and in winter, about midway between the two bridges on Calle Betis, tel. 954-331-499).

Near Recommended Hotels in Barrio Santa Cruz

These eateries—for tapas, dining, and cheap eats—are handy to my recommended Barrio Santa Cruz accommodations.

Tapas

For tapas, the Barrio Santa Cruz is trendy and *romántico*. Plenty of atmospheric-but-touristy restaurants fill the neighborhood near the cathedral and along Calle Santa María la Blanca. From the cathedral, walk up Mateos Gago, where several classic old bars—with the day's tapas scrawled on chalkboards—keep tourists and locals well-fed and watered. (Turn right at Mesón del Moro for several more.)

Cervecería Giralda is a long-established meeting place for locals. It's famous for its fine tapas (confirm prices, stick with straight items on menu rather than expensive trick specials proposed by waiters; open long hours daily, Mateos Gago 1).

A block farther, you'll find **Bodega Santa Cruz** (a.k.a. **Las Columnas**), a popular standby with good, cheap tapas and *montaditos* (little sandwiches). You can keep an eye on the busy kitchen from the bar, or hang out like a cowboy at the tiny stand-up tables out front. Separate chalkboards list €2 tapas and €2 *montaditos*.

Las Teresas is a characteristic small bar draped in fun photos. It serves good tapas from a tight little user-friendly menu. Prices at the bar and outside tables (for fun tourist-watching) are the same, but they serve tapas only at the bar. The hams (with little upside-down umbrellas to catch the dripping fat) are a reminder that they are enthusiastic about their cured-meat dishes (open daily but sometimes closed for the siesta, Calle Santa Teresa 2, tel. 954-213-069).

Dining

Corral del Agua Restaurante, a romantic pink-tablecloth place with a smart interior and charming courtyard seating, serves fine

Andalusian cuisine deep in the Barrio Santa Cruz (€18 entrées, 3-course lunch special with wine for €20, Mon–Sat 12:00–16:00 & 20:00–24:00, closed Sun, arrive early or reserve ahead, Calle Agua 6, tel. 954-224-841).

Restaurante Modesto is a local favorite serving pricey but top-notch Andalusian fare—especially fish—with a comfortable dining room and atmospheric outdoor seating in the bright, bustling square just outside the Barrio Santa Cruz. They offer creative, fun meals—look around before ordering—and a good €20 fixed-price lunch or dinner served by energetic, occasionally pushy waiters. Their mixed salad is a meal, and their *fritura modesto* (fried seafood plate) is popular (€14.50, inside open daily 12:00–17:00 & 20:00–24:00, outside tables open daily 12:00–24:00, near Santa María la Blanca at Cano y Cueto 5, tel. 954-416-811). Note that they have indoor dining areas on both sides of the street (busy bar at one, non-smoking zone—in other words, tourists—at the other).

Eating Cheaply in Barrio Santa Cruz and Plaza Santa María la Blanca

Freiduría Puerta de la Carne and **Bar Restaurante El 3 de Oro** are a fried-fish-to-go place, with great outdoor seating, and a restaurant across the street serving fine wine or beer. You can order a cheap cone of tasty fried fish with a tomato salad, and sip a nice drink (served by a waiter from the restaurant), all while enjoying a great outdoor setting—almost dining for the cost of a picnic. Study the photos of the various kinds of seafood available—*un quarto* (250 grams for about €5) serves one (Mon–Sat until 24:00, Sun lunch only, Santa María la Blanca 34, tel. 954-426-820).

Restaurante San Marco offers cheap pizza and fun, basic Italian cuisine under the arches of what was a Moorish bath in the Middle Ages (and a disco in the 1990s). The air-conditioned atmosphere is easygoing and family-friendly, yet not cheesy (good salads, pizza, and pasta for €8, daily 13:00–16:15 & 20:00–24:00, Calle Mesón del Moro 6, tel. 954-564-390).

Breakfast on Plaza Santa María la Blanca: Several nondescript places seem to keep travelers happy at breakfast time on the sunny main square near most of my recommended hotels. I like **Café Bar Carmela.** For the cost of a continental breakfast at your hotel (€6), you can have a hearty American-style breakfast on the square (easy menus, metal tables, open from 9:30, Calle Santa María la Blanca 6, tel. 954-540-590).

Between the Cathedral and the River

I don't like the restaurants surrounding the cathedral, but many good places are just across Avenida de la Constitución. In the area between the cathedral and the river, you can find tapas, cheap eats, and fine dining.

Tapas

Calle García de Vinuesa leads past several colorful and cheap tapas places to a busy corner surrounded with happy eateries.

Horno San Buenaventura, across from the cathedral, is slick, chrome-filled, spacious, and handy for tapas, coffee, pastries, and ice cream. They are understandably happy to be booming now, thanks to the newly pedestrianized boulevard (open daily, light meals are posted by the door, avoid the frozen paella, good quiet seating upstairs).

Bodega Morales is farther up Calle García de Vinuesa, at #11. The front area is more of a drinking bar—go in the back section (around the corner) to munch tiny sandwiches *(montaditos)* and tapas, and sip wine among huge kegs. Everything is the same price (€2 *montaditos*, €2 tapas, €6 half-*raciones*—order at the bar), with the selections chalked onto giant adobe jugs (Mon–Sat 12:00–16:00 & 20:00–24:00, closed Sun, tel. 954-22-1242).

Freiduría La Isla, next door, has been frying fish since 1938 (they just renovated...and changed the oil). Along with *pescado frito,* they also sell wonderful homemade potato chips and fried almonds. It's family-friendly, with an easy English menu. Try their €5 *adobo* (marinated shark) or *frito variado* for a fish sampler. It's pretty much all fried fish, except for a tomato and pepper dish and their €1.20 *gazpacho,* offered only in the summer (Mon 20:00–23:00, Tue–Sat 13:00–15:30 & 20:00–23:00, closed Sun).

Bodega Paco Góngora is colorful and a bit classier than most tapas bars, with a tight dining area and delightful tapas dishes served at the bar. Its sit-down meals are well-presented and reasonably priced (daily 13:00–16:00 & 20:00–24:00, sometimes closed on Wed, ask for the English menu, off Plaza Nueva at Calle Padre Marchena 1, tel. 954-214-139).

Cheap Eats Between the Cathedral and the River

Taberna Torre de la Plata is a handy-to-the-Alcázar eatery close to the sights, but tucked away enough that it's mostly patronized by locals who appreciate its tasty dishes. Local guides take lunch here in the cool, quiet back courtyard (€10 plates, wine list, midway between the cathedral and the Torre del Oro at Calle Santander 1, tel. 954-228-761).

Cafetería Mesón Serranito is a family-friendly diner full of bull lore and happily munching locals (€9 *platos combinados,* Antonia Díaz 11, tel. 954-211-243).

Mercado del Arenal, the covered fish-and-produce market, is ideal for both snapping photos and grabbing a cheap lunch.

As with most markets, you'll find characteristic little diners with prices designed to lure in savvy shoppers, not to mention a crispy fresh world of picnic goodies—and a riverside promenade with benches just a block away (Mon–Sat 9:00–14:30, closed Sun, sleepy on Mon, on Calle Pastor y Landero at Calle Arenal, just beyond bullring). There's also a fancier fish restaurant in the market with a great lunch deal (see Taberna del Alabardero, in next section).

Dining Between the Cathedral, Plaza Nueva, and the River

Marisquería Arenal Sevilla is a popular fish restaurant that thrives in the middle of the Arenal Market. When the market closes (daily at 14:30), this eatery stays open. You'll be eating in the empty Industrial Age market with workers dragging their crates around. It's a great family-friendly, finger-licking-good scene much appreciated by its enthusiastic local following. Fish is priced by weight, so be careful when ordering, and always double-check the bill (€8–20 fish plates, generally open 13:00–17:00 & 21:00–24:00, in summer closed Sat night and all day Sun, rest of year closed Mon, reservations smart for dinner, Mercado Arenal, enter on Calle Pastor y Landero 9, tel. 954-220-881).

Bar Restaurante Pepe Hillo serves upscale bar food with a bull motif, across from the bullring (and, therefore, riotous after fights). One side is a youthful tapas bar. But the other side is a delightful oasis serving big half-*raciones* from an inviting menu with creative house specialties and a good wine list (enter on Calle Pastor y Landero, Adriano 24, tel. 954-215-390).

Restaurante Enrique Becerra is a fancy little 10-table place popular with local foodies. It's well-known for its gourmet Andalusian cuisine and fine wine. Muscle past the well-dressed locals at their tapas bar for gourmet snacks and wine by the glass. While the restaurant satisfies its guests with quality food, given the tight seating and its popularity with tourists, it can feel like a trap (€40 dinners, Mon–Sat 13:00–16:30 & 20:00–24:00, closed Sun, reservations essentially required, Gamazo 2, tel. 954-213-049).

Taberna del Alabardero, one of Sevilla's finest restaurants, serves refined Spanish cuisine in chandeliered elegance just a couple of blocks from the cathedral. If you order à la carte it will add up to about €45 a meal, but for €60 you can have a fun seven-course fixed-price meal with lots of little surprises from the chef. Or consider their €18/person (no sharing) starter sampler, followed by an entrée. The service in the fancy upstairs dining rooms gets mixed reviews (carefully read and understand your bill)...but the setting is stunning (daily 13:00–16:30 & 20:00–24:00, closed Aug, air-con, reservations smart, Zaragoza 20, tel. 954-502-721).

Taberna del Alabardero Student-Served Lunch: Their ground-floor dining rooms (elegant but nothing like upstairs) are popular with local office workers for their great-value student-chef-prepared fixed-price sampler (€13 for three delightful courses Mon–Fri, €18 Sat–Sun, drink not included, open daily 13:00–16:30). To avoid a wait, arrive before 14:00 (no reservations possible).

Connections

Note that many destinations are well-served by both trains and buses.

From Sevilla by AVE Train to Madrid: The AVE express train is expensive (€78, €8 cheaper during off-peak times, €10 reservation fee with railpass) but fast (2.5 hrs to Madrid; departures 7:00–21:45, 22/day). Departures between 16:00 and 19:00 can book up far in advance, but surprise holidays and long weekends can totally jam up trains as well—reserve as far ahead as possible.

From Sevilla by Train to Córdoba: The fast 45-minute AVE train goes hourly, but it's pricey for such a short journey (€30, €47 round-trip—must reserve both ways when you book, with railpass you still must pay €10 reservation fee). The slower train to Córdoba takes 80 minutes, costs only €9 each way, and comes with no reservation headaches.

Other Trains from Sevilla to: Málaga (11/day, 2 hrs on AVE or AVANT, 2.5 hrs on other trains), **Ronda** (2/day, 4 hrs, transfer in Bobadilla), **Granada** (4/day, 3 hrs), **Jerez** (12/day, 1.25 hrs), **Barcelona** (3/day, 6–12 hrs), **Algeciras** (3/day, 5 hrs, transfer at Córdoba, Antequera, or Bobadilla). Trains run to **Lisbon,** Portugal, but they take a long time, since they go through Madrid; buses to Lisbon are far better (see below). Train info: tel. 902-240-202, www.renfe.es.

From Sevilla by Bus to: Madrid (departures generally on the hour, 6 hrs, €20, tel. 902-229-292), **Córdoba** (9/day, 2 hrs), **Málaga** (9/day, 7 direct, 2.5–3.5 hrs, connects to Nerja), **Ronda** (5/day, 2.5 hrs, fewer on weekends), **Tarifa** (4/day, 3 hrs), **La Línea/ Gibraltar** (4/day, 4 hrs), **Granada** (11/day, 3 hrs *directo*, 4 hrs *ruta*), **Arcos** (2/day, 2 hrs, more departures with a transfer in Jerez), **Jerez** (7/day, 1.5 hrs), **Barcelona** (2/day), **Algeciras** (Linesur runs the most frequent direct buses—11/day, 2 direct, fewer on weekends, 2.25–2.5 hrs). Bus info: tel. 954-908-040 but rarely answered, go to TI for latest schedule info.

By Bus to Portugal: The best way to get to **Lisbon,** Portugal, is by bus (Alsa and Eurolines share a service offering 2/day, departures at 15:00 and 24:00, 7 hrs, €42 by way of Faro, departs Plaza de Armas Station, tel. 954-907-800 or 902-422-242, www.alsa.es). The midnight departure continues past Lisbon to **Coimbra** (arriving 9:45) and **Porto** (arriving 11:30). Sevilla also has a direct bus

SEVILLA

service to **Lagos,** Portugal, on the Algarve (4/day in summer, 2/day off-season, about 6 hrs, €20, buy ticket a day or two in advance May–Oct, tel. 954-907-737, www.damas-sa.es). The bus departs from Sevilla's Plaza de Armas bus station and arrives at the Lagos bus station. If you'd like to visit Tavira on the way to Lagos, purchase a bus ticket to Tavira, have lunch there, then take the train to Lagos.

Vanessa Montoya
Could not Bull
Kill the Fighter
Bull

GRANADA

For a time, Granada was the grandest city in Spain. But in the end, with the tumult that came with the change from Moorish to Christian rule, it eventually lost its power and settled into a long slumber. Today, Granada seems to specialize in evocative history and good living. We'll keep things fun and simple, settling down in the old center and exploring monuments of the Moorish civilization and its conquest. And we'll taste the treats of a North African–flavored culture that survives here today.

Granada's magnificent Alhambra fortress was the last stronghold of the Moorish kingdom in Spain. The city's exotically tangled Moorish quarter, the Albayzín, invites exploration. From its viewpoints, romantics can enjoy the sunset and evening views of the grand, floodlit Alhambra.

There is an old saying: "Give him a coin, woman, for there is nothing worse in this life than to be blind in Granada." This city has much to see, yet it reveals itself in unpredictable ways. It takes a poet to sort through and assemble the jumbled shards of Granada. Peer through the intricate lattice of a Moorish window. Hear water burbling unseen among the labyrinthine hedges of the Generalife Gardens. Listen to a flute trilling deep in the swirl of alleys around the cathedral. Don't be blind in Granada—open all your senses.

Planning Your Time

Granada is worth one day and two nights at a minimum. To use your time efficiently, reserve in advance for the Alhambra.

Here's the best intense one-day plan: In the morning, stroll the Pescadería market streets, follow my self-guided walk of the old town (or catch the 10:30 Cicerone walking tour), grab lunch, do the Alhambra in the afternoon (reservation essential), and tour the cathedral and Royal Chapel (both open roughly 16:00–19:30). Hike the hippie lane into the Albayzín Moorish quarter (or catch minibus #31 or #32) to the San Nicolás viewpoint for the magic hour, then find the right place for a suitably late dinner (taxi home for safety if in the Albayzín late).

When you're ready to move on, the Costa del Sol's best beach town, Nerja, is just a 1.5-hour drive or 2.5-hour bus ride away. You can also get to White Hill towns such as Ronda (by train) in that time; Sevilla is an easy three-hour train ride away. The Madrid–Granada train service is slow (5 hours), but passes through beautiful countryside.

Orientation to Granada

Modern Granada sprawls (300,000 people), but its sights are all within a 20-minute walk of Plaza Nueva, where dogs wag their tails to the rhythm of modern hippies and street musicians. Most of my recommended hotels are within a few blocks of Plaza Nueva. Make this the hub of your Granada visit.

Plaza Nueva was a main square back when kings called Granada home. This historic center is in the Darro River Valley, which separates two hills (the river now flows under the square). On one hill is the great Moorish palace, the Alhambra, and on the other is the best-preserved Moorish quarter in Spain, the Albayzín. To the southeast are the cathedral, Royal Chapel, and Alcaicería (Moorish market), where the city's two main drags—Gran Vía de Colón (often just called "Gran Vía" by locals) and Calle Reyes Católicos—lead away into the modern city.

Tourist Information

The main TI is tucked away just above Plaza Nueva on Santa Ana (above the church, Mon–Fri 9:00–19:30, Sat–Sun 9:30–15:00, tel. 958-575-202). Another TI is at the entrance of the Alhambra (March–Oct Mon–Sat 8:00–20:00, Nov–Feb until 18:00, year-round Sun 8:00–13:30, tel. 958-544-003). Both cover Granada as well as all Andalucía. At either TI, get a free city map and the *Pocket Guía* magazine in easy Spanish (English magazines not always available), and verify your Alhambra plans. To save yourself

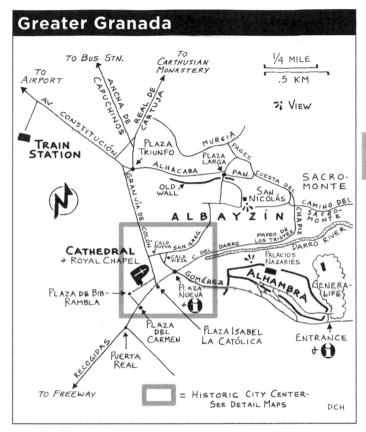

Greater Granada

a trip to the train or bus stations, get schedule information (both TIs list all departures on the wall). During peak season (April–Oct), TI kiosks sometimes pop up in Plaza Nueva and Plaza de Bib-Rambla.

Arrival in Granada

By Train: Granada's train station is connected to the center by frequent buses, a €5 taxi ride, or a 30-minute walk down Avenida de la Constitución and Gran Vía. The train station does not have luggage storage. If your itinerary is set, reserve your train out upon arrival.

Exiting the train station, walk straight ahead down the tree-lined Avenida Andaluces. At the first major intersection (Avenida de la Constitución), you'll see a series of bus stops on your right. Buses #3 through #9 (and most other buses—check the easy-to-read map at the stop) go to the cathedral, the nearest stop to Plaza Nueva—confirm by asking the driver, "¿Catedral?"

(kah-tay-DRAHL). Buy a €1.20 ticket from the driver. Get off at the cathedral; cross the busy Gran Vía and walk three short blocks to Plaza Nueva.

By Bus: Located on the city outskirts, Granada's bus station, Estación de Autobuses, has a good and cheap cafeteria, ATMs, luggage storage, and an info office (tel. 958-185-480 for the Alsa company, which serves Barcelona and east-coast destinations). To get to the center, either take a 10-minute taxi ride (€6) or bus #3 or #33 (€1.20, pay driver). It's about a 20-minute bus ride; nearing the center, the bus goes up Gran Vía. For Plaza Nueva, get off at the cathedral (cathedral not visible from bus), a half-block before the grand square called Plaza Isabel La Católica (a three-block walk from Plaza Nueva).

By Car: Driving in Granada's historic center is restricted to buses, taxis, and (technically) tourists with hotel reservations. Signs are posted to this effect, and entrance is strictly controlled—but generally not by an officer. Hidden cameras snap a photo of your license plate as soon as you enter the restricted zone. Getting into the old center and finding your hotel or a parking garage is a major frustration because of these strict controls and the many one-way streets. Your hotelier can contact the local police department to register your car (and prevent a nasty surprise when you return your rental car). Some hoteliers have deals with nearby garages and can give you detailed directions to those spots.

The *autovía* (freeway) circles the city with a *circunvalación* road (Ronda Sur). If you're heading for a hotel near Plaza Nueva, take exit #129, direction Centro, Recogidas. Calle Recogidas becomes Calle Reyes Católicos where it enters the restricted zone, and leads directly into the heart of town. There might be a police block at Puerta Real (Victoria Hotel) because driving down Calle Reyes Católicos is now heavily controlled. Technically, you can pull into Plaza Nueva if you have a hotel reservation, but the roadside posts—which have a list of hotels with button buzzers to gain drivers entry—generally do not work.

Granada has several parking garages. Parking San Agustín—near the cathedral, just off Gran Vía—costs more than the others, but is the only lot that's an easy walk to my recommended hotels (€25/day; as you approach Plaza Isabel La Católica on Gran Vía, follow blue *Parking* sign).

By Plane: Granada's sleepy airport, which serves only a dozen or so planes a day, is about 10 miles west of the city center. To get between the airport and downtown, you can take a taxi (€25) or, much cheaper, the airport bus, timed to leave when flights arrive and depart (€3, 12/day, 40 min). Use the bus stop at Gran Vía del Colón, nearly across from the cathedral. Airport info: tel. 958-245-223 (press "9" for English).

Helpful Hints

Theft Alert: Gypsy (Roma) women, usually hanging out near the cathedral and Alcaicería, will accost you with sprigs of rosemary. The twig is free...and then they grab your hand and read your fortune for a tip. Coins are bad luck, so the minimum payment they'll accept is €5. Don't make eye contact, don't accept a sprig, and say firmly but politely, *"No, gracias."* While aggressive (especially in the morning), these Spanish Roma are harmless. Locals warn that Gypsies from Romania (new arrivals who tend to have gold teeth) are more likely to be pickpockets. In general, be on guard for pickpockets, especially late at night in the Albayzín (see "Safety in the Albayzín"). Your biggest threat is being conned while enjoying drinks and music in Sacromonte.

City Pass: The **Bono Turístico** city pass covers the Alhambra, cathedral, Royal Chapel, Carthusian Monastery, sightseeing bus, and city buses, plus minor sights and discounts on others (€30, valid for five days). When you buy your pass, the vendor schedules a time for your Alhambra visit. Passes are sold at a kiosk on Plaza Nueva by the minibus stop. Or you can buy a pass and book your Alhambra palace visit in advance online (http://caja.caja-granada.es; click "Bono Turístico Info y Compra"). Note that some of the fancier hotels provide one free pass per room for stays of two or more nights.

Festivals and Concerts: From late June to early July, the International Festival of Music and Dance offers classical music, ballet, flamenco, and zarzuela (light opera) nightly in the Alhambra at reasonable prices. The ticket office is located in the Corral de Carbón (open mid-April–Oct). Beginning in February, you can also book tickets online at www.granadafestival.org. This festival is one of the most respected and popular in Spain, and tickets for major performers typically sell out months in advance. During the festival, flamenco is free every night at midnight; ask the ticket office or TI for the venue.

From fall through spring, the City of Granada Orchestra offers popular weekly concerts that generally sell out quickly (€5–20, Sept–May only, Auditorio Manuel de Falla, ticket office in Corral de Carbón, Mon–Fri 12:00–14:00 & 17:00–19:00, Sat 12:00–14:00, closed Sun, www.orquestaciudadgranada.es).

Granada at a Glance

▲▲▲**The Alhambra** The last and greatest Moorish palace, high-lighting the splendor of that civilization in the 13th and 14th centuries. Reservations are a must if you plan to visit during the day. **Hours:** The entire complex is open daily March–Oct 8:30–20:00, Nov–Feb 8:30–18:00. The Palacios Nazaries is open for night-time visits March–Oct Tue–Sat 22:00–23:30, closed Sun–Mon; Nov–Feb Fri–Sat 20:00–21:30, closed Sun–Thu. See page 65.

▲▲**Royal Chapel** Lavish 16th-century Plateresque Gothic chapel with the tombs of Queen Isabel and King Ferdinand. **Hours:** March–Oct Mon–Sat 10:30–13:30 & 16:00–19:30, opens Sun at 11:00; Nov–Feb Mon–Sat 10:30–13:30 & 15:30–18:30, opens Sun at 11:00. See page 87.

▲▲**San Nicolás Viewpoint** Breathtaking vista over the Alhambra and the Albayzín. **Hours:** Always open; best at sunset. See page 93.

▲**Cathedral** The second-largest cathedral in Spain, unusual for its bright Renaissance interior. **Hours:** April–Oct Mon–Sat 10:45–13:30 & 16:00–20:00, Sun 16:00–20:00; Nov–March until 19:00. See page 89.

Alcaicería Tiny shopping lanes filled with tacky tourist shops. **Hours:** Always open, with shops open long hours. See page 81.

Corral del Carbón Granada's only surviving caravanserai (inn for traveling merchants), with impressive Moorish door. **Hours:** Always viewable. See page 81.

Paseo de los Tristes A prime strolling strip above the Darro River lined with eateries and peppered with Moorish history. **Hours:**

Internet Access: Many Internet points are scattered throughout Granada, often part of *locutorios* (call centers). A handy, friendly place is just across from Hotel Anacapri (on Calle Joaquín Costa).

Post Office: It's on Puerta Real (Mon–Fri 8:30–20:30, Sat 9:30–14:00, closed Sun, tel. 958-221-138).

Travel Agencies: All travel agencies book flights, and many also sell long-distance bus and train tickets. **Viajes Bonanza** sells it all at Calle Reyes Católicos 30 (Mon–Fri 9:00–13:00 & 17:00–20:00, Sat 10:00–13:30, closed Sun, tel. 958-223-578). Mega-chain **El Corte Inglés** sells plane and train tickets, but doesn't handle bus travel (Mon–Sat 10:00–21:00, closed Sun, Acera del Darro, floor 2, tel. 958-220-425).

Always open; best in the evenings. See page 85.

Hammam El Bañuelo 11-century ruins of Moorish baths. **Hours:** Unreliably Tue–Sat 10:00–14:00, closed Sun–Mon. See page 86.

Albayzín Spain's best old Moorish quarter. **Hours:** Always open but use caution after dark. See page 91.

Great Mosque of Granada Islamic house of worship featuring a minaret with a live call to prayer, an information center for the Muslim perspective on Granada history, and a courtyard with commanding views. **Hours:** Daily 11:00–14:00 & 18:00–21:00. See page 94.

Hammam Baños Árabes Tranquil spot for soaks and massages in Arab baths. **Hours:** Daily 10:00–24:00. See page 97.

Zambra Dance Touristy flamenco-like dance performance in Sacromonte district. **Hours:** Shows generally daily at 22:00. See page 95.

Center for the Interpretation of Sacromonte Digs into geology and cave building, as well as Roma (Gypsy) crafts, food, and music. **Hours:** April–Oct Tue–Sun 10:00–14:00 & 17:00–21:00; Nov–March Tue–Sun 10:00–14:00 & 16:00–19:00, closed Mon. See page 96.

Carthusian Monastery Lavish Baroque monastery on the outskirts of town. **Hours:** Daily April–Oct 10:00–13:00 & 16:00–20:00, Nov–March 10:00–13:00 & 15:00–18:00. See page 97.

Getting Around Granada

With cheap taxis, frisky minibuses, good city buses, and nearly all points of interest an easy walk from Plaza Nueva, you'll get around Granada easily.

Tickets for minibuses and city buses cost €1.20 per ride (buy from driver). Credibus magnetic cards save you money if you'll be riding often—or, since they're shareable, if you're part of a group (€5/7 trips, €10/16 trips, plus €2 for each card issued, buy from driver, valid on minibuses and city buses, no fee for connecting bus if you transfer within 45 min).

By Minibus: Handy little red minibuses, which cover the city center, depart every few minutes from Plaza Nueva and Plaza Isabel La Católica until late in the evening (about 22:30). Here are a few handy minibus routes to look for:

Bus #32 is the best for a trip up to the Alhambra, connecting the Alhambra and Albayzín (from the cathedral and Plaza Isabel La Católica, the bus goes up to the Alhambra, returns to Plaza Isabel La Católica, then loops through the Albayzín and back down Gran Vía).

Bus #31 does the Albayzín loop, departing from Plaza Nueva.

Bus #34 is the same as #31, with a side-trip into Sacromonte.

Bus #30 would normally be the most direct and quickest bet for getting up to the Alhambra, but its route—up Cuesta de Gomérez—is closed through 2010 while the Granada Gate is being restored. Although Cuesta de Gomérez is closed to vehicle traffic, eager pedestrians can still hike up to the Alhambra.

By City Bus: These are handy if you're visiting the Carthusian Monastery (bus #8) or going to the bus station (#3 or #33) or train station (#3–#9).

Tours in Granada

Walking Tours—Cicerone, run by María and Rosa, offers informative 2.5-hour tours (€12, show this book to save €2, kids under 14 free, March–Oct daily at 10:30, Nov–Feb Wed–Sun at 11:00; to book a tour, visit the kiosk labeled *Meeting Points* on Plaza de Bib-Rambla, or call mobile 607-691-676, 670-541-669, or 600-412-051; www.ciceronegranada.com, info@ciceronegranada.com). Cicerone's excellent guides describe the fitful and fascinating changes the city underwent as it morphed from a Moorish capital to a Christian one 500 years ago. While it doesn't enter any actual sights, the tour weaves together bits of the Moorish heritage that survive around the cathedral and the Albayzín. Tours start on Plaza de Bib-Rambla and finish on Plaza Nueva. Groups are small (may cancel if less than five show up, although you have the option of paying more for it to go). Visits are generally only in English, but may be in both English and Spanish on slow days.

Local Guides—Margarita Ortiz de Landázuri, an English-speaking guide, is a charming and effective teacher (tel. 958-221-406, www.alhambratours.com, info@alhambratours.com). If Margarita is busy, her partner, Miguel Ángel, and her cousin, Patricia Ortiz de Landazuri Quero (patlandazuri@yahoo.es, tel. 619-053-972), are also very good. Guide rates are standard (€130/2.5 hours, €260/day).

This is Granada Audio Tour—This service provides you with a pre-loaded MP3 player and map, and covers the entire city including the Alhambra with a fine audio tour. Two people get the system for up to five days for €15 (rent from kiosk on Plaza Nueva).

Olive Oil Tour—This company helps you explore Granada's countryside and taste some local olive oil. The morning tours include lunch; the afternoon tours don't (€55 with lunch, €38 without, both in English, tel. 958-559-643, mobile 651-147-504, www.olive oiltour.com, reservas@oliveoiltour.com).

Self-Guided Tour

▲▲▲The Alhambra

This last and greatest Moorish palace is one of Europe's top sights. Attracting up to 8,000 visitors a day, it's the reason most tourists

come to Granada. Nowhere else does the splendor of Moorish civilization shine so beautifully.

The last Moorish stronghold in Europe is, with all due respect, really a symbol of retreat. Granada was only a regional capital for centuries. Gradually the Christian Reconquista moved south, taking Córdoba (1237) and Sevilla (1248). The Nazarids, one of the many diverse ethnic groups of Spanish Muslims, held together the last Moorish kingdom, which they ruled from Granada until 1492. As you tour their grand palace, remember that while Europe slumbered through the Dark Ages, Moorish magnificence blossomed—ornate stucco, plaster "stalactites," colors galore, scalloped windows framing Granada views, exuberant gardens, and water, water everywhere. Water—so rare and precious in most of the Islamic world—was the purest symbol of life to the Moors. The Alhambra is decorated with water: standing still, cascading, masking secret conversations, and dripdropping playfully.

Orientation: The Alhambra, not nearly as confusing as it might seem, consists of four sights clustered together atop a hill:

▲▲▲**Palacios Nazaries**—Exquisite Moorish palace, the one must-see sight.

▲**Generalife Gardens**—Fancy, manicured gardens with small summer palace.

▲**Charles V's Palace**—Christian Renaissance palace plopped on top of the Alhambra after the Reconquista, with a fine little Museo de la Alhambra (free entry).

Alcazaba—Empty old fort with tower and views.

These sights are described in more detail in "The Alhambra in Four Parts," below.

Cost: The Alcazaba fort, Palacios Nazaries, and Generalife Gardens require a €12 combo-ticket. Reservations are essential if you want to see Palacios Nazaries during the day (see sidebar). If the Palacios Nazaries is booked up, consider getting the €6 ticket that covers only the Generalife Gardens and Alcazaba, so you can view the garden and fort during the day, and then visit the palace at night (see "The Alhambra by Moonlight," below). Only Charles V's Palace is free.

Hours: The Alhambra is open daily March–Oct 8:30–20:00, Nov–Feb 8:30–18:00 (ticket office opens at 8:00, last entry one hour before closing, tel. 902-441-221). The Palacios Nazaries is also open most evenings (see below).

The Alhambra by Moonlight: If you're frustrated by the reservation system, or just prefer doing things after dark, late-night visits to the Alhambra are easy (reservations are generally unnecessary—just buy your ticket upon arrival) and magical (less crowded and beautifully lit). The night visits only include the Palacios Nazaries (not the Alcazaba fort or the

Generalife Gardens)—but, hey, the palace is 80 percent of the Alhambra's thrills anyway. For evening visits, it's open March–Oct Tue–Sat 22:00–23:30 (ticket office open 21:30–22:30), closed Sun–Mon; and Nov–Feb Fri–Sat 20:00–21:30 (ticket office open 19:30–20:30), closed Sun–Thu.

Getting to the Alhambra: There are three ways to get to the Alhambra:

1. From Plaza Nueva, hike 30 minutes up the street Cuesta de Gomérez. Keep going straight—you'll see the Alhambra high on your left. The ticket pavilion is on the far side of the Alhambra, near the Generalife Gardens.

2. From Plaza Isabel La Católica, catch a red #32 minibus, marked *Alhambra* (€1.20, runs every 15 min). There are three Alhambra stops: Justice Gate (below Palacios Nazaries and Charles V's Palace), Charles V, and Generalife (where you must pick up your tickets, closest to the gardens).

3. Take a taxi (€5, taxi stand on Plaza Nueva).

Don't drive. Though there's convenient parking near the entrance of the Alhambra (€1.50/hr), leaving via the one-way streets will send you into the traffic-clogged center of modern Granada.

Planning Your Visit: It's a 15-minute walk from the entry (at the top end) to Palacios Nazaries at the other end. Be sure to arrive at the Alhambra with enough time to make it to the palace before your allotted half-hour entry time slot ends. The ticket-checkers at Palacios Nazaries are strict. Remember that if you have an appointment for Palacios Nazaries after 14:00, you cannot get into the Alcazaba fort or the Generalife Gardens any earlier than 14:00. Once inside the Palacios Nazaries, you can stay as long as you want. Note that some rooms may be closed for renovation.

To minimize walking, see Charles V's Palace and the Alcazaba fort before your visit to Palacios Nazaries. When you finish touring the palace, you'll leave through the Partal Gardens near the Alhambra entrance, not far from the Generalife Gardens. Depending on the time, you can visit the Generalife Gardens before or after seeing Palacios Nazaries. If you have any time to kill before your palace appointment, do it luxuriously on the breezy view terrace of the parador bar (actually within the Alhambra walls). There are drinks, WCs, and guidebooks near the entrance of Palacios Nazaries, but none inside the actual palace.

If you're going to the Albayzín afterwards, catch minibus #32, which goes from the three Alhambra stops back through Plaza Isabel La Católica and then up into the Albayzín. Or, for a delightful escape, walk back into town along the Cuesta de los Chinos. (It starts near the ticket booth, by Restaurante La Mimbre and the minibus stop.) You'll walk on a desolate lane downhill along a stream, beneath the Alhambra ramparts, and past the sultan's cobbled horse lane leading up to Generalife Gardens. In 10 minutes you're back in town at Paseo de los Tristes. You can't get lost.

Audioguide: The €4 audioguide brings the palace to life, providing two hours of description for 48 stops (rent it at the entrance or at Charles V's Palace; you'll need to return it where you picked it up). Audioguides are not available for night visits.

Guidebooks: Consider getting a guidebook in town and reading it the night before to understand the layout and history of this remarkable sight before entering. The classic is *The Alhambra and the Generalife* (€10, includes great map, sold in town and throughout the Alhambra). I prefer the slick *Alhambra and Generalife in Focus*, which is more readable, has vibrant color photos, and costs less (€8, at bookstores). The "official guide" is not as good.

Eating: The only eateries within the Alhambra walls are the restaurant at the parador, the courtyard of the Hotel América (with pricey meals but affordable sandwiches and a great peaceful ambience), a small bar-café kiosk in front of the Alcazaba fort

Getting a Reservation for the Alhambra's Palacios Nazaries

Many tourists never get to see the Alhambra's Palacios Nazaries, because tickets sell out. Make a reservation as soon as you're ready to commit to a time (especially during Holy Week, on weekends, or on major holidays). During the off-season (July–Aug and winter), you might be able to walk right in. While things are improving, the crowds can still be unpredictable; luckily, getting a reservation is quite easy.

The Alhambra complex's top sight is the Moorish palace—Palacios Nazaries. Only 300 visitors are allowed to enter per half-hour (in 50-person spurts every five minutes). You must enter during the 30-minute time slot printed on your ticket. Once inside the palace, you can linger as long as you like. If your entry time to Palacios Nazaries is before 14:00, you can stroll the Alhambra grounds anytime in the morning, see the palace at your appointed time, and leave the Alhambra by 14:00 (although you can get away with staying longer in the fort, gardens, or palace, you won't be allowed to *enter* any of these sites after 14:00). If your ticket is stamped for 14:00 or later, you cannot go inside the Alhambra grounds any earlier than 14:00. For instance, if you have a reservation to visit Palacios Nazaries between 16:30 and 17:00, you can enter the Alhambra grounds starting at 14:00 and see the fort and Generalife Gardens before the palace. (Because of the time restriction on afternoon visits, morning tickets sell out the quickest. But for most travelers, an afternoon is ample time to see the site—the light is perfect, and there are fewer tour groups.)

Reserving in Advance: There are four options, each with a €1 surcharge.

• Order online at www.alhambra-tickets.es. This is easy and just takes a few minutes. You can reserve online up to three months in advance of your visit.

• Order by phone. Within Spain, dial 934-923-750 (cheaper), 902-888-001, or 902-505-061. To call internationally, dial the international access code first (00 from a European country, 011 from the US or Canada), then 34-934-923-750 (daily 8:00–24:00, can reserve between one day and a year in advance; while waiting for an operator, a recording tells you the date of the next available tickets). Pay with a credit card (Visa, MasterCard, or American Express).

• If you plan to stay at one of the fancier hotels, ask—when you book your hotel room—if the hotelier can make a reservation for you to visit the Alhambra the day after your arrival.

• If you buy a Bono Turístico city pass in advance, you can also book your Alhambra appointment then (explained earlier in "Helpful Hints," page 61).

Picking Up Tickets: On the day of your tour, make sure you arrive at the Alhambra about an hour before your palace appointment, since the ticket line may require up to a 20-minute wait, and walking from the ticket office to the palace takes 15 minutes. Bring a photo ID and the same debit/credit card that you used to make the reservation. If you have a foreign card, you will need to wait in line at the windows marked *Retirada de Reservas* to pick up your tickets. Be prepared to enter your credit or debit card's PIN (this is the code required to withdraw cash, not your credit card's security code).

If You're in Granada Without a Palace Reservation: You have a number of options.

• Your hotel may able to book a reservation for you on short notice.

• Wake up early and stand in line. The Alhambra admits 7,800 visitors a day. Six thousand tickets are sold in advance. The remaining 1,800 are sold each day at the Alhambra ticket window labeled *Venta Directa*. The ticket office opens at 8:00, and on busy peak-season days, tickets can sell out quickly. (You'll hear periodic updates over the PA system about how many tickets are left for the day, which can help you judge whether it's worth waiting in line.) Generally, if you're in line by about 7:30, you'll get an entry time, probably for later that day. On a slow day, you'll get in right away. If the Palacios Nazaries is booked up during the day, you can get the €6 ticket that covers only the Generalife Gardens and the Alcazaba fort, then return to visit the palace at night (see "The Alhambra by Moonlight," page 66).

• If you'll be staying in Granada at least two days, consider getting the Bono Turístico city pass, which comes with an entry time to the Alhambra.

• Take a tour of the Alhambra. The pricier hotels can book you on an expensive €49 GranaVisión tour that includes transportation to the Alhambra and a guided tour of the Palacios Nazaries (tel. 958-535-875, www.visitargranada.com).

• Easiest of all, simply go at night (Palacios Nazaries only; see "The Alhambra by Moonlight," page 66).

GRANADA

The Alhambra

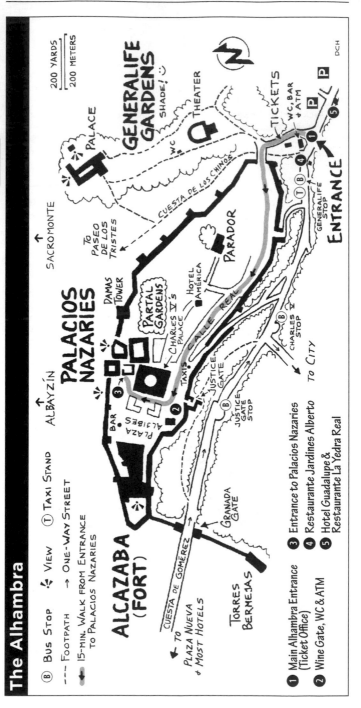

Ⓑ Bus Stop ⍨ View Ⓣ Taxi Stand

--- Footpath → One-Way Street

↓ 15-min. Walk from Entrance to Palacios Nazaries

200 YARDS
200 METERS

DCH

GENERALIFE GARDENS

PALACE

THEATER

SHADE! :)

WC

TICKETS

WC, BAR + ATM

P P

Ⓣ Ⓑ Ⓐ ①

GENERALIFE STOP

ENTRANCE

CUESTA DE LOS CHINOS

SACROMONTE

To PASEO DE LOS TRISTES

PARADOR

CALLE REAL

HOTEL AMÉRICA

CHARLES V STOP Ⓑ

DAMAS TOWER

PALACIOS NAZARIES

PARTAL GARDENS

CHARLES V'S PALACE

TAXIS

JUSTICE GATE

To CITY

ALBAYZÍN →

BAR

PLAZA ALCIBES

③ ②

JUSTICE GATE STOP Ⓑ

ALCAZABA (FORT)

GRANADA GATE

CUESTA DE GOMÉREZ

← To PLAZA NUEVA & MOST HOTELS

TORRES BERMEJAS

① Main Alhambra Entrance (Ticket Office)
② Wine Gate, WC & ATM
③ Entrance to Palacios Nazaries
④ Restaurante Jardines Alberto
⑤ Hotel Guadalupe & Restaurante La Yedra Real

(near Palacios Nazaries entrance), and vending machines (at the WC) near Charles V's Palace. You're welcome to bring in a picnic as long as you eat it in a public area. There are plenty of better-value options around the parking lot and ticket booth at the top of the complex. **Restaurante La Yedra Real** is your best economic sit-down eatery, and is located over the Alhambra parking lot (Tue–Sun 9:30–17:00, closed Mon, €3 sandwiches, easy photo menu, air-con, efficient, Paseo de la Sabica 28, tel. 958-229-145). Across from the breezy Restaurante La Mimbro, the **Restaurante Jardines Alberto,** with a nice courtyard and a more formal menu, feels a little less touristy.

GRANADA

Photography: Photos are permitted.

The Alhambra in Four Parts

I've listed these sights in the order you're likely to visit them.

▲▲Charles V's Palace and the Museo de la Alhambra

It's only natural for a conquering king to build his own palace over his foe's palace, and that's exactly what the Christian king Charles

V did. The Palacios Nazaries wasn't good enough for Charles, so he built this new home, which was financed by a salt-in-the-wound tax on Granada's defeated Muslim population. With a unique circle-within-a-square design by Pedro Machuca, a devotee of Michelangelo and Raphael, this is Spain's most impressive Renaissance building. Stand in the circular court-yard surrounded by mottled marble columns, then climb the stairs. Perhaps Charles' palace was designed to have a dome, but it was never finished—his son, Philip II, abandoned it to build his own much more massive palace, El Escorial. Even without the dome, acoustics are perfect in the center—stand in the middle and sing your best aria. The palace doubles as one of the venues for the popular International Festival of Music and Dance.

The **Museo de la Alhambra** (ground floor of Charles V's Palace, free) shows off some of the Alhambra's best surviving Moorish art, along with one of the lions from Palacios Nazaries' fountain. While scant, the artifacts (with English descriptions) do help humanize the Alhambra visit. If you're early for your palace entry, spend your time in here (Tue–Sun 8:30–14:30, closed Mon). The Museo de Bellas Artes (upstairs, also free) is of little interest to most.

Alcazaba

This fort—the original "red castle" or "Alhambra"—is the oldest and most ruined part of the complex, offering exercise and fine

city views. What you see is from the mid-13th century, but there was probably a fort here in Roman times. Once upon a time, this tower defended a town (or medina) of 2,000 Muslims living within the Alhambra walls. From the top (looking north), find Plaza Nueva and the San Nicolás viewpoint (in the Albayzín). To the south are the Sierra Nevada mountains. Is anybody skiing today?

Think of that day in 1492 when the Christian cross and the flags of Aragon and Castile were raised on this tower, and the fleeing Moorish king Boabdil (Abu Abdullah in Arabic) looked back and wept. His mom chewed him out, saying, "You weep like a woman for what you couldn't defend like a man." With this defeat, more than seven centuries of Muslim rule in Spain came to an end. Much later, Napoleon stationed his troops at the Alhambra, contributing substantially to its ruin when he left.

▲▲▲Palacios Nazaries

During the 30-minute entry time slot stamped on your ticket, enter the jewel of the Alhambra: the Moorish royal palace. Once you're in, you can relax—there are no more time constraints.

You'll walk through three basic sections: royal offices, ceremonial rooms, and private quarters. Built mostly in the 14th century, this palace offers your best possible look at the refined, elegant Moorish civilization of Al-Andalus (Arabic for the Iberian Peninsula).

You'll visit rooms decorated from top to bottom with carved wood ceilings, stucco "stalactites," ceramic tiles, molded-plaster walls, and filigree windows. Open-air courtyards in the palace feature fountains with bubbling water like a desert oasis. A garden enlivened by lush vegetation and peaceful pools is the Quran's symbol of heaven. The palace is well-preserved, but the trick is to imagine it furnished and filled with Moorish life...sultans with hookah pipes lounging on pillows upon Persian carpets, heavy curtains on the windows, and ivory-studded

The Alhambra's Palacios Nazaries

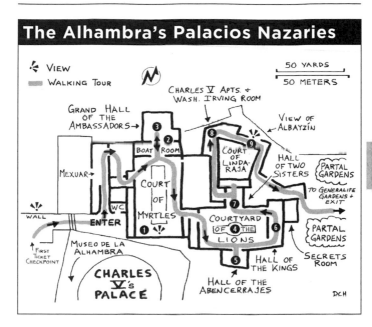

wooden furniture. The whole place was painted with bright colors, many suggested by the Quran—red (blood), blue (heaven), green (oasis), and gold (wealth). And throughout the palace, walls, ceilings, vases, carpets, and tiles were covered with decorative patterns, mostly poems and verses of praise from the Quran written in calligraphy. Much of what is known about the Alhambra is known simply from reading the inscriptions that decorate its walls.

As you wander, keep the palace themes in mind: water, almost no figural images (forbidden by the Quran), "stalactite" ceilings—and few signs telling you where you are. As tempting as it might be to touch the stucco, don't—it is very susceptible to the oils from your hand. Use the map on this page to locate the essential stops listed below.

• *Begin by walking through a few administrative rooms (the* mexuar*) with a stunning Mecca-oriented prayer room (the* oratorio, *with a niche on the right facing Mecca) and a small courtyard with a round fountain, until you hit the big rectangular courtyard with a fish pond lined by a myrtle-bush hedge.*

❶ Court of Myrtles

Moors loved their patios—with a garden and water, under the sky. Women rarely went out, so they stayed in touch with nature in courtyards like the Court of Myrtles (Patio de los Arrayanes)—named for the two fragrant myrtle hedges that added to the courtyard's charm. One exotic theory about the function of this

The Alhambra Grounds

As you wander the grounds, remember that the Alhambra was once a city of 2,000 people fortified by a 1.5-mile rampart and 30 towers. The zone within the walls was the medina, a town with a general urban scene. As you stroll from the ticket booth down the garden-like Calle Real de la Alhambra to the palace, you're walking through the ruins of the medina (destroyed by the French in 1812).

The Palacios Nazaries, Alcazaba fort, and Generalife Gardens all have turnstiles. But the medina—with Charles V's Palace, a line of shops showing off traditional woodworking techniques, and the fancy Alhambra parador—is wide open to anyone with an Alhambra ticket.

It's especially fun to snoop around the historic **Parador de Granada San Francisco,** which—as a national monument— must technically be open to the public. Once a Moorish palace within the Alhambra, it was later converted into a Franciscan monastery, with a historic claim to fame: Its church is where the Catholic Monarchs (Ferdinand and Isabel) chose to be buried. For a peek, step in through the arch leading to a small garden area and reception. Enter to see the tomb, located in the open-air ruins of the church (just before the reception desk and the guests-only-beyond-this-point sign). The slab on the ground near the altar—a surviving bit from the mosque that was here before the church—marks the place where the greatest king and queen of Spain were buried until 1521 (when they were moved to the Royal Chapel). The next room is a delightful former cloister. Now a hotel, the parador has a separate restaurant and café for non-guests.

The medina's main road dead-ended at the **Wine Gate** (Puerta del Vino), which protected the fortress. When you pass through the Wine Gate, you enter a courtyard that was originally a moat, then a reservoir (in Christian times). The well—now encased in a bar-kiosk—is still a place for cold drinks. If you're done with your Alhambra visit, you can exit down to the city from the Wine Gate.

complex is that the living quarters for the women (harem) were upstairs—the Quran let a man have four wives and an unlimited number of concubines—"all the women you can maintain with dignity." Notice the wooden screens (erected by jealous husbands) that allowed the cloistered women to look out without being clearly seen. The less interesting, but more likely, theory is that the upstairs was for winter use, and the cooler ground level was for the hotter summer.

• *Head left from the entry through gigantic wooden doors into the long narrow antechamber to the throne room, called the...*

❷ Boat Room

It's understandable that many think the Boat Room (Sala de la Barca) is named for the upside-down-hull shape of its fine cedar ceiling. But the name is actually derived from the Arab word *baraka*, meaning "divine blessing and luck" (which was corrupted to *barca*, the Spanish word for "boat"). As you passed through this room, blessings and luck are exactly what you'd need—because in the next room, you'd be face-to-face with the sultan.

• *Oh, it's your turn. Enter the ornate throne room.*

❸ Grand Hall of the Ambassadors

The palace's largest room, the Gran Salón de los Embajadores, functioned as the throne room. It was here that the sultan, seated on a throne opposite the entrance, received foreign emissaries. Ogle the room—a perfect cube—from top to bottom. The star-studded, domed wooden ceiling (8,017 inlaid pieces like a giant jigsaw puzzle) suggests the complexity of Allah's infinite universe. Wooden "stalactites" form the cornice, running around the entire base of the ceiling. The stucco walls, even without their original paint and gilding, are still glorious, decorated with ornamental flowers made by pressing a mold into the wet plaster. The filigree windows once held stained glass and had heavy drapes to block out the heat. Some precious 16th-century tiles survive in the center of the floor.

A visitor here would have stepped from the glaring Court of Myrtles into this dim, cool, incense-filled world, to meet the silhouetted sultan. Imagine the alcoves functioning busily as work stations, and the light at sunrise or sunset, rich and warm, filling the room.

Note the finely carved Arabic script. Muslims avoided making images of living creatures—that was God's work. But they could carve decorative religious messages. One phrase—"only Allah is victorious"—is repeated 9,000 times throughout the palace. Find the character for "Allah"—it looks like a cursive W with a nose on its left side. The swoopy toboggan blades underneath are a kind of artistic punctuation setting off one phrase.

Islamic Art

Rather than making paintings and statues, Islamic artists expressed themselves with beautiful but functional objects. Ceramics (often blue and white, or green and white), carpets, glazed tile panels, stucco-work ceilings, and glass tableware are covered with complex patterns. The intricate interweaving, repetition, and unending lines suggest the complex, infinite nature of God, known to Muslims as Allah.

You'll see only a few pictures of humans or animals, since the Islamic religion was wary of any "graven images" or idols forbidden by God. However, secular art by Muslims for their homes and palaces was not bound by this restriction; you'll get an occasional glimpse of realistic art featuring men and women enjoying a garden paradise, a symbol of the Muslim heaven.

Look for floral patterns (twining vines, flowers, and arabesques) and geometric designs (stars and diamonds). The most common pattern is calligraphy—elaborate lettering of an inscription in Arabic, the language of the Quran. A quote from the Quran on a vase or lamp combines the power of the message with the beauty of the calligraphy.

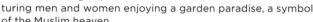

In 1492, two historic events likely took place in this room. Culminating a 700-year-long battle, the Reconquista was completed here as the last Moorish king, Boabdil, signed the terms of his surrender before eventually leaving for Africa.

And it was here that Columbus made his pitch to Isabel and Ferdinand to finance a sea voyage to the Orient. Imagine the scene: The king, the queen, and the greatest minds from the University of Salamanca gathered here while Columbus produced maps and pie charts to make his case that he could sail west to reach the East. Ferdinand and the professors laughed and called Columbus mad—not because they thought the world was flat (most educated people knew otherwise), but because they thought Columbus had underestimated the size of the globe, and thus the length and cost of the journey.

But Isabel said "Sí, señor." Columbus fell to his knees (promising to pack light, wear a money belt, and use the most current guidebook available).

Opposite the Boat Room entrance, photographers pause for a picture-perfect view of the tower reflected in the Court of Myrtles pool. This was the original palace entrance (before Charles V's Palace was built).

· *Continue deeper into the palace, to a courtyard where, 600 years ago, only the royal family and their servants could enter. It's the much-photographed...*

❹ Courtyard of the Lions

The Patio de los Leones features a fountain that's usually ringed with 12 lions; however, they've been missing for the past two years

as they undergo restoration (they'll probably be back in place sometime in 2010). One of the lions is on display in the Museo de la Alhambra inside Charles V's Palace.

Why did the fountain have 12 lions? Since the fountain was a gift from a Jewish leader celebrating good relations with the sultan (Granada had a big Jewish community), the lions probably represent the 12 tribes of Israel. During Moorish times, the fountain functioned as a clock, with a different lion spouting water each hour. (Conquering Christians disassembled the fountain to see how it worked, and it's never worked since.) From the center, four streams went out—figuratively to the corners of the earth and literally to various apartments of the royal family. Notice how the court, with its 124 columns, resembles the cloister of a Catholic monastery. The craftsmanship is first-class. For example, the lead fittings between the pre-cut sections of the columns allow things to flex during an earthquake, preventing destruction during shakes.

Six hundred years ago, the Muslim Moors could read the Quranic poetry that ornaments this court, and they could understand the symbolism of this lush, enclosed garden, considered the embodiment of paradise or truth. ("How beautiful is this garden / where the flowers of Earth rival the stars of Heaven. / What can compare with this alabaster fountain, gushing crystal-clear water? / Nothing except the fullest moon, pouring light from an unclouded sky.") Imagine—they appreciated this part of the palace even more than we do today.

· *On the right, off the courtyard, is a square room called the...*

❺ Hall of the Abencerrajes

This was the sultan's living room, with an exquisite ceiling based on the eight-sided Muslim star. According to legend, the father of Boabdil took a new wife and wanted to disinherit the children of his first marriage—one of whom was Boabdil. In order to deny power to Boabdil and his siblings, the sultan killed nearly the entire pre-Boabdil Abencerraje family. He thought this would pave the way for the son of his new wife to be the next sultan. He happily stacked 36 Abencerraje heads in the pool under the sumptuous honeycombed stucco ceiling in this hall, called the Sala de los Abencerrajes. But his scheme failed, and Boabdil ultimately assumed the throne. Bloody power struggles like this were the norm here in the Alhambra.

• *At the end of the court opposite where you entered is the...*

❻ Hall of the Kings

Notice the ceilings of the three chambers branching off this gallery, the Hall of the Kings (Sala de los Reyes). Breaking from the tradition of imageless art, paintings on the goat-leather ceiling depict scenes of the sultan and his family. The center room's group portrait shows the first 10 of the Alhambra's 22 sultans. The scene is a fantasy, since these people lived over a span of many generations. The two end rooms display scenes of princely pastimes, such as hunting and shooting skeet. In a palace otherwise devoid of figures, these offer a rare look at royal life in the palace.

• *As you exit, you'll pass doors leading right and left to a 14th-century WC plumbed by running water and stairs up to the harem. Next is the...*

❼ Hall of Two Sisters

The Sala de Dos Hermanas—nicknamed for the giant twin slabs of white marble on the floor flanking the fountain—has another oh-wow stucco ceiling lit from below by clerestory windows. The room features geometric patterns and stylized Arabic script quoting verses from the Quran. If the inlaid color tiles look "Escheresque," you've got it backwards: Escher is Alhambra-esque. M. C. Escher was inspired by these very patterns on his visit. Study the patterns—they remind us of the Moorish expertise in math. The sitting room (farthest from the entry) has low windows, because Moorish people sat on the floor. Some rare stained glass survives in the ceiling. From here the sultana enjoyed a grand view of medieval city (before the 16th-century wing was added that blocks the view today).

• *That's about it for the palace. From here, you wander past the domed roofs of the old baths down a hallway to a pair of rooms decorated with a mahogany ceiling. Marked with a large plaque is the...*

❽ Washington Irving Room

Washington Irving wrote *Tales of the Alhambra* in this room. While living in Spain in 1829, Irving stayed in the Alhambra. It was a romantic time, when the palace was home to Gypsies and donkeys. His "tales" kindled interest in the Alhambra, causing it to become recognized as a national treasure. A plaque on the wall thanks Irving, who later served as the US ambassador to Spain (1842–1846). Here's a quote from Irving's *The Alhambra by Moonlight:* "On such heavenly nights I would sit for hours at my window inhaling the sweetness of the garden, and musing on the checkered fortunes of those whose history was dimly shadowed out in the elegant memorials around."

• *As you leave, stop at the open-air...*

❾ Hallway with a View

Here you'll enjoy the best-in-the-palace view of the labyrinthine Albayzín—the old Moorish town on the opposite hillside. Find

the famous San Nicolás viewpoint (below where the white San Nicolás church tower breaks the horizon). Creeping into the mountains on the right are the Gypsy neighborhoods of Sacromonte. Still circling old Granada is the Moorish wall (built in the 1400s to protect the city's population, swollen by Muslim refugees driven south by the Reconquista).

The Patio de Lindaraja (with its maze-like hedge pattern garden) marks the end of the palace visit. Before exiting, you can detour right into the adjacent "Secrets Room"—stark brick rooms of the former bath with fun acoustics. Whisper into a corner, and your friend—with an ear to the wall—can hear you in the opposite corner. Try talking in the exact center.

• *Leaving the palace, you enter the Partal Gardens (El Partal), where you can enjoy the reflecting pond of the Partal Palace. Climb a few stairs, continue through the gardens, and follow signs directing you left to the Generalife Gardens or right to the exit. If you're interested in poking around the Alhambra grounds, exit and do it now before entering the Generalife (because you can't easily backtrack into the Alhambra grounds after leaving the gardens).*

▲ Generalife Gardens

If you have a long wait before your entry to the Palacios Nazaries, tour these gardens first, then the Alcazaba fort and Charles V's Palace.

The sultan's vegetable and fruit garden and summer palace, called the Generalife (hen-eh-raw-LEEF-ay), are a short hike uphill past the ticket office. The 2,000 residents of the Alhambra enjoyed the fresh fruit and veggies grown here. But most

importantly, this little palace provided the sultan with a cool and
quiet summer escape.

Follow the simple one-
way path through the sprawling gardens (planted only in the
1930s—in Moorish times, there
were no cypress trees here). The
sleek, modern amphitheater was
recently renovated and continues
to be an important concert venue for Granada. It sees most activity
during the International Festival of Music and Dance. Many of
the world's greatest artists have performed here, including Arthur
Rubenstein, Rudolf Nureyev, and Margot Fonteyn. At the small
palace, pass through the dismounting room (imagine dismounting
onto the helpful stone ledge, and letting your horse drink in the
trough here). Step past the guarded entry into the most perfect
Arabian garden in Andalucía.

This summer home of the Moorish kings, the closest thing on
earth to the Quran's description of heaven, was planted more than
600 years ago—remarkable longevity for a European garden. Five-
hundred-year-old paintings show it looking essentially the same as
it does today. The flowers, herbs, aromas, and water are exquisite...
even for a sultan. Up the Darro River, the royal aqueduct diverted
a life-giving stream of water into the Alhambra. It was channeled
through this extra-long decorative fountain to irrigate the bigger
garden outside, then along an aqueduct into the Alhambra for its
2,000 thirsty residents. While the splashing fountains are a delight,
they are a 19th-century addition. The Moors liked a peaceful pond
instead.

At the end of the pond, you enter the sultan's tiny three-room
summer palace. From the end, climb 10 steps into the Christian
Renaissance gardens. The ancient decrepit tree rising over the
pond inspired Washington Irving, who wrote that this must be the
"only surviving witness to the wonders of that age of Al-Andalus."

Exiting left to the top floor of the palace reveals a stunning
view of the Albayzín. Don't climb the *Escalera del Agua* unless you
need the exercise...it only goes up and then back down. Pass the
turnstile (pausing for a view back down into the palace garden) and
follow *salida* (exit) signs as you circle back to where you entered the
Generalife.

Your visit to the Alhambra is complete, and you've earned
your reward. "Surely Allah will make those who believe and do
good deeds enter gardens beneath which rivers flow; they shall be
adorned therein with bracelets of gold and pearls, and their gar-
ments therein shall be of silk" (Quran 22.23).

Sights in Granada

▲▲ Old Town Walk:
The Transition from Moorish to Christian

This short walk orients you to the old town, and covers all the essential sights beyond the Alhambra. At the same time it helps you grasp the dramatic changes brought about as the Reconquista finished expelling Muslim culture and re-established Christian rule here.

• *Start at Corral del Carbón, near the Plaza de Carmen.*

❶ **Corral del Carbón:** A caravanserai (of Silk Road fame) was a protected place for merchants to rest their camels, spend the night, get a bite to eat, and spin yarns. This, the only surviving caravanserai of Granada's original 14, was just a block away from the silk market (Alcaicería; the next stop on this walk). Stepping through the caravanserai's fine Moorish door, you find a square with 14th-century Moorish brickwork surrounding a water fountain. This plain-yet-elegant structure evokes the times when traders would gather here with exotic goods and tales from across the Muslim world.

It's a common mistake to think of the Muslim Moors as somehow not Spanish. They lived here for seven centuries and were really just as "indigenous" as the Romans, Goths, and Celts. While the Moors were Muslim, they were no more connected to Arabia than they were to France.

After the Reconquista, this space was used as a coal storage facility (hence the name "Carbón"). These days it houses two offices where you can buy tickets for musical events.

• *From the caravanserai, walk down Puente del Carbón to the big street named Calle Reyes Católicos (for the "Catholic monarchs" Ferdinand and Isabel, who finally conquered the Moors). The street covers a river that once ran openly here, with a series of bridges (like the* carbón *bridge...Puente del Carbón) lacing together the two parts of town. Continue one block farther to the yellow gate marked "Alcaicería." The pedestrian street, Zacatín, was the main drag, which ran parallel to the river before it was covered. Today it's a favorite paseo destination, busy each evening with strollers. Pass through the Alcaicería gate and walk 20 yards into the old market to the first intersection.*

❷ **Alcaicería:** Originally a Moorish silk market with 200 shops, the Alcaicería (al-kai-thay-REE-ah) was filled with precious salt, silver,

GRANADA

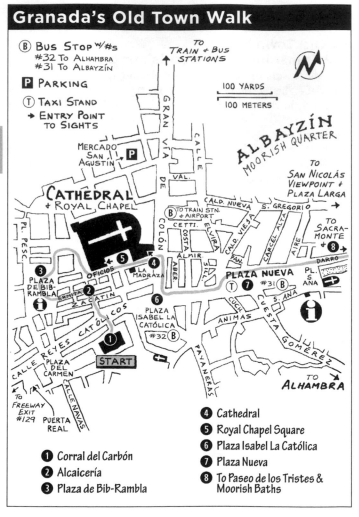

Granada's Old Town Walk

ⓑ **BUS STOP** w/#s
#32 TO ALHAMBRA
#31 TO ALBAYZÍN

🅿 **PARKING**

ⓣ **TAXI STAND**

→ **ENTRY POINT TO SIGHTS**

TO TRAIN & BUS STATIONS

100 YARDS
100 METERS

MERCADO SAN AGUSTÍN 🅿

CATHEDRAL + ROYAL CHAPEL

GRAN VÍA DE COLÓN

CALLE

VAL.

ALBAYZÍN
MOORISH QUARTER

TO SAN NICOLÁS VIEWPOINT + PLAZA LARGA

CALD. NUEVA   S. GREGORIO

ⓑ TO TRAIN STN. + AIRPORT

CETTI.

ELVIRA

CALD. VIEJA

CARCEL ALTA

AIRE

TO SACRAMONTE → ⑧

PL. PESC.

COSTA

ALMIR.

PAN.

DARRO

③ PLAZA DE BIB-RAMBLA
ⓘ

OFICIOS

LA MADRAZA

④

ABER.

ⓣ ⑦ #31 ⓑ

PLAZA NUEVA

PL. S. ANA

ⓘ

⑤

②

ZACATÍN

⑥

S. ANA

CUCH.

CUESTA GOMÉREZ

PLAZA ISABEL LA CATÓLICA

ANIMAS

REYES CATÓLICOS

ERMITA

#32 ⓑ

CALLE NAVAS

PLAZA DEL CARMEN

① **START**

PAVANERAS

TO ALHAMBRA →

TO FREEWAY EXIT #129

PUERTA REAL

① Corral del Carbón
② Alcaicería
③ Plaza de Bib-Rambla

④ Cathedral
⑤ Royal Chapel Square
⑥ Plaza Isabel La Católica
⑦ Plaza Nueva
⑧ To Paseo de los Tristes & Moorish Baths

spices, and silk. It had 10 armed gates and its own guards. Silk was huge in Moorish times (silkworm-friendly mulberry trees flourished in the countryside), a product so important that the sultans controlled and guarded it by constructing this fine, fortified market. After the Reconquista, the Christians realized this market was good for business and didn't mess with it. Later, the more zealous Philip II had it shut down. A terrible fire in 1850 destroyed what was left. Today's Alcaicería was rebuilt in the late 1800s as a tourist souk (marketplace) to complement the romantic image of Granada popularized by the writings of Washington Irving.

Explore the mesh of tiny shopping lanes: overpriced trinkets, popcorn machines popping, men selling balloons, leather goods spread out on streets, kids playing soccer, barking dogs, dogged shoe-shine boys, and the whirring grind of bicycle-powered knife sharpeners. You'll invariably meet obnoxious and persistent Gypsy women pushing their sprigs on innocents in order to extort money. Be strong.

• *Turn left down Ermita lane. In 50 yards you leave the market via another fortified gate and enter a big square. The Neptune fountain marks the center of the...*

❸ **Plaza de Bib-Rambla:** This exuberant square, just two blocks behind the cathedral (from the fountain you can see its blocky spire peeking above the big red building) was once the center of Moorish Granada. While Moorish rule of Spain lasted 700 years, the last couple of centuries were a period of decline as Muslim culture split under weak leadership and Christian forces grew more determined. The last remnants of the Moorish kingdom united and ruled from Granada. As Muslims fled south from reconquered lands, Granada was flooded with refugees. By 1400 Granada had 120,000 people, huge for Europe. This was the main square, the focal point of market and festivals, but it was much smaller then than now, pushed in by the jam-packed city.

Under Christian rule, Moors and Jews were initially recognized as good for business and tolerated, and this area became the Moorish ghetto. Then, with the Inquisition (Philip II, c. 1550), ideology trumped pragmatism, and Jews and Muslims were evicted or forced to convert. The elegant square you see today was built, and built big. In-your-face Catholic processions started here. To assert Christian rule, all the trappings of Christian power were layered upon what had been the trappings of Moorish power. Between here and the cathedral were the Christian University (the big red building) and the adjacent archbishop's palace.

Today Plaza de Bib-Rambla is fine for coffee or a meal amid the color and fragrance of flower stalls and the burbling of its Neptune-topped fountain. It remains a multi-generational hangout where it seems everyone is enjoying a peaceful retirement. A block away (if Neptune turned 180 degrees and walked 100 yards), the Pescadería square is a smaller, similarly lively version of Bib-Rambla.

• *Leave the square toward the cathedral, heading down the lane between the big red building and Bar Manolo. In a block you come to a small square fronting a very big church.*

❹ **Cathedral:** Wow, the cathedral facade just screams triumph. In fact, its design is based on a triumphal arch and it was built over a destroyed mosque. Five hundred yards away, there was open space outside the city wall with good soil. But the Christian conquerors said, "No way." Instead, they destroyed the mosque and built their cathedral right here on difficult, sandy soil. This was the place where the people of Granada traditionally worshipped—and now they would worship as Christians.

The church has a Gothic foundation and was built mostly in the Renaissance style. Hometown artist Alonso Cano finished it, at the king's request, in Baroque. Accentuating the power of the Roman Catholic Church, the emphasis here is on Mary rather than Christ. The facade declares *Ave Maria*. (This was Counter-Reformation time and the Church was threatened by Protestant Christians. Mary was also more palatable to Muslim converts—she is revered in the Quran.)

• *The cathedral entrance is on the opposite side (and the interior is described in the self-guided cathedral tour, later in this chapter). Walk around to the right, popping into the Baroque chapel if open. Then circle around the cathedral until you reach the small square facing the Royal Chapel.*

❺ **Royal Chapel Square:** This square was once ringed by important Moorish buildings. A hammam (public bath), madrassa (school), caravanserai (Day's Inn), the silk market, and the leading mosque were all right here. With Christian rule, the madrassa (the building with the walls painted in 3-D Baroque style) because Granada's first City Hall. The royal coffins were moved from the Alhambra's parador to the oval Royal Chapel in 1521. (For a self-guided tour of the Royal Chapel, see next section.)

• *Continue up the cobbled, stepped lane to the big street, Gran Vía. With the arrival of cars and the modern age, the people of Granada wanted a Parisian-style boulevard. In the early 20th century they mercilessly cut through the old town and created the Gran Vía with its French-style buildings—in the process destroying everything in its path, including many historic convents.*

From here you could enter the cathedral, catch minibus #32 to the Alhambra, or go left two blocks, cross the street, and walk up Calle Cárcel Baja into the Albayzín. But for now, let's continue our orientation tour. Turn right and walk down Gran Vía to the big square ahead.

❻ **Plaza Isabel La Católica:** Granada's two grand boulevards, Gran Vía and Calle Reyes Católicos, meet a block off Plaza Nueva

at Plaza Isabel La Católica. Above the fountain, a fine statue shows Columbus unfurling a long contract with Isabel. It lists the terms of Columbus' *mcccclxxxxii* voyage: "Forasmuch as you, Columbus, are going by our command to discover and subdue some Islands and Continents in the ocean...."

The two reliefs show the big events in Granada of 1492: Isabel and Ferdinand accepting Columbus' proposal and a stirring battle scene (which never happened) at the walls of the Alhambra.

Isabel was driven by her desire to spread Catholicism. Columbus was driven by his desire for money. As a reward for adding territory to Spain's Catholic empire, Isabel promised Columbus the ranks of Admiral of the Oceans and Governor of the New World. To sweeten the pie, she tossed in one-eighth of all the riches he brought home. Isabel died thinking that Columbus had found India or China. Columbus died poor and disillusioned.

Calle Reyes Católicos leads from this square to the busy intersection with Puerta Real. From there, Acera del Darro takes you through modern Granada to the river via the huge El Corte Inglés department store and lots of modern commerce. This area erupts with locals out strolling each night. For the best Granada paseo, wander the streets around here around 19:00.

• *Follow Calle Reyes Católicos a couple of blocks to the left where you'll find another square.*

❼ **Plaza Nueva:** Long a leading square in Granada, Plaza Nueva is dominated by the Palace of Justice (grand Baroque facade with green Andalusian flag). The fountain is capped by a stylized pomegranate—the symbol of the city, always open and fertile. The main action here is the comings and goings of the busy little shuttle buses serving the Alhambra and Albayzín. The local hippie community, nicknamed the *pies negros* (black feet) for obvious reasons, hangs out here and on Calle Elvira. They squat—with their dogs and guitars—in abandoned caves above those the Gypsies occupy in Sacromonte. Many are the children of rich Spanish families from the north, hell-bent on disappointing their high-achieving parents.

• *Our tour continues with a stroll up Paseo de los Tristes. Leave Plaza Nueva opposite where you entered and walk up the Darro River Valley. This is particularly enjoyable in the cool of the evening. If you're tired, note that minibuses #31 and #32 run from Plaza Nueva, up this lane, and then hook into and through the Albayzín quarter.*

❽ **Paseo de los Tristes:** This "Walk of the Sad Ones" was once the route of funeral processions to the cemetery at the edge of town. Leaving Plaza Nueva you pass the Church of Santa Ana. This was originally a mosque—the church tower replaced a minaret. Notice the ceramic brickwork. This is Mudejar art, a technique of Moorish craftsmen later employed by Christians. Inside you'll see a fine Alhambra-style cedar ceiling.

Follow Carrera del Darro high above the River Darro at the base of the Alhambra (look down by the river for a glimpse of feral cats). Six miles upstream, part of the Darro is diverted to provide water for the Alhambra's many fountains. Past the church on the left is Santa Catalina de Zafra, a convent of cloistered nuns (they worship behind a screen that divides the church's rich interior in half).

Farther ahead is the broken nub of a once-grand 11th-century bridge over the river, leading to the Alhambra. Notice two slits in the column: One held an iron portcullis to keep bad guys from entering the town via the river. The second held a solid door that was lowered to build up water, then released to flush out the river-bed and keep it clean.

• *Across from the remains of the bridge (and the stop for minibuses #31 and #34) is the brick facade of an evocative Moorish bath, the Hammam El Bañuelo.*

❾ Hammam El Bañuelo (Moorish Baths): In Moorish times, hammams (public baths) were a big part of the community (working-class homes didn't have bathrooms). Baths were strictly segregated (as they are today) and functioned as more than a place to wash: Business was done here, and it was a social meeting point. In Christian times, it was assumed that conspiracies brewed in these baths—therefore, only a few of them survive. This place gives you the chance to explore the stark but evocative ruins of an 11th-century Moorish public bath (free, unreliably Tue–Sat 10:00–14:00, closed Sun–Mon, borrow the English description at the door).

Entering the baths, you pass the house of the keeper and the foyer, then visit the cold room, the warm room (where services like massage were offered), and finally the hot or steam room. Beyond that, you can see the oven that generated the heat, which flowed under the hypocaust-style floor tiles (getting less hot with distance). The romantic little holes in the ceiling once had stained-glass louvers that attendants opened and closed with sticks to regulate the heat and steaminess. While Romans soaked in their pools, Muslims just doused. Rather than being totally immersed, people scooped and splashed water over themselves. Imagine attendants stoking the fires under the metal boiler…while people in towels and wooden slippers (to protect their feet from the heated floors) enjoyed all the spa services you can imagine as beams of light slashed through the mist. This was a great social mixer. As all were naked, class distinctions disappeared—elites learned the latest from commoners. Mothers found matches for their kids. The popular Muslim phrase summed up the attraction of the baths: "This is where anyone would spend their last coin."

• *Continuing straight ahead, you see the Church of San Pedro, the parish church of Sacromonte's Gypsy community (across from the Archaeological Museum). Within its rich interior is an ornate oxcart used to carry the host on the annual pilgrimage to Rocío near the Portuguese border. This walk ends at Paseo de los Tristes—with its restaurant tables spilling out under the floodlit Alhambra. From here, the road arcs up into Sacromonte.*

▲▲Royal Chapel (Capilla Real)

Without a doubt Granada's top Christian sight, this lavish chapel holds the dreams—and bodies—of Queen Isabel and King Ferdinand. The "Catholic Monarchs" were all about the Reconquista. Their marriage united the Aragon and Castile kingdoms, allowing an acceleration of the Christian and Spanish push south. In its last 10 years, the Reconquista snowballed. This last Moorish capital—symbolic of their victory—was their chosen burial place.

Cost, Hours, Location: €3.50; March–Oct Mon–Sat 10:30–13:30 & 16:00–19:30, opens Sun at 11:00; Nov–Feb Mon–Sat 10:30–13:30 & 15:30–18:30, opens Sun at 11:00; no photos, entrance on Calle Oficios, just off Gran Vía—go through iron gate, tel. 958-227-848.

❍ Self-Guided Tour: In the lobby, before you show your ticket and enter the chapel, notice the **painting of Boabdil** (on the black horse) giving the key of Granada to the conquering King Ferdinand. Boabdil wanted to fall to his knees, but the Spanish king, who had great respect for his Moorish foe, embraced him instead. They fought a long and noble war (for instance, respectfully returning the bodies of dead soldiers). Ferdinand is in red, and Isabel is behind him wearing a crown. The painting is flanked by two large portraits of Ferdinand and Isabel. Two small exhibits celebrate the 500th anniversaries of the death of Isabel in 2004 and of Philip the Fair (her son-in-law) in 2006.

Isabel decided to make Granada the capital of Spain (and burial place for Spanish royalty) for three reasons: 1) With the conquest of this city, Christianity had finally overcome Islam in Europe; 2) her marriage with Ferdinand, followed by the conquest of Granada, had marked the beginning of a united Spain; and 3) in Granada, she agreed to sponsor Columbus.

Show your ticket and step into the **chapel.** It's Plateresque Gothic—light and lacy silver-filigree style, named for and inspired by the fine silverwork of the Moors. The chapel's interior was originally austere, with fancy touches added later by Ferdinand and Isabel's grandson Charles V. Five hundred years ago, this was the most lavish interior money could buy. Ferdinand and Isabel spent a quarter of their wealth on it. Because of its speedy completion (1506–1521), the architecture is unusually harmonious.

The **four royal tombs** are Renaissance-style. Carved in Italy in 1521 out of Carrara marble, they were sent by ship to Spain. The faces—based on death masks—are considered accurate. If you're looking at the altar, **Ferdinand** and **Isabel** are on the right. (Isabel fans attribute the bigger dent she puts in the pillow to her larger brain.) Isabel's contemporaries described the queen as being of medium height, with auburn hair and blue eyes, and possessing a serious, modest, and gentle personality. (Compare Ferdinand and Isabel's tomb statues with the painted and gilded wood statues of them kneeling in prayer, flanking the altarpiece.)

Philip the Fair and **Juana the Mad** (who succeeded Ferdinand and Isabel) lie on the left. Philip was so "Fair" that it drove the insanely jealous Juana "Mad." Philip died young, and for two years Juana kept his casket at her bedside, kissing his embalmed body good night. Philip and Juana's son, Charles V (known as Carlos I in Spain), was a key figure in European history, as his coronation merged the Holy Roman Empire (Philip the Fair's Habsburg domain) with Juana's Spanish empire. Europe's top king, Charles V ruled a vast empire stretching from Holland to Sicily, from Bohemia to Bolivia (1519–1556, see sight listing for his palace within the Alhambra).

When Philip II, the son of Charles V, decided to build El Escorial and establish Madrid as the single capital of a single Spain, Granada lost power and importance. More importantly, Spain began to decline. After the reign of Charles V, Spain squandered her vast wealth trying to maintain this impossibly huge empire. The country's rulers did it not only for material riches, but to defend the romantic, quixotic dream of a Catholic empire—ruled by one divinely ordained Catholic monarch—against an irrepressible tide of nationalism and Protestantism that was sweeping across the vast Habsburg holdings in Central and Eastern Europe. Spain's relatively poor modern history can be blamed, in part, on its people's stubborn unwillingness to accept the end of this old-regime notion. Even Franco borrowed symbols from the Catholic Monarchs to legitimize his dictatorship and keep the 500-year-old legacy alive. Today's Spaniards reflect that the momentous marriage that created their country also sucked them into centuries of European squabbling, eventually leaving Spain impoverished.

Look at the fine carving on the tombs. It's a humanistic statement, with these healthy, organic, realistic figures rising out of the Gothic age.

From the feet of the marble tombs, step downstairs to see the actual **coffins.** They are plain. Ferdinand and Isabel were originally buried in the Franciscan monastery (in what is today the parador, up at the Alhambra). You're standing in front of the two people who created Spain. The fifth coffin (on right, marked *PM*) belongs to a young Prince Michael, who would have been king of a united Spain and Portugal. (A sad—but too long—story...)

The **high altar** is one of the finest Renaissance works in Spain. It's dedicated to two Johns: the Baptist and the Evangelist.

In the center, you can see the Baptist and the Evangelist chatting as if over tapas—an appropriately humanistic scene. Scenes from the Baptist's life are on the left: John beheaded after Salomé's fine dancing, and (below) John baptizing Jesus. Scenes from the Evangelist's life are on the right: John's martyrdom (a failed attempt to boil him alive in oil), and John on Patmos (where he wrote the last book of the Bible, Revelation). John is talking to the eagle that, according to tradition, flew him to heaven. A colorful series of reliefs at the bottom level recalls the Christian conquest of the Moors (left to right): Ferdinand, Boabdil with army and key to Alhambra, Moors expelled from Alhambra (right of altar table), conversion of Muslims by tonsured monks, and Ferdinand again.

A finely carved Plateresque arch, with the royal initials "F" and "Y," leads to a small glass pyramid in the **treasury.** This holds Queen Isabel's silver crown ringed with pomegranates (symbolizing Granada), her scepter, and King Ferdinand's sword. Beside the entry arch (on right) you'll see the devout Isabel's prayer book, in which she followed the Mass. The book and its sturdy box date from 1496. According to legend, the fancy box on the other side of the door is supposedly the one that Isabel (cash-poor because of her military expenses) filled with jewels and gave to Columbus. Columbus sold these to finance his journey. In the corner (and also behind glass) is the ornate silver-and-gold cross that Cardinal Mendoza, staunch supporter of Queen Isabel, carried into the Alhambra on that historic day in 1492. Next, the big silk, silver-and-gold tapestry is the altar banner for the mobile campaign chapel of Ferdinand and Isabel, who always traveled with their army. In the next case, you'll see the original Christian army flags raised over the Alhambra in 1492.

The room holds the first great art collection ever established by a woman. Queen Isabel amassed more than 200 important paintings. After Napoleon's visit, only 30 remained. Even so, this is a fine collection, all on wood, featuring works by Sandro Botticelli, Pietro Perugino, the Flemish master Hans Memling, and some less-famous Spanish masters.

Finally, at the end of the room, the two carved sculptures of Ferdinand and Isabel were the originals from the high altar. Charles V considered these primitive and replaced them with the ones you saw earlier.

To reach the cathedral (described next), exit behind Isabel, out through one iron gate and then immediately through the neighboring iron gate.

▲Cathedral

One of only two Renaissance churches in Spain (the other is in Córdoba), Granada's cathedral is the second-largest in Spain after

Sevilla's. While it was started as a Gothic church, it was built using Renaissance elements, and then decorated in Baroque style.

Cost, Hours, Location: €3.50; April–Oct Mon–Sat 10:45–13:30 & 16:00–20:00, Sun 16:00–20:00; Nov–March until 19:00; 45-min audioguide-€3, entrance off Gran Vía through iron gateway, tel. 958-222-959.

❸ Self-Guided Tour: You'll start your visit (after the ticket checker, step right) in the priests' wardrobe room. It's lush and wide-open; the gilded ceilings, mirrors, and wooden cabinets give this room a light, airy feel. Two grandfather clocks made in London (one with Asian motifs) ensured that everyone got dressed on time. The highlight of this room: the delicate painted wood statue of the *Immaculate Conception* by Granada's own Alonso Cano (1601–1667).

Wandering out, you'll be behind the main altar. A fine series of paintings by Cano, moved from under arches high above, now encircle the back of the altar. Their distortion was intentional, since the paintings were designed to look natural when viewed from floor level. As you walk around the pews and gigantic Baroque organs, you'll see the cathedral at its most beautiful.

Standing in front of the high altar, look up at the spread of vacant niches (with squares now filled with paintings). These were intended to hold the royal coffins. But Phillip II changed focus, abandoning Granada for El Escorial, and these sit empty to this day. Only four royals are buried in Granada (at the Royal Chapel). The cathedral's cool, spacious, bright interior is a refreshing break from the dark Gothic of so many Spanish churches. In a modern move back in the 18th century, the choir walls (the big heavy wooden box that dominates the center of most Spanish churches) were taken out so that people could be involved in the worship. At about the same time, a bishop ordered the interior painted with lime (for hygienic reasons, during a time of disease). The people liked it, and it stayed white. As you explore, remember that the abundance of Marys is all part of the Counter-Reformation. Most of the side chapels are decorated in Baroque style. To the right of the high altar is a politically incorrect version of St. James the Moor-Slayer, with his sword raised high and an armored Moor trampled under his horse's hooves.

Wander back through the pews toward the cathedral's main doors. A small sacristy museum is tucked away in the right corner (as you face the doors). There may be no detailed descriptions for any of the items, but a beautiful bust of St. Peter (with a flowing beard) by Cano is worth seeking out. Also on display is the confusing accounting book for the cathedral's construction. As you head out, look for the music sheets behind the main altar; they're mostly 16th-century Gregorian chants. Notice the sliding C clef. Rather than a fixed G or F clef, the monks knew that this clef—which could be located wherever worked best on the staff—marked middle C, and they chanted to notes relative to that. Go ahead—try singing a few verses of the Latin.

Immediately in front of the cathedral is the stop for minibus #32 to the Alhambra. And four blocks away (if you head left up the busy street, then turn right) is the Albayzín.

The Albayzín

Explore Spain's best old Moorish quarter, with countless colorful corners, flowery patios, and shady lanes. Climb high to the San Nicolás church for the best view of the Alhambra. Then wander through the mysterious backstreets. (I've listed these sights roughly in order from the San Nicolás viewpoint.)

Getting to the Albayzín: A handy city **minibus** threads its way around the Albayzín from Plaza Nueva (see "Albayzín Circular Bus Tour," next), getting you scenically and sweatlessly to the San Nicolás viewpoint. You can also **taxi** to the San Nicolás church and explore from there. Consider having your cabbie take you on a Sacromonte detour en route.

To **walk** up, leave the west end of Plaza Nueva on Calle Elvira. After about 200 yards, bear right on Calle Calderería Nueva. Follow this stepped street past Moroccan eateries and pastry shops, vendors of imported North African goods, *halal* butchers, and *teterías* (Moorish tea rooms). The lane bears right, then passes to the left of the church (becoming San Gregorio), and slants, winds, and zigzags uphill. San Gregorio eventually curves left and is regularly signposted. When you reach the Moorish-style house, La Media Luna, stop for a photo and a breather, then follow the wall, continuing uphill. At the next intersection, turn right on Aljibe del Gato. Farther on, this street takes a 90-degree turn to the left, becoming Calle Atarasana Vieja. It's confusing, but keep going up, up, up. At the crest, turn right on Camino Nuevo de San Nicolás, then walk 300 yards to the street that curves up left (look for a bus stop sign—this is where the minibus would have dropped you off). Continue up the curve and soon you'll see feet hanging from the plaza wall. Steps lead up to the church's viewpoint. Whew! You made it!

Albayzín Circular Bus Tour—The handy Albayzín minibus #31 gallops the 15-minute loop as if in a race, departing from Plaza

GRANADA

Albayzín Neighborhood

STREET WIDTH IS
EXAGGERATED
FOR CLARITY

NOTE: NOT TO SCALE
➡ 20 MIN. UPHILL WALK FROM
PLAZA NUEVA to SAN NICOLÁS

❶ Hotel Santa Isabel la Real
❷ La Casa de Rafa (Apts.)
❸ Casa Torcuato (2 Locations)
❹ Restaurante El Ladrillo
❺ Bar Kiki
❻ Paseo de los Tristes Bars
❼ Carmen de las Tomasas &
   Carmen Mirador de Aixa
❽ Carmen Mirador de Morayma
❾ Carmen de Aben Humeya
❿ Arrayanes Restaurante
⓫ Calle Calderería Nueva Eateries
⓬ Great Mosque of Granada
⓭ Hammam El Bañuelo
   (Moorish Baths)
⓮ Hammam Baños Árabes
   (Arab Baths)
⓯ To Center for the Interpretation
   of Sacromonte, Roma Caves &
   Zambra Dance Clubs

Nueva about every 15 minutes (pay driver €1.20, minibus #32 does the same loop but—depending on where you catch it—goes to the Alhambra first). While good for a lift to the top of the Albayzín (buzz when you want to get off), I'd stay on for an entire circle and return to the Albayzín later for dinner—either on foot or by bus again. (Note: Minibus #34 does same trip with a side-trip up into Sacromonte.)

Here's the route: You'll go along up above the Darro River,

GRANADA

Safety in the Albayzín

With tough economic times, young ruffians are making the dark back lanes of the labyrinthine Albayzín quarter more dangerous. The big discussion in Granada is whether it's reckless to be out after dark in this charming Moorish district. While the area is certainly safe by day, it is questionable how safe it is after dark. There have been muggings, and they have been violent. I hate to hurt the business of the many fine little restaurants and hotels in this area. But if you want to play it safe—stay away after dark. And if you do venture in, leave your valuables at your hotel.

past the ruins of a bridge and gate and the Paseo de los Tristes square. Turning uphill, you pass Sacromonte on the right (entrance to the neighborhood marked by a statue of a popular Gypsy guide). Then, turning left, you enter the actual Albayzín. After stopping at the church of San Salvador, you plunge into the thick of it, with stops below the San Nicolás church (famous viewpoint, and the jumping-off point for my suggested "Exploring the Albayzín" stroll—described later in this section) and at Plaza San Miguel Bajo (cute square with recommended eateries and another viewpoint). Then you descend, enjoying a commanding view of Granada on the left as you swing through the modern city. Hitting the city's main drag, Gran Vía, you make a U-turn at the Garden of the Triumph, celebrating the Immaculate Conception of the Virgin Mary (notice her statue atop a column). Behind Mary stands the old Royal Hospital—built in the 16th century for Granada's poor by the Catholic kings after the Reconquista, in hopes of winning the favor of the city's conquered residents. From here, you zip back into town, stopping at the cathedral, and back home to Plaza Nueva.

▲▲San Nicolás Viewpoint (Mirador de San Nicolás)—For one of Europe's most romantic viewpoints, be here at sunset, when the Alhambra glows red and the Albayzín widows share the benches with local lovers, hippies, and tourists (free, always open). In 1997, President Clinton made a point to bring his family here—a favorite spot from a trip he made as a student. For a drink with the same view, step into the El Huerto de Juan Ranas Bar

(just below and to the left, at Calle de Atarazana 8).

Great Mosque of Granada—Granada's Muslim population is on the rebound, and now numbers 8 percent of the city's residents. A striking and inviting mosque is just next to the San Nicolás viewpoint (to your left as you face the Alhambra). Local Muslims write, "The Great Mosque of Granada signals, after a hiatus of 500 years, the restoration of a missing link with a rich and fecund Islamic  contribution to all spheres of human enterprise and activity." Built in 2003 (with money from the local community and Islamic Arab nations), it has a peaceful view courtyard and a minaret that comes with a live call to prayer five times a day (printed schedule inside). It's stirring to see the muezzin holler "God is Great" from the minaret without amplification (locals didn't want it amplified). Visitors are welcome in the courtyard, which offers Alhambra views without the hedonistic ambience of the more famous San Nicolás viewpoint (free, daily 11:00–14:00 & 18:00–21:00).

While tourists come to Granada to learn about the expulsion of the Moors in 1492, local Muslims are frustrated by the "errors, nonsense, and lies local guides perpetuate without knowledge nor shame which flocks of passive tourists accept without questioning." A flier at the mosque tries to set the record straight, from the Muslim perspective: Muslims were as indigenous as any other group. After living here for seven centuries, the Muslims of Granada and Andalucía were as Iberian as the modern Spaniards of today. Islam is not a religion of immigrants. Islam is not a culture of the Orient and Arabs. Muslims and Arabs are different. The Muslims of Al-Andalus were not hedonistic. The Reconquista did not liberate Spain. Harems were not just full of sexy women. (For more on the Muslim perspective, visit the info desk at the mosque.)

The European Union sees Granada as a center for Muslim-Christian integration—or, at least, co-existence. To Muslims, the city is a symbol of the "holocaust" of the Reconquista, when 135,000 of their people were brutally expelled and many more suffered "forced conversion" in the 16th century. Today there are about 700,000 Muslims in Spain (and about 5 million in France).

Exploring the Albayzín—From the San Nicolás viewpoint and the Great Mosque, you're at the edge of a hilltop neighborhood even the people of Granada recognize as a world apart. Each of the district's 20 churches sits on a spot once occupied by a mosque. When the Reconquista arrived in Granada, the Christians attempted to coexist with the Muslims. But after seven years, this idealistic attempt ended in failure, and the Christians forced the Muslims to convert. In 1567, Muslims were expelled, leading to 200 years of economic depression for the city. Eventually, large walled noble manor houses with private gardens were built here in the depopulated Albayzín. These survive today in the form of the characteristic *carmen* restaurants so popular with visitors.

From the San Nicolás viewpoint, turn your back to the Alhambra and walk north (passing the church on your right and the Biblioteca Municipal on your left). A lane leads past a white stone arch (on your right)—now a chapel built into the old Moorish wall. You're walking past the scant remains of the pre-Alhambra fortress of Granada. At the end of the lane, step down to the right through the 11th-century "New Gate" (Puerta Nueva—older than the Alhambra) and into **Plaza Larga.** In medieval times, this tiny square (called "long," because back then it was) served as the local marketplace. It still is a busy market each morning. Casa Pasteles, at the near end of the square, serves good coffee and cakes.

Leave Plaza Larga on **Calle Agua de Albayzín** (as you face Casa Pasteles, it's to your right). The street, named for the public baths that used to line it, shows evidence of the Moorish plumbing system: gutters. Back when Europe's streets were filled with muck, Granada actually had Roman Empire–style gutters with drains leading to clay and lead pipes.

You're in the heart of the Albayzín. Explore. Poke into an old church. They're plain by design to go easy on the Muslim converts, who weren't used to being surrounded by images as they worshipped. You'll see lots of real Muslim culture living in the streets, including many recent Spanish converts.

Sacromonte

The Sacromonte district is home to Granada's thriving Roma community (see sidebar). Marking the entrance to Sacromonte is a statue of Chorrohumo (literally, "Exudes Smoke," and a play on the slang word for "thief"...*chorro*). He was a Roma from Granada, popular in the 1950s for guiding people around the city.

Sacromonte has one main street: Camino del Sacromonte is lined with caves primed for tourists and restaurants ready to fight over the bill. (Don't come here expecting to get a deal on anything.) Intriguing lanes run above and below this main drag.

Zambra Dance—A long flamenco tradition exists in Granada. Sacromonte is a good place to see *zambra*, a flamenco variation with a more Oriental feel in which the singer also dances. Two popular—or at least well-established—*zambra* venues are Zambra Cueva del Rocio (€25, includes a drink and a bus ride from hotel, €20 without

Granada's Roma (Gypsies)

Both the English word "Gypsy" and its Spanish counterpart, *gitano*, come from the word "Egypt"—where Europeans used to mistakenly believe these nomadic people originated. Today, the preferred term is "Roma," since the term "Gypsy" has acquired negative connotations (I've used both names throughout this book).

After migrating from India in the 14th century, the Roma people settled mostly in the Muslim-occupied lands in the south (such as the Balkan Peninsula, then controlled by the Ottoman Turks). Under the Muslims, the Roma enjoyed relative tolerance. They were traditionally good with crafts and animals.

The first Roma arrived in Granada in the 15th century—and they've remained tight-knit ever since. Today 50,000 Roma call Granada home, many of them in the district called Sacromonte. In most of Spain, Roma are more assimilated into the general population, but Sacromonte is a large, distinct Roma community. (After the difficult Civil War era, they were joined by many farmers who, like the Roma, appreciated Sacromonte's affordable, practical cave dwellings—warm in the winter and cool in the summer.)

Spaniards, who consider themselves accepting and not racist, claim that in maintaining such a tight community, the Roma segregate themselves. The Roma call Spaniards *payos* ("whites"). Recent mixing of Roma and *payos* has given birth to the term *gallipavo* (rooster-duck), although who's who depends upon whom you ask.

Are Roma thieves? Sure, some of them are. But others are honest citizens, trying to make their way in the world just like anyone else. It's wise to be cautious when dealing with a Roma person—but it's also important to keep an open mind.

transport, daily show at 22:00, 60 min, Camino del Sacromonte 70, tel. 958-227-129) and María la Canastera (€25, includes a drink and transportation from hotel, €17 without transport, daily show at 22:00, Camino del Sacromonte 89, tel. 958-121-183). I'd just go and explore late at night (with no wallet and €30 in my pocket) rather than booking an evening through my hotel (they'll likely offer to reserve for you).

Center for the Interpretation of Sacromonte (Centro de Interpretación del Sacromonte)—This facility is a kind of Roma open-air folk museum, offering an insight into Sacromonte's geology and environment, cave building, and Roma crafts, food, and musical traditions (with English explanations). There are also great views over Granada and the Alhambra. As you wander, imagine this in the 1950s, when it was still a bustling community

of Roma cave-dwellers. Today, hippies squat in abandoned caves higher up. The center also features €12 flamenco shows and classical guitar concerts in its wonderfully scenic setting (details at TI), 300 yards up the steep hill from the Venta El Gallo restaurant on the main Sacromonte lane (€5; April–Oct Tue–Sun 10:00–14:00 & 17:00–21:00, Nov–March Tue–Sun 10:00–14:00 & 16:00–19:00, closed Mon; Barranco de los Negros, tel. 958-215-120, www.sacromontegranada.com). The closest a taxi can get you is the Venta El Gallo restaurant. From there, you climb on foot, following the signs.

Hammam Baños Árabes (Arab Baths)—For an intimate and subdued experience, consider some serious relaxation at the Arab Baths. A maximum of 16 people are allowed in the baths at one time. The 90-minute soak and a 15-minute massage cost €28; for a 90-minute bath only, it's €19 (daily 10:00–24:00, appointments scheduled every even-numbered hour, co-ed with mandatory swimsuits, quiet atmosphere encouraged, free lockers and towels available, just off Plaza Nueva at Santa Ana 16; from Plaza Nueva, it's the first right, over a bridge and past the church; 50 percent paid reservation required, tel. 958-229-978, www.hammamspain.com/granada).

Near Granada

Carthusian Monastery (La Cartuja)—A church with an interior that looks as if it squirted out of a can of whipped cream, La Cartuja is nicknamed the "Christian Alhambra" for its elaborate white Baroque stucco work. In the rooms just off the cloister, notice the gruesome paintings of martyrs placidly meeting their grisly fates (€3.50, daily April–Oct 10:00–13:00 & 16:00–20:00, Nov–March 10:00–13:00 & 15:00–18:00, tel. 958-161-932). It's a mile north of town on the way to Madrid. Drive north on Gran Vía de Colón and follow the signs, or take bus #8 from Gran Vía.

Sleeping in Granada

In July and August, when Granada's streets are littered with sunstroke victims, rooms are plentiful and prices soft. In the crowded months of April, May, September, and October, prices can spike up 20 percent. Except for the hotels in the Albayzín and near the Alhambra, most of my listings are within a five-minute walk of Plaza Nueva.

GRANADA

Sleep Code

(€1 = about $1.40, country code: 34)
S = Single, **D** = Double/Twin, **T** = Triple, **Q** = Quad, **b** = bathroom, **s** = shower only. Unless otherwise noted, credit cards are accepted and English is spoken. Prices include the 7 percent tax. Breakfast may or may not be included.

To help you easily sort through these listings, I've divided the rooms into three categories based on the price for a standard double room with bath during high season:

$$$ Higher Priced—Most rooms €100 or more.
 $$ Moderately Priced—Most rooms between €50–100.
  $ Lower Priced—Most rooms €50 or less.

Given all the restrictions, it is difficult to drive into Granada even when you know the system (see "Arrival in Granada"). While few hotels have parking facilities, any of them can direct you to a garage (such as Parking San Agustín, just off Gran Vía, €25/day).

On or near Plaza Nueva

Each of these is big, professional, plenty comfortable, and perfectly located. Prices vary with demand.

$$$ Casa del Capitel Nazarí, just off the church end of Plaza Nueva, is a restored 16th-century Renaissance palace transformed into 17 small but tastefully decorated rooms facing a courtyard (Db-€115, extra bed-€38, breakfast-€8, includes afternoon tea/coffee and pastry, air-con, free Internet access, parking-€18.50/day, Cuesta Aceituneros 6, tel. 958-215-260, fax 958-215-806, www.hotelcasacapitel.com, info@hotelcasacapitel.com).

$$$ Hotel Maciá Plaza, right on the colorful Plaza Nueva, has 44 clean, modern, and classy rooms. Choose between an on-the-square view or a quieter interior room (Sb-€75, Db-€110, Tb-€123, 10 percent discount in 2010 when you show this book at check-in or reserve directly through their website, good buffet breakfast-€8, air-con, elevator, free Wi-Fi, Plaza Nueva 4, tel. 958-227-536, fax 958-227-533, www.maciahoteles.com, maciaplaza @maciahoteles.com).

$$ Hotel Inglaterra is a modern and peaceful chain hotel, with 36 rooms offering all the comforts (Db-€77–97, extra bed-€30, buffet breakfast-€12, air-con, elevator to third floor only, 20 parking spaces at €13/day, Cetti Merien 6, tel. 958-221-559, fax 958-227-100, www.nh-hotels.com, nhinglaterra@nh-hotels.com).

$$ Hotel Anacapri is a bright, cool marble oasis with 49 modern rooms and a quiet lounge (Sb-€55–65, Db-€75–97, Tb-€95–117, extra bed-€20, includes breakfast with direct bookings in 2010,

Granada Hotels and Restaurants

1. Casa del Capitel Nazarí
2. Hotel Maciá Plaza
3. Hotel Inglaterra
4. Hotel Anacapri
5. Pensión Landazuri
6. Hotel Puerta de las Granadas, Pensión Viena & Pensión Austria
7. Hostal Residencia Britz
8. Hostal Navarro Ramos
9. To Hotel Reina Cristina & Zurita Pensión
10. Hotel Los Tilos
11. Hotel Lisboa
12. Bodegas Castañeda
13. Restaurante Sevilla
14. La Cueva De 1900
15. Los Italianos Ice Cream
16. To Paseo de los Tristes Eateries
17. Market Scene

air-con, elevator, 2 blocks toward Gran Vía from Plaza Nueva at Calle Joaquín Costa 7, just a block from cathedral bus stop, tel. 958-227-477, fax 958-228-909, www.hotelanacapri.com, reservas @hotelanacapri.com, helpful Kathy speaks Iowan).

Cheap Sleeps on Cuesta de Gomérez

These are inexpensive and ramshackle lodgings on the street leading from Plaza Nueva up to the Alhambra. A restoration project is currently blocking the end of the road, making it quieter and almost traffic-free. There are plans to make this a pedestrian-only street.

$$ Hotel Puerta de las Granadas is a basic value with 16 simple rooms, no-frills comforts, an inviting cafeteria courtyard, and a handy location (Db-€60–85, ask for 5 percent Rick Steves discount, air-con, free Internet access and Wi-Fi, free tea in cafeteria all day, Cuesta de Gomérez 14, tel. 958-216-230, fax 958-216-231, www.hotelpuertadelasgranadas.com, reservas@hotelpuertadelas granadas.com).

$ Pensión Landazuri is run by friendly English-speaking Matilde Landazuri and her son, Manolo. Some of their 18 rooms are well-worn, while others are renovated. It boasts hardworking, helpful management and a great roof garden with an Alhambra view (S-€24, Sb-€36, D-€34, Db-€45, Tb-€60, cheap eggs-and-bacon breakfast, cash only, parking-€10/day, Cuesta de Gomérez 24, tel. & fax 958-221-406). The Landazuris also run a good, cheap café.

$ Hostal Residencia Britz, overlooking Plaza Nueva, is simple and no-nonsense. All of its 22 basic rooms are streetside— bring earplugs (S-€25, D-€36, Db-€48, elevator, Plaza Nueva y Gomérez 1, tel. & fax 958-223-652).

$ Hostal Navarro Ramos is a little cash-only cheapie, renting seven stark rooms facing an interior airshaft with mostly shared bathrooms (S-€20, D-€27, Db-€36, Cuesta de Gomérez 21, tel. 958-250-555, Carmen).

$ Pensión Viena and **Pensión Austria,** run by English-speaking Austrian Irene (ee-RAY-nay), rent 32 basic backpacker-type rooms on a quiet side street (S-€26, Sb-€36, D-€36, Db-€46, T-€53, Tb-€62, family rooms, air-con, next-door bar noisy on weekends, 10 yards off Cuesta de Gomérez at Hospital de Santa Ana 2, tel. & fax 958-221-859, www.hostalviena.com, hostal viena@hostalviena.com, reception at Pensión Austria).

Near the Cathedral

$$$ Hotel Reina Cristina has 58 quiet, elegant rooms a few steps off Plaza Trinidad, a park-like square near the lively Pescadería and Bib-Rambla squares. Check out the great Mudejar ceiling and the painting at the entrance of this house, where the famous Spanish poet Federico García Lorca hid until he was captured and executed by the Guardia Civil (Sb-€53–78, Db-€75–114, Tb-€107–135, breakfast-€13, air-con, elevator, near Plaza de la Trinidad at Tablas 4, tel. 958-253-211, fax 958-255-728, www.hotelreinacristina.com, clientes@hotelreinacristina.com).

$$ Hotel Los Tilos offers 30 comfortable rooms (some with balconies) on the charming traffic-free Plaza de Bib-Rambla behind the cathedral. All clients are welcome to use the fourth-floor view terrace overlooking the great café, shopping, and people-watching neighborhood. The hall carpets are well-trafficked, but the in-room flooring has been renovated (Sb-€40–55, Db-€55–80, Tb-€77–100, prices may be cheaper if you reserve online, air-con, parking-€18/day, Plaza de Bib-Rambla 4, tel. 958-266-712, fax 958-266-801, www.hotellostilos.com, clientes@hotellostilos.com, friendly José María).

$ Zurita Pensión is a well-run 14-room place facing a big and delightful square. Even with its double-paned windows it may come with night noise (S-€21, D-€34, Db-€42, Tb-€63, air-con, Plaza de la Trinidad 7, tel. 958-275-020, www.pensionzurita.com, pensionzurita@gmail.com, Francisco and Loli).

$ Hotel Lisboa, overlooking Plaza del Carmen and the start of the busy pedestrianized Calle Navas with its popular tapas bars, offers 28 simple but well-maintained rooms with friendly owners (S-€25, Sb-€36, D-€36, Db-€49, T-€44, Tb-€66, elevator, free Internet access, Plaza del Carmen 27, tel. 958-221-414, fax 958-221-487, www.lisboaweb.com, Mary).

In the Albayzín

Note that some consider this area unsafe after dark (see the "Safety in the Albayzín" sidebar, earlier).

$$ Hotel Santa Isabel la Real, an elegant medieval mansion, has 11 rooms ringing a noble courtyard. Buried deep in the Albayzín and furnished in a way that gives you the old Moorish Granada ambience, it offers a warm welcome and rich memories (Db-€85–105 with breakfast, air-con, free Internet access and Wi-Fi, midway between San Nicolás viewpoint and Plaza San Miguel Bajo on Calle Santa Isabel la Real, immediately at a bus stop, tel. 958-294-658, fax 958-294-645, www.hotelsantaisabella real.com, info@hotelsantaisabellareal.com).

$$ La Casa de Rafa is a traditional house in the heart of the Albayzín that's been converted into four small, funky kitchenette apartments with an eclectic, ever-evolving artistic feel (Chicago-raised owner Rafa lives on-site). You'll share two tiny patios and a rooftop terrace with a spectacular in-your-face view of the Alhambra (Sb-€35–45, Db-€45–60, extra person-€10–12.50, 2-night minimum, 5-min walk from Plaza Nueva at tiny Plaza

Virgen del Carmen, tel. 958-220-682, mobile 610-322-216, www.
elnumero8.com, casaocho@gmail.com). Call Rafa to get (initially
tricky) directions and set up a time to meet and check in.

In or near the Alhambra

If you want to stay on the Alhambra grounds, there are two popular options (famous, overpriced, and generally booked up long in
advance) and one practical and economic place above the parking
lot. All are a half-mile up the hill from Plaza Nueva.

$$$ Parador de Granada San Francisco offers 40 designer
rooms in a former Moorish palace that was later transformed into a
15th-century Franciscan monastery. It's considered Spain's premier
parador...and that's saying something (Db-€310, breakfast-€20,
air-con, free parking, Calle Real de la Alhambra, tel. 958-221-440,
fax 958-222-264, www.parador.es, granada@parador.es). You must
book months ahead to spend the night in this lavishly located,
stodgy, and historic palace. Any peasant, however, can drop in for
a coffee, drink, snack, or meal. For details about the history of the
building, see "The Alhambra Grounds" sidebar.

$$$ Hotel América is classy and cozy, with 17 rooms next
to the parador (Sb-€70, Db-€115, breakfast-€8, closed Dec–Feb,
Calle Real de la Alhambra 53, tel. 958-227-471, fax 958-227-470,
www.hotelamericagranada.com, reservas@hotelamericagranada
.com). Book well in advance.

$$ Hotel Guadalupe, big and modern with 57 rooms, is qui-
etly and conveniently located overlooking the Alhambra parking
lot. While a 20-minute hike above the town, many (especially
drivers) find this to be a practical option (Sb-€50–60, Db-€60–
80, Tb-€80–100, more during festivals, pricey "double superiors"
aren't worth it, air-con, parking in Alhambra lot-€13, Paseo de la
Sabica 30, tel. 958-225-730, www.hotelguadalupe.es, info@hotel
guadalupe.es).

Eating in Granada

Many of Granada's bars still serve a small tapas plate free with
any beer or wine—a tradition
that's dying out in most of Spain.
Restaurants generally serve lunch
from 13:00 to 16:00 and din-
ner from 20:00 until very late
(Spaniards don't start dinner until
about 21:00).

In search of an edible mem-
ory? A local specialty, *tortilla
Sacromonte*, is a spicy omelet with

pig's brain and other organs. *Berenjenas fritas* (fried eggplant) and *habas con jamón* (small green fava beans cooked with cured ham) are worth seeking out. *Tinto de verano*—a red-wine spritzer with lemon and ice—is refreshing on a hot evening. For tips on eating near the Alhambra, see page 67.

In the Albayzín

The most interesting meals hide out deep in the Albayzín (Moorish quarter). The easy way to get there is by taking minibus #31 from Plaza Nueva or #32 from Plaza Isabel La Católica. To find a particular square, ask any local, or follow my directions. If dining late, take the minibus or a taxi back to your hotel; Albayzín back streets can be dangerous because of pickpockets.

Part of the charm of the quarter is the lazy ambience on its squares: **Plaza Larga** is extremely characteristic, with tapas bar tables spilling out onto the square, a morning market, and a much-loved pastry shop. The farthest hike into the Albayzín, **Plaza San Miguel el Bajo** is a neighborhood square boasting my favorite funky, local scene—kids kicking soccer balls, old-timers warming benches, and women gossiping under the facade of a humble church. Its four square-side bars serve serious tapas and its good little restaurant offers a €10 fixed-price meal. This is a fine spot to end your Albayzín visit, as there's a viewpoint overlooking the modern city a block away. Minibuses #31 and #32 rumble by every few minutes, ready to zip you back to Plaza Nueva.

Casa Torcuato is a hardworking eatery serving straightforward yet creative food in a smart upstairs dining room. They serve a good €8 fixed-price meal. Plates of fresh fish run €8–12 and their tropical salad includes a Tahitian wonderland of fruits (closed Sun, 2 blocks beyond Plaza Larga at Calle Aqua 20, second location on nearby Calle Pagés, tel. 958-202-039).

Restaurante El Ladrillo, with outdoor tables on a peaceful square, is *the* place for piles of fish. Their popular €12 *barco* ("boatload" of mixed fried fish) is a fishy feast that stuffs two to the gills. The smaller €8.50 half *barco* fills one person adequately, or, when combined with a salad, can feed two (daily, on Plaza Fátima, just off Calle Pages).

***Near the San Nicolás Viewpoint:* Bar Kiki,** a laid-back and popular bar-restaurant on an unpretentious square, serves simple tapas. Try their tasty fried eggplant (long hours, closed Wed, just behind viewpoint at Plaza de San Nicolás 9).

Paseo de los Tristes: This is like a stage set of outdoor bars on a terrace over the river gorge. While there is no serious restaurant here and the food values are mediocre at best, the scene—cool along a stream under trees, with the floodlit Alhambra high above, and a happy crowd of locals enjoying a meal or drink out—is a winner. As this is at the base of the Albayzín, there is no issue of danger after dark here. You're a simple, level five-minute walk back to Plaza Nueva.

Carmens: For a more memorable but expensive experience, consider fine dining with Alhambra views in a *carmen,* a typical Albayzín house with a garden (buzz to get in). Following the Reconquista, the Albayzín became depopulated. Wealthy families took larger tracts of land and built fortified mansions with terraced gardens within their walls. Today, rather than growing produce, the gardens of many of these *carmens* host dining tables and romantic restaurants.

Carmen Mirador de Aixa, small and elegant, has the dreamiest Alhambra views among the *carmens.* You'll pay a little more, but the food is exquisitely presented and the view makes the splurge worthwhile (plan on €45 plus wine for dinner, next to Carmen de las Tomasas at Carril de San Agustín 2, tel. 958-223-616).

Carmen de las Tomasas serves gourmet traditional Andalusian cuisine with killer views in a dressy/stuffy atmosphere (€40 meals, Wed–Sun 21:00–24:00, generally closed Mon–Tue, call ahead as they sometimes close on Sun instead, reservations required, Carril de San Agustín, tel. 958-224-108, Cristina).

Carmen Mirador de Morayma boasts great atmosphere and fine rustic cuisine, but no commanding Alhambra views. This is where famous visitors dine to the sounds of classical guitar. For seating, choose between outdoor—on one of three garden terraces—or inside the noble mansion, where it's bright and nice, but not romantic (€30 tasting *menus,* closed Sun, Calle Pianista García Carrillo 2, tel. 958-228-290).

Carmen de Aben Humeya is the least expensive, least stuffy, and least romantic. Its outdoor-only seating lets you enjoy a meal or just a long cup of coffee while gazing at the Alhambra. This is a rare place enthusiastic about dinner salads (€10–15 plates, daily 13:00–24:00, food served 13:00–16:00 & 19:30–22:30—or until 24:00 in heat of summer, Cuesta de las Tomasas 12, tel. 958-226-665).

Near Plaza Nueva

For people-watching, consider the many restaurants on Plaza Nueva or Plaza de Bib-Rambla (south of cathedral). For a happening scene, check out the bars on and around Calle Elvira. It's best to wander and see where the biggest crowds are.

Bodegas Castañeda is the best mix of lively, central, untouristy, and cheap among the tapas bars I visited. Just a block off Plaza Nueva, it requires a bit of self-service: When crowded, you need to power your way to the bar to order; when quiet, you can order at the bar and grab a little table (same budget prices). Consider their *tablas combinadas*—variety plates of cheese, meat, and *ahumados* (four different varieties of smoked fish)—and tasty *croquetas* (breaded and fried mashed potatoes and ham). The big kegs tempt you with different local sherries. Tapas can be ordered from an easy menu and cost €2–3 apiece (daily 11:30–16:30 & 17:00–24:00, Calle Almireceros 1, tel. 958-215-464). Don't be confused by a different "Castaneda" restaurant nearby (unless you're hankering for stuffed potatoes).

Restaurante Sevilla, with its tight and charming little dining room behind a high-energy tapas bar, has been a favorite of well-dressed natives for 75 years. Specialties include paella, other rice dishes, soups, and salads. You'll eat surrounded by old photos of local big shots who've dined here. On hot nights, tables pour out onto the little square facing the Royal Chapel. It's a local-feeling, elegant, urban scene (€20 meals, summer closed Sun, rest of year closed Sun–Mon; across from Royal Chapel at Calle Oficios 12, tel. 958-221-223). *Great paella*

La Cueva de 1900 is a fresh family-friendly deli-like place on the main drag appreciated for its simple dishes and quality ingredients. It's proud of its homemade hams, sausages, and cheeses—sold in 100-gram lots and served with checkered-tablecloth style. If you've had enough meat, they have good €5 salads (Calle Reyes Católicos 42, tel. 958-229-327). *no liquor ***

At Arrayanes, a good Moroccan restaurant, Mostafa will help you choose among the many salads, the *pastela* (a chicken-and-cinnamon pastry appetizer), the couscous, or *tajin* dishes. He treats you like an old friend...especially the ladies (Wed–Mon 13:30–16:30 & 19:30–23:30, closed Tue, Cuesta Marañas 4, where Calles Calderería Nueva and Vieja meet, tel. 958-228-401).

Hippie Options on Calle Calderería Nueva: From Plaza Nueva, walk two long blocks down Calle Elvira and turn right onto the wonderfully hip and Arabic-feeling Calle Calderería Nueva, which leads uphill into the Albayzín. The street is lined with trendy *teterías.* These small tea shops, open all day, are good places to linger, chat, and imagine you're in Morocco. Some are conservative and unmemorable, and others are achingly romantic, filled with incense, beaded cushions, live African music, and effervescent young hippies. They sell light meals such as crêpes, and a worldwide range of teas, all marinated in a candlelit snake charm.

Dessert: **Los Italianos,** Italian-run and teeming with locals, is popular for its ice cream, *horchata* (*chufa*-nut drink), and shakes (mid-March–mid-Oct daily 8:00–24:00, closed mid-Oct–mid-March, across the street from cathedral and Royal Chapel at Gran Vía 4, tel. 958-224-034).

Markets: Though heavy on meat, **Mercado San Agustín** also sells fruits and veggies. Throughout the EU, locals lament the loss

---

Cheap Tricks in Granada

- Buy some drinks and snacks near Plaza Nueva, and sling them up to the Albayzín. This makes for a great cheap date at the San Nicolás viewpoint or one of the scattered squares and lookout points.
- Have a drink at the Carmen de Aben Humeya—it's an inexpensive way to soak up great Alhambra views.
- Do a tapas crawl on Calle Navas right off Plaza del Carmen. Claim your "right" to a free tapa with every drink.

---

of the characteristic old market halls as they are replaced with new hygienic versions. If nothing else, it's as refreshingly cool as a meat locker (Mon–Sat 8:00–15:30, closed Sun, a block north of cathedral and a half-block off Gran Vía on Calle Cristo San Agustín). Tucked away in the back of the market is a very cheap and colorful little eatery: **Cafeteria San Agustín.** They make their own *churros* and give a small tapa free with each drink (menu on wall). If waiting for the cathedral or Royal Chapel to open, kill time in the market. The **Pescadería** square, downhill from the actual market and a block from Plaza de Bib-Rambla, is actually more popular with locals looking to buy produce.

Connections

From Granada by Train to: Barcelona (1/day Wed, Thu, and Sat only, 11.5 hrs; also 1/night daily, 12 hrs), **Madrid** (2/day, 5 hrs), **Toledo** (all service is via Madrid, nearly hourly AVE connections to Toledo), **Algeciras** (3/day, 4.25–5 hrs), **Ronda** (3/day, 2.5 hrs), **Sevilla** (4/day, 3 hrs), **Córdoba** (2/day, 2.5 hrs), **Málaga** (3/day, 2.5–3.25 hrs on AVE, transfer in Bobadilla or Antequera). Train info: tel. 902-240-202. Many of these connections have a more frequent (and sometimes much faster) bus option—see below.

By Bus to: Nerja (5/day, 2.5 hrs, more with transfer in Motril),

Sevilla (11/day, 3 hrs *directo*, 4 hrs *ruta*), **Córdoba** (8/day, 2.5–3 hrs), **Madrid** (18/day, 5.25 hrs), **Málaga** (hourly, 1.5–2 hrs), **Algeciras** (5/day, 4–5.5 hrs, some are *directo*, others are the slow *ruta*), **La Línea/Gibraltar** (2/day, 5 hrs), **Jerez** (1/day, 4.5 hrs). All of these buses are run by the Alsina Graells company (tel. 958-185-480, www.movelia.es).

By Car: To drive to Nerja (1.5 hours away), take the exit for the coastal town of Motril. You'll wind through 50 scenic miles south of Granada, then follow signs for Málaga. Note that you can also hop a taxi to Nerja (€125 fixed rate).

CÓRDOBA

Straddling a sharp bend of the Guadalquivir River, Córdoba has a glorious Roman and Moorish past, once serving as a regional capital for both empires. It's home to Europe's best Islamic sight after Granada's Alhambra: the Mezquita, a splendid and remarkably well-preserved mosque that dates from A.D. 784. When you step inside the mosque, which is magical in its grandeur, you can imagine Córdoba as the center of a thriving and sophisticated culture. During the Dark Ages, when much of Europe was barbaric and illiterate, Córdoba was a haven of enlightened thought—famous for religious tolerance, artistic expression, and dedication to philosophy and the sciences.

Planning Your Time

Ideally, Córdoba is worth two nights and a day. Don't rush the magnificent Mezquita, but also stick around to experience the city's other pleasures: Wander the evocative Jewish Quarter, enjoy the tapas scene, and take the TI's guided town walk in the evening.

However, if you're tight on time, it's possible to do Córdoba more quickly—especially since it's conveniently located on the AVE bullet-train line (and because, frankly, Córdoba is less interesting than the other two big Andalusian cities, Sevilla and Granada). To see Córdoba as an efficient stopover between Madrid and Sevilla (or as a side-trip from Sevilla—hourly trains, 45-min trip), focus on the Mezquita: Taxi from the station, spend two hours there, explore the old town for an hour...and then scram.

Orientation to Córdoba

Córdoba's big draw is the mosque-turned-cathedral called the Mezquita (for pronunciation ease, think female mosquito). Most of the town's major sights are nearby, including the Alcázar, a former royal castle. While the town seems to ignore its river, there is a Renaissance triumphal arch on the riverbank next to a stout "Roman Bridge" which spans the marshy Guadalquivir River (a prime bird-watching area). The bridge leads to the town's old fortified gate (which now houses a fascinating museum on Moorish culture, the Museum of Al-Andalus Life). The Mezquita is buried in the characteristic medieval town. North of that stretches the Jewish Quarter, then the modern city—which feels much like any other in Spain, but with some striking Art Deco buildings at Plaza de las Tendillas and lots of Art Nouveau lining Avenida del Gran Capitán.

Tourist Information

Córdoba has three helpful TIs: at the train station, Mezquita, and Alcázar (all open daily 9:30–14:00 & 16:30–19:30, Alcázar TI open through midday break Fri–Sun, tel. 902-201-774, www.turismo decordoba.org). A small TI kiosk is on **Plaza de las Tendillas** (similar hours but until 21:30 in summer).

The TIs **Córdoba Card** is unlikely to be a good value for any short visit (€30–45, valid for one year).

Arrival in Córdoba

By Train or Bus: Córdoba's train station is located on Avenida de América. The bus station is across the street from the train station (on Avenida Vía Augusta, to the north). It's about a 25-minute walk from either station to the old town. There is no luggage storage at the train station, but you can stow your bag at the bus station for €3.20.

Built in 1991 to accommodate the high-speed AVE train line, the train station has ATMs, restaurants, a variety of shops, a TI booth, an information counter, and a small lounge for first-class AVE passengers. Taxis and local buses are just outside.

To get to the old town, hop a **taxi** (€6 to the Mezquita) or catch bus #3 or #4 (get off at San Fernando, ask driver for "Mezquita").

To **walk** the 25 minutes from the train station to the Mezquita, turn left onto Avenida de América, then right on Avenida del Gran Capitán, which becomes a pedestrian zone. At the end, ask someone, *"¿Dónde está la Mezquita?"* You'll be directed downhill, through the whitewashed old Jewish Quarter.

Córdoba

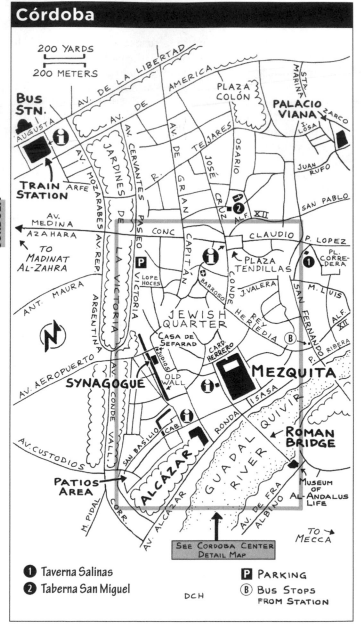

200 YARDS
200 METERS

Bus Stn.

AUGUSTA

Train Station

ARFE

AV. DE LA LIBERTAD

AV. DE AMERICA

PLAZA COLÓN

STA. MARINA

PALACIO VIANA

ZARCO

I. LOSA

AV. DE

AV. CERVANTES

JARDINES

AV. MOZARABES

R. DE GRAN

JOSÉ CRUZ

TEJARES

OSARIO

JUAN RUFO

SAN PABLO

AV. MEDINA
AZAHARA

TO MADINAT
AL-ZAHRA

ANT. MAURA

DE LA VICTORIA

AV. REP. ARGENTINA

CONC

CAPITÁN

CLAUDIO

P. LOPEZ

PL. CORREDERA

PLAZA TENDILLAS

CONDE HERIEDIA

J. VALERA

REY

M. LUIS

ALF. XII

P. RIBERA

ALF. XII

PASEO VICTORIA

P

LOPE HOCES

BARROSO

JEWISH QUARTER

CASA DE SEFARAD

CARD. HERRERO

SAN FERNANDO

B

MEZQUITA

AV. AEROPUERTO

JUDIOS
OLD WALL

SYNAGOGUE

AV. CONDE VALL.

SAN BASILIO

CAB.

RONDA

ISASA

ROMAN BRIDGE

AV. CUSTODIOS

PATIOS AREA

M. PIDAL

CORR.

ALCÁZAR

AV. ALCAZAR

GUADAL QUIVIR RIVER

AV. DE FRA ALBINO

MUSEUM OF AL-ANDALUS LIFE

TO MECCA

SEE CORDOBA CENTER DETAIL MAP

N

1 Taverna Salinas
2 Taberna San Miguel

DCH

P PARKING
B BUS STOPS
FROM STATION

CÓRDOBA

Helpful Hints

Closed Days: The synagogue and Madinat Al-Zahra are closed on Monday, while the Palacio de Viana is closed Sunday. The Mezquita is open daily.

Festival: During the first half of May, Córdoba hosts the Concurso Popular de Patios Cordobeses—a patio contest (see "Patios" sidebar later in this chapter).

Cheap Tricks: Some minor sights, including the Baths of the Caliphate Alcázar and the Alcázar de los Reyes Cristianos, are free all day Wednesday. The Mezquita is free from Monday through Saturday, but only if you get there before 10:00.

Internet Access: Chat-is is a block down from Plaza de las Tendillas at Calle Claudio Marcelo 15 (Mon–Fri 9:30–13:30 & 17:00–20:30, closed Sat–Sun, tel. 957-475-500).

Laundry: The helpful staff at **Sol y Mar** will wash, dry, and fold your laundry (€12.50/load, usually same-day service, cheaper for self-service, Mon–Fri 9:00–13:30 & 17:00–20:30, Sat 9:30–13:30, closed Sun, Calle del Doctor Fleming 8, tel. 957-298-929).

Tours in Córdoba

Guided Walks—In summer, two-hour nighttime walks start at the TI on Plaza de las Tendillas and finish at a typical bar near the Mezquita (€15, includes a drink and tapa, April–Oct daily at 21:30, no tours Nov–March, prepay at TI, request English).

Local Guide—**Isabel Martinez Richter** is a charming archaeologist who loves to make the city come to life for curious Americans (mobile 669-369-645, isabmr@terra.es). **Angel Lucena** is also a good teacher and a joy to be with (€95/2.5 hours, mobile 607-898-079, aluc@eresmas.com).

Sights in Córdoba

▲▲▲The Mezquita *Fabuloso!!*

This massive former mosque—now with a 16th-century church rising up from the middle—was once the center of Western Islam and the heart of a cultural capital that rivaled Baghdad and Istanbul. A wonder of the medieval world, it's remarkably well-preserved, giving today's visitors a chance to soak up the ambience of Islamic Córdoba in its 10th-century prime.

Cost and Hours: €8, ticket kiosk inside the Patio de los Naranjos, free entry until 10:00 (because they don't want to charge a fee to attend Mass), dry €3.50 audioguide; open Mon–Sat 8:30–19:00, Sun 8:30–10:30 & 14:00–19:00, Christian altar accessible only after 10:30 unless you attend Mass, try to avoid midday

The Mezquita

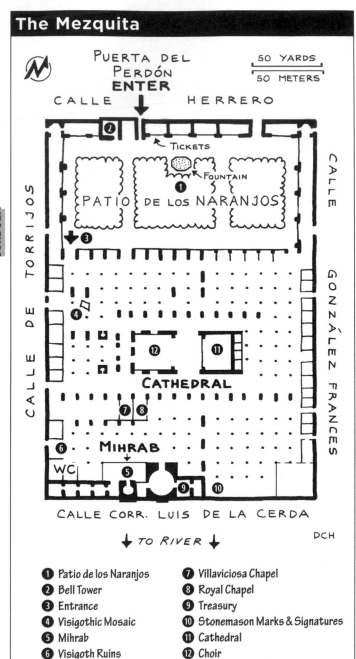

PUERTA DEL PERDÓN
ENTER

CALLE HERRERO

50 YARDS

50 METERS

Tickets

CALLE

PATIO DE LOS NARANJOS

Fountain

CÓRDOBA

CALLE DE TORRIJOS

GONZÁLEZ FRANCES

CATHEDRAL

MIHRAB

WC

CALLE CORR. LUIS DE LA CERDA

↓ TO RIVER ↓

DCH

1 Patio de los Naranjos
2 Bell Tower
3 Entrance
4 Visigothic Mosaic
5 Mihrab
6 Visigoth Ruins
7 Villaviciosa Chapel
8 Royal Chapel
9 Treasury
10 Stonemason Marks & Signatures
11 Cathedral
12 Choir

crowds (11:00–15:00) by coming early or late; tel. 957-470-512, www.mezquitadecordoba.org.

◑ Self-Guided Tour: Before entering the patio, take in the exterior of the Mezquita. The mosque's massive footprint is clear when you survey its sprawling walls from outside. At 600 feet by 400 feet, it seems to dominate the higgledy-piggledy medieval town that surrounds it.

Patio de los Naranjos: The Mezquita's big and welcoming courtyard is free to enter. When this was a mosque, the Muslim faithful would gather in this courtyard to perform ablution—ritual washing before prayer, as directed by Muslim law. Historians believe this was the first such courtyard with trees for shade. The trees (probably olive, palm, or orange) were planted in rows that line up with the colonnades inside the mosque, symbolically extending the place of worship through the courtyard. The courtyard walls display many of the mosque's carved ceiling panels and beams, which date from the 10th century. Gaze up through the trees for views of the **bell tower** (c. 1600), built over the remains of the original Muslim minaret. For four centuries, five times a day, a cleric (called a muezzin) would climb the minaret that once stood here to call Muslims to face Mecca and pray.

• *Buy your ticket and enter the mosque, passing through the keyhole gate at the far right corner (pick up an English map-brochure as you enter).*

Interior: Entering the former mosque from the patio, you pass from an orchard of orange trees into a forest of delicate

columns dating from 786. The 850 red-and-blue columns are topped with double arches—a round Romanesque arch above a Visigothic horseshoe arch—made from alternating red brick and white stone. The columns and capitals (built of marble, granite, and alabaster) were recycled from ancient Roman ruins and conquered Visigothic churches. (Arabs excelled at absorbing both the technology and the building materials of the people they conquered.) The columns seem to recede to infinity, as if reflecting the immensity and complexity of Allah's creation. Supporting such a tall ceiling with thin columns required extra bracing with the double arches you see—a

Islamic Córdoba (756–1236): Medieval Europe's Cultural Capital

After his family was slaughtered by political rivals (A.D. 750), 20-year-old Prince Abd Al-Rahman fled the royal palace at Damascus, headed west across North Africa, and went undercover among the Berber tribesmen of Morocco. For six years, he avoided assassination while building a power base among his fellow Arab expatriates and the local Muslim Berbers. As an heir to the title of "caliph," or ruler of Islam, he sailed north and claimed Moorish Spain as his own, confirming his power by decapitating his enemies and sending their salted heads to the rival caliph in Baghdad. This split in Islam is much like the divide in Christianity between Protestants and Catholics.

Thus began an Islamic flowering in southern Spain under Abd Al-Rahman's family, the Umayyads. They dominated Sevilla and Granada, ruling the independent state of "Al-Andalus," with their capital at Córdoba.

By the year 950—when the rest of Europe was mired in poverty, ignorance, and superstition—Córdoba was Europe's greatest city, rivaling Constantinople and Baghdad. It had well over 100,000 people (Paris had a third that many), with hundreds of mosques, palaces, and public baths. The streets were paved and lighted at night with oil lamps, and running water was piped in from the outskirts of the city. Medieval visitors marveled at the size and luxury of the Mezquita mosque, a symbol that the Umayyads of Spain were the equal of the caliphs of Baghdad.

This Golden Age was marked by a remarkable spirit of tolerance and cooperation among the three great monotheistic religions: Islam, Judaism, and Christianity. Giving that society a positive spin, my guide explained, "Umayyad Al-Andalus was

beautiful solution to a practical problem.

Although it's a vast room, the low ceilings and dense columns create an intimate and worshipful atmosphere. The original mosque was brighter before Christians renovated the place for their use and closed in the arched entrances from the patio and street. The giant cathedral sits in the center of the mosque. For now, pretend it doesn't exist. We'll visit it after exploring the mosque.

The mosque sits on the site of an early-Christian church built during the Visigothic period (sixth century). Five columns in from the entrance, a wooden railing marks a hole where you can look down to see a Visigothic **mosaic** from that original church. This is important to the locals, proving there was a church here before the mosque and making it defensible for this newer church to have "violated" the great mosque. There's a little tension lately as some local Muslims are calling to have the Mezquita become a mosque again. The local bishop is responding by changing the tourist not one country with three cultures. It was one culture with three religions...its people shared the same food, dress, art, music, and language. Different religious rituals within the community were practiced in private. But clearly, Muslims ruled. No church spire could be taller than a minaret and while the call to prayer rang out five times daily, there was no ringing of church bells."

The university rang with voices in Arabic, Hebrew, and Latin, sharing their knowledge of *al-jibra* (algebra), medicine, law, and literature. The city fell under the enlightened spell of the ancient Greeks, and Córdoba's 70 libraries bulged with translated manuscripts of Plato and Aristotle, works that would later inspire medieval Christians.

Ruling over the Golden Age were two energetic leaders—Abd Al-Rahman III (912–961) and Al-Hakam II (961–976)—who conquered territory, expanded the Mezquita, and boldly proclaimed themselves caliphs.

Córdoba's Y1K crisis brought civil wars that toppled the caliph (1031), splintering Al-Andalus into several kingdoms. Córdoba came under the control of the Almoravids (Berbers from North Africa), who were less sophisticated than the Arab-based Umayyads. Then a wave of even stricter Islam swept through Spain, bringing the Almohads to power (1147) and driving Córdoba's best and brightest into exile. The city's glory days were over, and it was replaced by Sevilla and Granada as the centers of Spanish Islam. On June 29, 1236, Christians conquered the city. That morning Muslims said their last prayers in the great mosque. That afternoon, the Christians set up their portable road altar and celebrated the church's first Mass. Córdoba's days as a political and cultural superpower were over.

information to make it clear...this is a living church and will stay that way.

• *Walk to the center of the far wall (opposite the entrance), where you'll find the focal point of the mosque, the...*

Mihrab: The mosque equivalent of a church's high altar, this was the focus of the mosque and is the highlight of the Mezquita today. Picture the mosque at prayer time. Each floor stone is about the size of a prayer rug...more than 20,000 people could pray at once here. Imagine the multitude kneeling in prayer, facing the mihrab, rocking forward to touch their heads to the ground, and saying, *"Allahu Akbar, La illa a il Allah, Muhammad razul Allah"*— "Allah is great, there is no god but Allah, and Muhammad is his prophet."

The mihrab, a feature found in all mosques, is a decorated "niche"—in this case, more like a small room with a golden-arch entrance. During a service, the imam (prayer leader) would stand here to read scripture and give sermons. He spoke loudly into the niche, his back to the assembled crowd, and the architecture worked to amplify his voice so all could hear. Built in the mid-10th century by Al-Hakam II, the exquisite room reflects the wealth of Córdoba in its prime. Three thousand pounds of multicolored glass-and-enamel cubes panel the walls and domes in mosaics designed by Byzantine craftsmen, depicting flowers and quotes from the Quran. Gape up. Overhead rises a colorful, starry dome with skylights and interlocking lobe-shaped arches.

• *In the far-right corner, you'll find...*

Visigoth Ruins: On display in the corner to the right of the mihrab are bits of carved stone from the Visigothic Christian church of San Vicente that stood here in the sixth century. (The Christian symbolism was scratched off so the stones could be reused by Muslims.) Abd Al-Rahman I bought the church from his Christian subjects before leveling it to build the mosque. From here, pan 90 degrees to enjoy a view that reveals the vastness of the mosque. (Perhaps you might also appreciate a hidden WC and drinking fountain—in the corner.)

• *Immediately in front of the mihrab, in about the center of the mosque, is an open area that was the...*

Villaviciosa Chapel: In 1236, Saint-King Ferdinand III conquered the city and turned the mosque into a church. Still, the locals continued to call it "La Mezquita," and left the structure virtually unchanged (70 percent of the original mosque structure survives to this day). Sixteen columns were removed and replaced by Gothic arches to make this chapel. It feels as if the church architects appreciated the opportunity to incorporate the sublime architecture of the pre-existing mosque into their church. Notice how the floor was once almost entirely covered with the tombs of nobles and big shots eager to make this their final resting place.

• *Behind the wall, face the mihrab and look to the left to see the...*

Royal Chapel: The chapel—designed for the tombs of Christian kings—is completely closed off. While it was never open to the public, the tall, well-preserved Mudejar walls and dome are easily visible. The lavish Arabic-style decor dates from the 1370s, done by Muslim artisans after the Reconquista. The fact that a Christian king chose to be buried in a tomb so clearly Moorish in design indicates the mutual respect between the cultures (before the Inquisition changed all that).

• *Return to the mihrab. To your immediate left, enter the Baroque...*

Treasury (Tesoro): The treasury is filled with display cases of religious artifacts and the enormous monstrance that is paraded through the streets of Córdoba each Corpus Christi, 60 days after Easter (notice the handles). The monstrance was an attempt by 16th-century Christians to create something exquisite enough to merit being the holder of the Holy Communion wafer. As locals believed the wafer actually was the body of Christ, this trumped any relics. The monstrance is designed like a seven-scoop ice-cream cone, held together by gravity. While the bottom is silver-plated 18th-century Baroque, the top is late Gothic—solid silver with gold plating courtesy of 16th-century conquistadors.

The big canvas nearest the entrance shows Saint-King Ferdinand III, who conquered Córdoba in 1236, accepting the keys to the city's fortified gate from the vanquished Muslims. The victory ended a six-month siege and resulted in a negotiated settlement: The losers' lives were spared, providing they evacuated. Most went to Granada, which remained Muslim for another 250 years. The same day (exhibiting the same spirit of military glee enjoyed by American troops who set up camp in Saddam Hussein's palace), the Spaniards celebrated Mass in a makeshift chapel right here in the great mosque.

Among the other Catholic treasures, don't miss the ivory crucifix (next room, body carved from one tusk, arms carefully fitted on) from 1665. Get close to study Jesus' mouth—it's incredibly realistic. The artist? No one knows.

Just outside the treasury exit, a glass case shows off casts of the many **stonemason marks and signatures** found in this one building. Try to locate the actual ones on nearby columns. (I was five for six.) This part of the mosque has the best light for photography, thanks to skylights put in by 18th-century Christians.

The mosque grew over several centuries under a series of rulers. Remarkably, each ruler kept to the original vision—rows and rows of multicolored columns topped by double arches. Then came the Christians.

Cathedral: Rising up in the middle of the forest of columns is the bright and newly restored cathedral, oriented in the Christian tradition, with its altar at the east end. This doesn't jibe with the mihrab, which normally also faces east (but to Mecca not Jerusalem), because this mihrab actually faces south—as mosques in Syria do in order to face Mecca. (Syria was the ancestral home of Córdoba's jealous Umayyad branch of Islam.) Gazing up at the rich decoration, it's easy to forget that you were in a former mosque just seconds ago. While the mosque is about 30 feet high, the cathedral's ceiling soars 130 feet up. Look at the glorious ceiling.

In 1523, Córdoba's bishop proposed building this grand church in the Mezquita's center. The town council opposed it, but King Charles V ordered it done. According to a false but believable legend, when the king saw the final product, he declared that they'd destroyed something unique to build something ordinary. For a more positive take on this, acknowledge that it would have been quicker and less expensive for the Christian builders to destroy the mosque, but they respected its beauty and built their church into it.

It's interesting to ponder the aesthetics and psychology of the Catholic church versus Islam in the styles of these two great places of worship (horizontal, vertical, intimate, power, fear, love, guilt, dark, bright, simple, elaborate, feeling close to God, feeling small before God).

The basic structure is late Gothic with fancy Isabelline-style columns. The nave's towering Renaissance arches and dome emphasize the triumph of Christianity over Islam in Córdoba. The twin pulpits feature a marble bull, lion, angel, and eagle—symbols of the four evangelists. The cathedral's new Carrara marble throne is the seat of the bishop.

Choir: The Baroque-era choir stalls were added much later—made in 1750 of New World mahogany. While cluttering up a previously open Gothic space, the choir is considered one of the masterpieces of 18th-century Andalusian Baroque. Each of the 109 stalls (108 plus the throne—*catedra*—of the bishop) features a scene from the Bible: Mary's life on one side facing Jesus' life on the other. The lower chairs feature carved reliefs of the 49 martyrs of Córdoba (from Roman, Visigothic, and Moorish times), each with a palm frond symbolizing martyrdom and the scene of their death in the background. The medieval church strayed from the inclusiveness taught by Jesus. Choirs (which seem to consume otherwise-spacious church interiors throughout Spain) were only for canons, priests, and the bishop. Those days are long gone. In fact, a public Mass is now held right here (Mon–Sat at 9:30 in the morning).

Near the Mezquita

Just downhill from the mosque is the Guadalquivir River (which flows on to Sevilla and eventually out to the Atlantic). While silted up today, it was once navigable from here. The town seems to turn its back on the Guadalquivir, but the arch next to the Roman Bridge (with its ancient foundation surviving) and the fortified gate on the far bank (now a museum, described below) evoke a day when the river was key to the city's existence.

Triumphal Arch and Plague Monument—The unfinished Renaissance arch was designed to give King Philip II a royal welcome, but he arrived before its completion—so the job was canceled. The adjacent monument with the single column is an 18th-century plague monument dedicated to St. Raphael (he was in charge of protecting the population from the main scourges in this region at that time: plague, hunger, and floods).

Roman Bridge—The bridge sits on its first-century-A.D. foundations and retains its 16th-century arches, but was poorly restored in 2009. It feels like so much other modern work along this riverbank—done on the cheap. As it was the first bridge over this river, it established Córdoba as a strategic point. Walk across the bridge for a fine view of the city—especially the huge mosque with its cathedral busting through the center. You'll be steps away from the fascinating museum described next.

▲**Museum of Al-Andalus Life**—The Museo Vivo de Al-Andalus fills the fortified gate (built in the 14th century to protect the Christian city) at the far side of the Roman Bridge. It is a velvety, philosophical, almost evangelical attempt to humanize the Muslim Moorish culture funded by the Fundación Roger Garaudy (started by Garaudy, a former French politician and writer controversial for Holocaust revisionism). You don headsets and wander through simple displays with a clear, engrossing soundtrack letting you sit at the feet of the great poets and poke into Moorish living rooms. Garaudy's "How Man Became Human" 60-minute video is a flowery story taking you from prehistory to the formation of the great monotheistic religions...the greatest of which—in his opinion—is Islam (€4.50, daily May–Sept 10:00–14:00 & 16:30–20:30, Oct–April 10:00–18:00, "Multivision" is €1 extra, played in English, 6/day, generally on the hour—ask about next showing as you enter, Torre de la Calahorra, tel. 957-293-929, www.torrecalahorra.com).

Baths of the Caliphate Alcázar (Banos Califales)—The scant but evocative remains of these 10th-century royal baths are all that's left from the caliph's palace complex. They date from a time when the city had hundreds of baths and a population of several hundred thousand. The exhibit teaches about Arabic baths in general and the caliph's in particular. A 10-minute video (normally in Spanish, English on request) tells the story well (€2, May–June and Sept–mid-Oct Tue–Sat 10:00–14:00 & 17:30–19:30; July–Aug Tue–Sat 8:30–14:30; mid-Oct–April Tue–Sat 10:00–14:00 & 16:30–18:30; year-round: Sun 9:30–14:30, closed Mon; just outside the wall near the Alcázar).

Jewish Córdoba

Córdoba's Jewish Quarter dates from the late Middle Ages, after Muslim rule and during the Christian era. Now little remains. For a sense of it in its thriving heyday, visit the synagogue and the cultural center located a few steps away (both described in this section). For a pretty picture, find **Calle de las Flores** (a.k.a. "Blossom Lane"). This narrow flower-bedecked street frames the cathedral's bell tower as it hovers in the distance (the view is a favorite for local guidebook covers).

Synagogue (Sinagoga)—The small yet beautifully preserved synagogue was built in 1315, under Christian rule, but the Islamic decoration has roots way back to Abd Al-Rahman I (see "Islamic Córdoba" sidebar earlier in this chapter). During Muslim times,

Central Córdoba

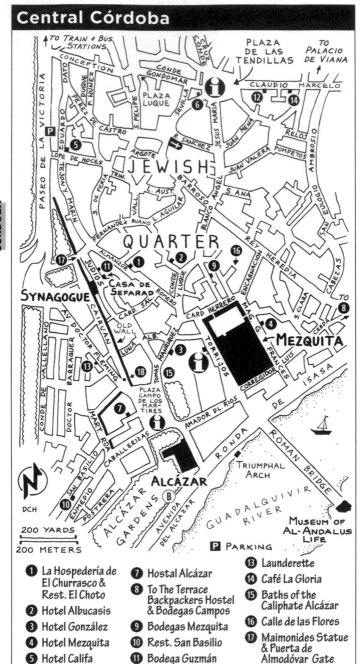

CÓRDOBA

1. La Hospedería de El Churrasco & Rest. El Choto
2. Hotel Albucasis
3. Hotel González
4. Hotel Mezquita
5. Hotel Califa
6. Hotel Boston
7. Hostal Alcázar
8. To The Terrace Backpackers Hostel & Bodegas Campos
9. Bodegas Mezquita
10. Rest. San Basilio
11. Bodega Guzmán
12. Internet Café
13. Launderette
14. Café La Gloria
15. Baths of the Caliphate Alcázar
16. Calle de las Flores
17. Maimonides Statue & Puerta de Almodóvar Gate
18. Averroes Statue

Córdoba's sizable Jewish community was welcomed, though they paid substantial taxes to the city—money that enlarged the Mezquita and generated goodwill. That goodwill came in handy when Córdoba's era of prosperity and mutual respect ended with the arrival of the intolerant Almohad Berbers. Christians and Jews were repressed, and brilliant minds—such as the rabbi and philosopher Maimonides—fled for their own safety.

The Christian Reconquista of Córdoba (1236) brought another brief period of religious tolerance. That's when this synagogue was built—the result of a joint effort by Christians, Jews, and Muslim (Mudejar) craftsmen. By the end of the 14th century, however, Spain's Jews were again persecuted. They were finally expelled or forced to convert in 1492; this is one of only three surviving synagogues in Spain built before that year.

Rich Mudejar decorations of intertwined flowers, arabesques, and Stars of David plaster the walls. What appear to be quotes from the Quran in Arabic are actually quotes from the Bible in Hebrew. On the east wall (the symbolic direction of Jerusalem), find the niche for the Ark, which held the scrolls of the Torah (the Jewish scriptures). The upstairs gallery was reserved for women. This synagogue, the only one that survives in Córdoba, was left undisturbed because it was used as a church until the 19th century—in fact, you can see a cross painted into a niche (€0.30, Tue–Sat 9:30–14:00 & 15:30–17:30, Sun 9:30–13:30, closed Mon, Calle de los Judíos 20, tel. 957-202-928). To learn more about the synagogue and its community, head next to the Casa de Sefarad (described next), just 10 steps uphill.

Casa de Sefarad—Set inside a restored 14th-century home directly across from the synagogue, this interpretive museum brings to life Córdoba's rich Jewish past. Five rooms around a central patio are themed to help you understand different aspects of daily life for Spain's former Jewish community. The rooms focus on contributions from women in the community, Jewish holidays, musical traditions, and more. Upstairs is an interpretive center for the synagogue, along with rooms dedicated to Maimonides and to the synagogue. The Casa de Sefarad is a cultural center for Sephardic (the Hebrew word for "Spanish") Jewish heritage. Jaime and his staff stress that the center's purpose is not political or religious, but cultural. Along with running this small museum, they teach courses, offer a library, and promote an appreciation of Córdoba's Sephardic heritage (€4, Mon–Sat 11:00–19:00, Sun

11:00–14:00, 30-minute guided tours in English are available by request if a guide is available, next to the synagogue at the corner of Calle de los Judíos and Calle Averroes, tel. 957-421-404, www .casadesefarad.es). The Casa de Sefarad hosts weekly concerts—acoustic, Sephardic, and Andalusian, but no flamenco—on its patio (€10, most Saturdays in season at 20:00, reservations smart).

City Wall—Built upon the foundation of Roman Córdoba's wall, these fortifications date mostly from the 12th century. While the city stretched beyond the wall in Moorish times, this wall protected its political, religious, and commercial center. There were seven gates. Today the Puerta de Almodóvar (near the synagogue) is best preserved. Just outside the gate you'll find statues of Córdoba's great thinkers: Seneca (the Roman philosopher and adviser to Nero), Maimonides, and Averroes.

Statues of Maimonides and Averroes—Statues honor two of Córdoba's deepest-thinking homeboys—one Jewish, one Muslim, both driven out during the wave of Islamic intolerance after the fall of the Umayyad caliphate. (Maimonides is 30 yards downhill from the synagogue; Averroes is at the end of the old wall, where Cairuán and Doctor Fleming streets meet.)

Maimonides (1135–1204) was born in Córdoba and raised on both Jewish scripture and Aristotle's philosophy. Like many tolerant Córdobans, he saw no conflict between the two. Maimonides—sometimes called the "Jewish Aquinas"—wrote the *Guide of the Perplexed* (in Arabic), in which he asserted (as the Christian philosopher St. Thomas Aquinas later would) that secular knowledge and religious faith could go hand-in-hand.

Córdoba changed in 1147, when the fundamentalist Almohads assumed power. (Imagine Pat Robertson taking over the US.) Maimonides was driven out, eventually finding work in Cairo as the sultan's doctor. Today tourists, Jewish scholars, and fans of Aquinas rub the statue's foot in the hope that some of Maimonides' genius and wisdom will rub off on them.

The story of **Averroes** (1126–1198) is a near match of Maimonides', except that Averroes was a Muslim lawyer, not a Jewish doctor. He became the medieval world's number-one authority on Aristotle, influencing Aquinas. Averroes' biting tract *The Incoherence of the Incoherence* attacked narrow-mindedness, asserting that secular philosophy (for the elite) and religious faith (for the masses) both led to truth. The Almohads banished him from the city and burned his books, ending four centuries of Córdoban enlightenment.

Córdoba's Jewish Quarter: A Ten-Point Scavenger Hunt

While most of the area around the big mosque is commercial and touristy, the neighborhood to the east seems somehow almost untouched by tourism and the modern world (as you leave the Mezquita, turn right and exit the orange-grove patio). To catch a whiff of Córdoba before the onslaught of tourism and the affluence of the 21st century, explore this district. Just wander and observe. Here are a few characteristics to look for:

1. **Narrow streets.** Skinny streets make sense in hot climates, as they provide much-appreciated shade.

2. **Thick, whitewashed walls.** Both features serve as a kind of natural air-conditioning—and the chalk "bugs" bugs.

3. **Colorful doors and windows.** What little color there is in this famously white city helps counter the boring white-wash.

4. **Iron grilles.** Historically, these were more artistic, but modern ones are more practical. Their continued presence is a reminder of the persistent gap through the ages between rich and poor. The wooden latticework covering many windows is a holdover from days when women were extremely modest and wanted privacy.

5. **Stone bumpers on corners.** These protected buildings against reckless drivers. Scavenged second-hand ancient Roman pillars worked well.

6. **Scuff guards.** Made of harder materials, these guards sit at the base of the whitewashed walls—and, from the looks of it, are serving their purpose.

7. **Riverstone cobbles.** These stones were cheap and local, and provided drains down the middle of a lane. They were flanked by smooth stones that stayed dry for walking (and now aid the rolling suitcases of modern-day tourists).

8. **Pretty patios.** Córdobans are proud of their patios. Walk up to the inner iron gates of the wide-open front doors and peek in (see "Patios" sidebar later in this chapter).

9. **Remnants of old towers from minarets.** Muslim Córdoba peaked in the 10th century with an estimated 400,000 people, which meant lots of neighborhood mosques.

10. **A real neighborhood.** People really live here. There are no tacky shops, and just about the only tourist...is you.

More Sights in Córdoba

Alcázar de los Reyes Cristianos—Tourists line up to visit Córdoba's overrated fortress, the "Castle of the Christian Monarchs," which sits strategically next to the Guadalquivir River. Upon entering, look to the right to see a big, beautiful garden rich with flowers and fountains. To the left is a modern-feeling, unimpressive fort. While it was built along the Roman walls in Visigothic times, constant reuse and recycling has left it sparse and barren (with the exception of a few interesting Roman mosaics on the walls). Crowds squeeze up and down the congested spiral staircases of "Las Torres" for meager views. Ferdinand and Isabel donated the castle to the Inquisition in 1482, and it became central in the church's effort to discover "false converts to Christianity"—mostly Jews who had decided not to flee Spain in 1492 (€4, Tue–Fri 8:30–19:30, closes at 15:00 in summer, Sat–Sun 8:30–15:00, closed Mon). On Fridays and Saturdays you're likely to see civil wedding parties here.

Plaza de las Tendillas—While most tourists leave Córdoba having seen just the Mezquita and the cute medieval quarter that surrounds it, the modern city offers a good peek at urban Andalucía. Perhaps the best way to sample this is to browse Plaza de las Tendillas and the surrounding streets. The square, with an Art Deco charm, acts like there is no tourism in Córdoba. On the hour, a clock here chimes the guitar chords of Juan Serrano, a Córdoban classic.

Characteristic cafés and shops abound. For example, **Café La Gloria** provides an earthy Art Nouveau experience. Located just down the street from Plaza de las Tendillas, it has an unassuming entrance, but a sumptuous interior. Carved floral designs wind around the bar, mixing with *feria* posters and bullfighting memories. Pop in for a quick beer or coffee (daily from 8:30, quiet after lunch crowd clears out, Calle Claudio Marcelo 15, tel. 957-477-780).

Palacio de Viana—Decidedly off the beaten path, this former palatial estate is a 20-minute walk northeast from the cluster of sights near the Mezquita. A guided tour whisks you through each room of an exuberant 16th-century estate, while an English handout drudges through the dates and origin of each important piece. But the house is best enjoyed by ignoring the guide and gasping at the massive collection of—for lack of a better word—stuff. Decorative-art fans will have a field day. The sight is known as the "patio museum" for its 12

Patios

In Córdoba, patios are taken very seriously, as shown by the fiercely fought contest that takes place the first half of every

May to pick the city's most picturesque. Patios, a common feature of houses throughout Andalucía, have a long history here. The Romans used them to cool off, and the Moors added lush, decorative touches. The patio functioned as a quiet outdoor living room, an oasis from the heat. Inside elaborate ironwork gates, roses, geraniums, and jasmine spill down whitewashed walls, while fountains play and caged birds sing. Some patios are owned by individuals, some are communal courtyards for several homes, and some grace public buildings like museums or convents.

Today, homeowners take pride in these mini-paradises, and have no problem sharing them with tourists. Keep an eye out for square metal signs that indicate historic homes. As you wander Córdoba's back streets, pop your head into any wooden door that's open. The proud owners (who keep inner gates locked) enjoy showing off their picture-perfect patios. A concentration of patio-contest award-winners runs along Calle de San Basilio and Calle Martín Roa, just across from the Alcázar gardens.

connecting patios, each with a different theme (house-€6, patios only-€3; June–Sept Mon–Sat 9:00–14:00, closed Sun; Oct–May Mon–Fri 10:00–13:00 & 16:00–18:00, Sat 10:00–13:00, closed Sun; no photos inside, Plaza Don Gome 2, tel. 957-496-741).

Away from the Center

Madinat Al-Zahra (Medina Azahara)—Five miles northwest of Córdoba, these ruins of a once-fabulous palace of the caliph were completely forgotten until excavations began in the early 20th century. Built in A.D. 929 as a power center to replace Córdoba, Madinat Al-Zahra was both a palace and an entirely new capital city—the "City of the Flower"—covering nearly half a square mile (only about 10 percent has been uncovered). Extensively planned

with an orderly design, Madinat Al-Zahra was meant to symbolize and project a new discipline on an increasingly unstable Moorish empire in Spain. It failed. Only 75 years later, the city was looted and destroyed.

The site is underwhelming—a jigsaw puzzle waiting to be reassembled by patient archaeologists. Upper terrace excavations have uncovered stables and servants' quarters. Farther downhill, the house of a high-ranking official has been partially reconstructed. At the lowest level, you'll come to the remains of the mosque— placed at a diagonal, facing true east. The highlight of the visit is an elaborate reconstruction of the caliph's throne room, capturing a

moody world of horseshoe arches and delicate stucco. Legendary accounts say the palace featured waterfall walls, lions in cages, and—in the center of the throne room—a basin filled with mercury, reflecting the colorful walls. The effect likely humbled anyone fortunate enough to see the caliph.

Cost and Hours: €1.50, Tue–Sat 10:00–20:30, Sun 10:00–14:00, closed Mon.

Getting There: Madinat Al-Zahra is located on a back road five miles from Córdoba. By **car,** head to Avenida de Medina Azahara (one block south of the train station), following signs for *A-431*; the site is well-signposted from the highway. Though the ruins aren't accessible via regular public transportation, the TI runs a **shuttle bus** that leaves each morning and returns two hours later (€6.50, buy ticket at Alcázar or Plaza Tendillas TIs, runs year-round Tue–Fri at 11:00, Sat–Sun at 10:00 and 11:00, informative English booklet provided). Catch the bus near the Mezquita at Avenida Alcázar, along the river.

Sleeping in Córdoba

The first four listings and Hostal Alcázar are within a five-minute stroll of the Mezquita. The others are still central, but not buried in all that tangled medieval cuteness. If it's hot and you've got a lot of luggage, don't bother with the inconvenient city buses; just hop in a taxi.

$$$ La Hospedería de El Churrasco is a nine-room jewel box of an inn, featuring plush furniture, tasteful traditional decor, and hardwood floors. Quiet and romantic, it's tucked in the old quarter just far enough away from the tourist storm, yet still handy for sightseeing (Sb-€120, Db-€140, superior Db-€180, €20 more

---

Sleep Code

(€1 = about $1.40, country code: 34)
S = Single, **D** = Double/Twin, **T** = Triple, **Q** = Quad, **b** = bathroom,
s = shower only. Unless otherwise noted, credit cards are
accepted, English is spoken, and breakfast generally costs
extra.

To help you easily sort through these listings, I've divided
the rooms into three categories, based on the price for a
standard double room with bath during high season:

$$$ Higher Priced—Most rooms €100 or more.
  $$ Moderately Priced—Most rooms between €60-100.
    $ Lower Priced—Most rooms €60 or less.

---

per room in April–May and Oct, website shows off each distinct
room, no twin rooms, includes breakfast, air-con, Internet access,
parking-€20, midway between Puerta de Almodóvar and the
Mezquita at Calle Romero 38, tel. 957-294-808, fax 957-421-661,
www.elchurrasco.com, hospederia@elchurrasco.com).

$$ Hotel Albucasis, at the edge of the tourist zone, features
15 basic, clean rooms, all of which face quiet interior patios. The
friendly, accommodating staff and cozy setting make you feel right
at home (Sb-€55, Db-€85, breakfast-€6, air-con, parking-€12,
Calle del Buen Pastor 11, tel. 957-478-625, www.hotelalbucasis
.com, hotelalbucasis@hotmail.com).

$$ Hotel González, with many of its 17 basic rooms facing
its cool and peaceful patio, is sparse but sleepable. It's clean and
well-run, with a fine location and price (Sb-€43, Db-€78, Tb-€110,
includes breakfast, air-con, Wi-Fi, Manríquez 3, tel. 957-479-
819, fax 957-486-187, www.hotel-gonzalez.com, hotelgonzalez
@wanadoo.es).

$$ Hotel Mezquita, just across from the main entrance of
the Mezquita, rents 31 modern and comfortable rooms. The grand
entrance lobby elegantly recycles an upper-class mansion (Sb-€36,
Db-€74, Tb-€100, breakfast-€4, air-con, Plaza Santa Catalina
1, tel. 957-475-585, fax 957-476-219, www.hotelmezquita.com,
hotelmezquita@wanadoo.es).

$$ Hotel Califa, a modern business-class hotel from the
NH chain, sits on a quiet street a block off busy Paseo Victoria,
on the edge of the jumbled old quarter (65 rooms, vast price range
depending on demand but Db generally €80–90, around €70 in
heat of summer, air-con, parking-€15, Lope de Hoces 14, tel. 957-
299-400, www.nh-hotels.com, nhcalifa@nh-hotels.com).

$$ Hotel Boston, with 30 rooms, is a decent budget bet if you
want a reliable basic hotel away from the touristy Mezquita zone.

It's a taste of workaday Córdoba (Db-€60–72, Málaga 2, just off Plaza de las Tendillas, tel. 957-474-176, www.hotel-boston.com).

$ Hostal Alcázar is your best cheapie. Run-down and budget-priced, without a real reception desk, this friendly place is just outside the old city wall on a quiet cobbled traffic-free street known for its prize-winning patios. Its 16 rooms are split between two homes on opposite sides of the lane, conveniently located 50 yards from a taxi and bus stop (Sb-€18, small Db-€30, bigger Db-€45, Tb-€45–54, two-room apartment-€60 for two or €80 for four, breakfast-€3, air-con, Wi-Fi, parking-€6, near Alcázar at Calle de San Basilio 2, tel. 957-202-561, www.hostalalcazar.com, hostalalcazar@hotmail.com, ladies' man Fernando and family, son Demitrio speaks English).

$ The Terrace Backpackers Hostel rents dorm beds and simple doubles in a great neighborhood (dorm beds-€15–19, D-€40–50, includes breakfast, air-con, Internet access, terrace, kitchen, lots of hostel-type info and help, at San Fernando bus stop—take #3 or #4 from station—at Calle Lucano 12, tel. 957-492-966, theterracebackpackershostel@yahoo.com).

Eating in Córdoba

Local specialties include *salmorejo,* Córdoba's version of *gazpacho.* It's creamier, with more bread and olive oil and generally served with pieces of ham and hard-boiled egg. Most places serve white wines from the nearby Montilla-Moriles region; these *finos* are slightly less dry but more aromatic than the sherry produced in Jerez de la Frontera.

Restaurants generally serve lunch from 13:00 to 16:00 and dinner from 20:00 until very late (Spaniards don't start dinner until about 21:00).

Many smaller places have "bar menus" with *raciones* and half-*(media) raciones* rather than typical first and second courses. Enjoy this as an opportunity to explore the regional cuisine. Ordering half-*raciones* may cost a bit more per ounce, but you'll broaden your tasting experience. Two people can fill up on four *media-raciones.* Don't be intimidated by the language barrier. Ask for the *lista de tapas* in English (there's usually one around somewhere). For a good value and truly local scene, explore the little characteristic bars in the lanes around Plaza de la Corredera.

Near the Mezquita

There are plenty of touristy options around the Mezquita, designed for out-of-towners and tour groups. By walking a couple blocks away along Calle del Cardenal González, you get into a district of cheap, accessible little places offering a better value. Listed here, in order, are a bright and efficient diner about 50 yards from the mosque, a colorful neighborhood restaurant, a down-and-dirty wine bar, a steak house, and (a 10-min walk away) my favorite place in town.

Bodegas Mezquita is a good bet for a bright, not-too-touristy, air-conditioned place a block from the mosque. They have a good *menu del dia,* or you can try the two-person special—eight tapas for €20—on weekdays (one block immediately in front of the Mezquita garden at Calle de Céspedes 12, tel. 957-498-117).

Restaurante San Basilio is the local hangout on Calle de San Basilio, just outside the wall. While there's no seating outside, the restaurant still offers great "patio ambience"—with a view of the kitchen action. No tourists, no pretense...it's understandably the neighborhood favorite (classic €18 fixed-priced meal, €8 lunch special weekdays, lots of €10 fish dishes, closed Sun, Calle de San Basilio 19, tel. 957-297-007). If this doesn't work for you, there's a fancier restaurant a block farther toward the church. And for something rougher—rustic meals, tapas, and crowds—go to the church and head a block left to Bodega San Basilio (Calle de Enmedio, tel. 957-297-832).

Bodega Guzmán, which proudly displays the heads of brave-but-unlucky bulls, serves cold, very basic tapas to locals who burst into song when they feel the flamenco groove. Arrive early to get a table. While it feels like a drinking place, they have rustic tapas and *raciones* (ask for the list in English). Choose a table or belly up to the bar and try a white wine: dry *(blanco seco)* or sweet *(blanco dulce)* for €1 a glass. For grape juice, ask for *mosto* (closed Thu; if entering the old town from Puerta de Almodóvar take the first right—it's 100 yards from the gate at Calle de los Judíos 7).

Restaurante El Choto is bright, formal, and dressy, with a small leafy patio, buried deep in the Jewish Quarter. It's touristy yet intimate, serving well-presented international dishes with an emphasis on grilled meat. The favorite is kid goat with garlic—*choto al ajillo* (€17 house menu, €33 tasting menu, closed Mon, Calle de Almanzor 10, tel. 957-760-115).

Bodegas Campos is a historic and venerable house of eating, attracting so many locals it comes with its own garage. They have a stuffy formal restaurant upstairs, but I'd eat in the more relaxed tavern on the ground floor. The service is great and the menu is inviting. In two visits I nearly ate my way through the offerings, half-*ración* at a time, and enjoyed each €5–8 dish. Experiment—you can't go wrong. House specialties are bull-tail stew (*rabo de toro*—rich, tasty, and a good splurge) and cod with tomato. Don't leave without exploring the sprawling complex. Behind the WC you'll discover a virtual museum of classic, original *feria* posters and great photos (closed Sun; from river end of Mezquita walk east along Cardenal González, continue 10 min straight to Calle de Lineros 32; tel. 957-497-500).

In the Modern City

Taverna Salinas feels like a movie set designed to give you the classic Córdoba scene. While all the seating is indoors, it's still pleasantly patio-esque, and popular with locals for its traditional cuisine and exuberant bustle. The fun menu features a slew of enticing €6 plates (spinach with chick peas is a house specialty). Study what locals are eating before ordering. There's no drink menu—just basic beer or inexpensive wine. If there's a line (as there often is later in the evening), leave your name and throw yourself into the adjacent tapas-bar mosh pit for a drink (closed Sun; from Plaza de las Tendillas walk 3 blocks to the Roman temple, then go 1 more block and turn right to Tendidores 3; tel. 957-480-135).

Taberna San Miguel is nicknamed Casa el Pisto for its famous *pisto,* the local ratatouille-like vegetable stew. Well-respected, it's packed with locals who appreciate regional cuisine, a good value, and a place with a long Córdoban history. Go to the bar to be seated (€8–10 plates, closed Sun–Mon and Aug, 2 blocks north of Plaza de las Tendillas at Plaza San Miguel 1, tel. 957-470-166). Walking here, you feel a world apart from the touristy scene.

Connections

From Córdoba by Train: Córdoba is on the slick AVE train line (reservations required), making it an easy stopover between **Madrid** (28/day, 1.75 hrs) and **Sevilla** (hourly, 45 min, €30 one-way, €47 round-trip—must reserve both ways when you book, with railpass you still must pay €10 reservation fee). The slow train to **Sevilla** doesn't require a reservation and is much cheaper (80 min, €9 one-way). Other trains go to **Granada** (2/day, 2.5 hrs), **Ronda** (2/day direct, 1.75 hrs; more with transfer in Bobadilla, 3.5 hrs), **Málaga** (15/day, 1 hr on fast AVE train; 2/day, 2.25–3 hrs on slower train), and **Algeciras** (2/day, 3.5 hrs). Train info: tel. 902-240-202.

By Bus to: Granada (8/day, 2.5–3 hrs), **Sevilla** (9/day, 2 hrs), **Madrid** (6/day, 5 hrs), **Málaga** (5/day, 3–3.5 hrs *directo*), **Barcelona** (2/day, 10 hrs). The efficient staff at the information desk prints bus schedules for you. Bus info: tel. 957-404-040.

CÓRDOBA

ANDALUCÍA'S WHITE HILL TOWNS

Arcos de la Frontera • Ronda • Zahara •
Grazalema • Jerez

Just as the American image of Germany is Bavaria, the Yankee dream of Spain is Andalucía. This is the home of bullfights, flamenco, gazpacho, pristine whitewashed hill towns, and glamorous Mediterranean resorts. The big cities of Andalucía (Granada, Sevilla, and Córdoba) and the South Coast (Costa del Sol) are covered in separate chapters. This chapter explores its hill-town highlights.

The Route of the White Hill Towns (Ruta de los Pueblos Blancos), Andalucía's charm bracelet of cute towns perched in the sierras, gives you wonderfully untouched Spanish culture. Spend a night in the romantic queen of the white towns, Arcos de la Frontera. (Towns with "de la Frontera" in their names were established on the front line of the centuries-long fight to recapture Spain from the Muslims, who were slowly pushed back into Africa.) The hill towns—no longer strategic, no longer on any frontier—are now just passing time peacefully. Join them. Nearby, the city of Jerez, while teeming with traffic and lacking in charm, is worth a peek for its famous horses and a glass of sherry.

To study ahead, visit www.andalucia.com for information on hotels, festivals, museums, nightlife, and sports in the region.

Planning Your Time

On a three-week vacation in Spain, the region is worth two nights and up to two days sandwiched between visits to Sevilla and Tarifa. Arcos makes the best home base, as it's near Jerez, close to interesting smaller towns, and conveniently situated halfway between Sevilla and Tarifa. The towns can also be accessed from the Costa del Sol resorts via Ronda.

ANDALUCÍA'S HILL TOWNS

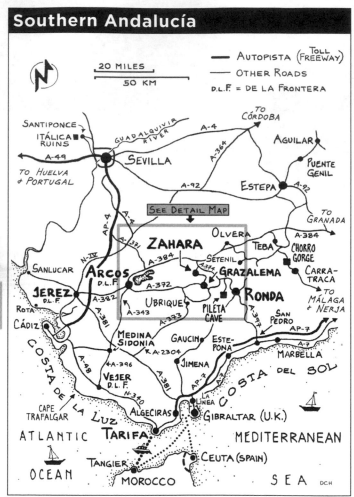

Southern Andalucía

See Jerez on your way in or out, spend a day hopping from town to town in the more remote interior (Grazalema and Zahara, at a minimum), and enjoy Arcos early and late in the day. For more details on exploring this region by car, see "Route Tips for Drivers" at the end of this chapter.

Without a car, you might keep things simple and focus only on Arcos and Jerez (both well-served by public buses). Another option, if you're staying in Sevilla, is to use Andalusian Minibus Tours for an all-day excursion to Olvera, Zahara, Grazalema, and Setenil de las Bodegas.

Spring and fall are high season throughout this area. In summer you'll find intense heat, but empty hotels and no crowds.

Arcos de la Frontera

Arcos smothers its long, narrow hilltop and tumbles down the back of the ridge like the train of a wedding dress. It's larger than most other Andalusian hill towns, but equally atmospheric. Arcos consists of two towns: the fairy-tale old town on top of the hill and the fun-loving lower, or new, town. The old center is a labyrinthine wonderland, a photographer's feast. Viewpoint hop through town. Feel the wind funnel through the narrow streets as cars inch around tight corners. Join the kids' soccer game on the churchyard patio. Enjoy the moonlit view from the main square.

Though it tries, Arcos doesn't have much to offer other than its basic whitewashed self. The locally produced English guidebook on Arcos waxes poetic and at length about very little. You can arrive late and leave early and still see it all.

Orientation to Arcos

Tourist Information

The TI, on the main square across from the parador, is helpful and loaded with information, including bus schedules (summer Mon–Fri 10:00–14:30 & 17:00–20:00, Sat 10:00–13:30 & 17:00–19:00, Sun 10:30–13:30; rest of year Mon–Fri 10:00–14:30 & 16:00–19:00, Sat 10:00–14:30 & 16:00–18:00, Sun 10:30–13:30; Plaza del Cabildo, tel. 956-702-264, www.ayuntamientoarcos.org).

The TI organizes a one-hour **walking tour** of the old town, which describes the church and the town's history, lifestyles, and Moorish influences. You also get a peek at some private courtyard patios. Call or drop by the TI to make sure a tour is scheduled and to book in advance (€7, Mon–Fri at 11:00, leave from main square, in Spanish and/or English; for private tours call TI).

Arrival in Arcos

By Bus: The bus station is on Calle Corregidores, at the foot of the hill. To get up to the old town, catch the shuttle bus marked *Centro* (€1, pay driver, 2/hr, Mon–Fri 8:15–21:15, Sat 8:15–14:15, doesn't run on Sun), hop a taxi (€5 fixed rate), or hike 20 uphill minutes (see map).

By Car: The old town is a tight squeeze with a one-way traffic flow from west to east (coming from the east, circle south under town). The TI and my recommended hotels are in the west. If you miss your target, you must drive out the other end, double back, and try again. Driving in Arcos is like threading needles. Turns are tight, parking is frustrating, and congestion can lead to long jams.

Cheap Tricks in the White Hill Towns

Good news: In general, the south of Spain is cheaper than the north (especially in the small towns).

In Arcos de la Frontera
For an inexpensive (€1) and scenic loop around town, take the minibus joyride described in "Getting Around Arcos" (below).

In Ronda
Instead of going for the big meal with views, either grab a *bocadillo* (sandwich) from a bar or get picnic fixings at the supermarket, and eat your lunch in the Alameda del Tajo park. Then have a coffee at the Hotel Don Miguel terrace, where you feel like you're falling into the gorge.

In Jerez
Rather than attending the horse show, watch the cheaper training sessions. Afterwards, take the Sandeman sherry tour (without tapas), or just go to the Sandeman shop and buy a bottle to chill and drink at your hotel.

Small cars can park in the main square of the old town at the top of the hill (Plaza del Cabildo). Get a €3.50 all-day pass from your hotel or buy a ticket from the machine (€0.70/hr, 2-hr maximum, only necessary Mon–Fri 9:00–14:00 & 17:00–21:00 and Sat 9:00–14:00—confirm times on machine). If checking in, tell the uniformed parking attendant the name of your hotel. If there's no spot, wait until one opens up (he'll help...for a little tip). Once you grab a spot, tell him you'll be back from your hotel with a ticket.

It's less stressful (and better exercise) to park in the modern underground lot at Plaza de España in the new town. From this lot, catch a taxi or the shuttle bus up to the old town (2/hr; as you're looking uphill, the bus stop is to the right of the traffic circle), or hike 15 minutes.

Getting Around Arcos
The old town is easily walkable, but it's fun and relaxing to take a circular **minibus** joyride. The little shuttle bus constantly circles through the town's one-way system and around the valley (€1, 2/hr, Mon–Sat 8:15–21:15, may stop running after 14:00 on Sat, doesn't run on Sun). For a 30-minute tour, hop on. You can catch it just below the main church in the old town near the mystical stone circle (generally departs roughly at :20 and :50 past the hour). Sit in the front seat for the best view of the tight squeezes and the school kids hanging out in the plazas as you wind through the old town. After passing under a Moorish gate, you enter a modern

Arcos de la Frontera Overview

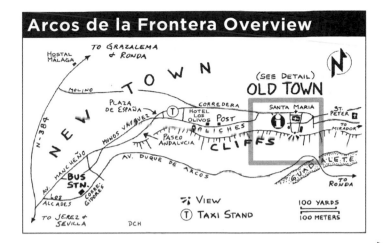

residential neighborhood, circle under the eroding cliff, and return to the old town by way of Plaza de España.

Helpful Hints

Internet Access: Try the single computer at the TI (€1/15 min).

Post Office: It's in the old town at Paseo de los Boliches 24, a few doors up from Hotel Los Olivos (Mon–Fri 8:30–14:30, Sat 9:30–13:00, closed Sun).

Viewpoint: For drivers, the best town overlook is from a tiny park just beyond the new bridge on the El Bosque road. In town, there are some fine viewpoints (for instance, from the main square), but the church towers are no longer open to the public.

Self-Guided Walk

Welcome to Arcos' Old Town

This walk will introduce you to virtually everything worth seeing in Arcos.

• *Start at the top of the hill, in the main square dominated by the church. (Avoid this walk during the hot midday siesta.)*

Plaza del Cabildo: Stand at the viewpoint opposite the church on the town's main square. Survey the square, which in the old days doubled as a bullring. On your right is the parador, a former palace of the governor. It flies three flags: Europe, Spain, and the

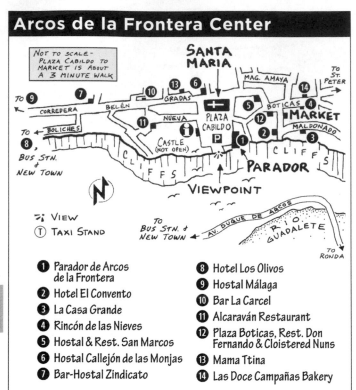

Arcos de la Frontera Center

NOT TO SCALE—
PLAZA CABILDO TO
MARKET IS ABOUT
A 3 MINUTE WALK

SANTA MARIA

TO ST. PETER

MAG. AMAYA

CORREDERA

BELÉN

GRADAS

BOTICAS

MARKET

NUEVA

PLAZA CABILDO

MALDONADO

BOLICHES

CASTLE
(NOT OPEN)

PARADOR

BUS STN.
&
NEW TOWN

C L I F F S

C L I F F S

VIEWPOINT

VIEW

TAXI STAND

TO
BUS STN. &
NEW TOWN

AV. DUQUE DE ARCOS

RIO
GUADALETE

TO
RONDA

1 Parador de Arcos
de la Frontera

2 Hotel El Convento

3 La Casa Grande

4 Rincón de las Nieves

5 Hostal & Rest. San Marcos

6 Hostal Callejón de las Monjas

7 Bar-Hostal Zindicato

8 Hotel Los Olivos

9 Hostal Málaga

10 Bar La Carcel

11 Alcaraván Restaurant

12 Plaza Boticas, Rest. Don
Fernando & Cloistered Nuns

13 Mama Ttina

14 Las Doce Campañas Bakery

green Andalusian flag. On your left are the City Hall and the TI, below the 11th-century Moorish castle where Ferdinand and Isabel held Reconquista strategy meetings (castle privately owned and closed to the public).

Now belly up to the railing and look down. The people of Arcos boast that only they see the backs of the birds as they fly. Ponder the parador's erosion concerns (it lost part of its lounge in the 1990s—dropped right off), the orderly orange groves, and fine views toward Morocco. The city council considered building an underground parking lot to clear up the square, but nixed it because of the land's fragility. You're 330 feet above the Guadalete River. This is the town's suicide departure point for men (women jump from the other side).

• *Looming over the square is the...*

Church of Santa María: After Arcos was retaken from the Moors in the 13th century, this church was built atop a mosque. Notice the church's fine but chopped-off bell tower. The old one fell in the earthquake of 1755 (famous for destroying Lisbon). The replacement was intended to be the tallest in Andalucía after Sevilla's—but money ran out. It looks like someone lives on an upper floor. Someone does—the church guardian resides there in a room strewn with bell-ringing ropes.

The church may be closed for restoration through 2010; if it's open, buy a ticket and enter (€1.50, Mon–Fri 10:00–13:00 & 16:00–19:00, Sat 10:00–14:00, closed Sun and Jan–Feb). Once inside, step into the center, where you can see the finely carved choir. The organ was built in 1789 with that many pipes. The fine Renaissance high altar—carved in wood—covers up a Muslim prayer niche that survived from the older mosque. The altar shows God with a globe in his hand (on top), and scenes from the life of Jesus (on the right) and Mary (left). Circle the church counterclockwise and notice the elaborate chapels. While most of the architecture is Gothic, the chapels are decorated in Baroque and Rococo styles. The ornate statues are used in Holy Week processions. Sniff out the "incorruptible body" (miraculously never rotting) of St. Felix—a third-century martyr. Felix may be nicknamed "the incorruptible," but take a close look at his knee. He's no longer skin and bones...just bones and the fine silver mesh that once covered his skin. Rome sent his body here in 1764, after recognizing this church as the most important in Arcos. In the back of the church, under a huge fresco of St. Christopher (carrying his staff and baby Jesus), is a gnarly Easter candle from 1767.

• *Back outside, examine the...*

Church Exterior: Circle clockwise around the church, down four steps, to find the third-century Roman votive altar with a carving of the palm tree of life. Though the Romans didn't build this high in the mountains, they did have a town and temple at the foot of Arcos. This carved stone was discovered in the foundation of the original Moorish mosque, which stood here before the first church was built.

Head down a few more steps and come to the main entrance (west portal) of the church (closed until restoration is complete). This is a fine example of Plateresque Gothic—Spain's last and most ornate kind of Gothic.

In the pavement, notice the 15th-century magic circle with 12 red and 12 white stones—the white ones have various "constellations" marked (though they don't resemble any of today's star charts). When a child would come to the church to be baptized, the parents would stop here first for a good Christian exorcism. The exorcist would stand inside the protective circle and cleanse the baby of any evil spirits. While locals no longer do this (and a modern rain drain now marks the center), Sufis, members of a sect of Islam, still come here in a kind of pilgrimage every November. (Down a few more steps and 10 yards to the left, you can catch the public bus for a circular minibus joyride through Arcos; see "Getting Around Arcos.")

Continue around the church to the intersection below the flying buttresses. These buttresses were built to shore up the church when it was damaged by an earthquake in 1699. (Thanks to these supports, the church survived the bigger earthquake of 1755.) The spiky security grille (over the window above) protected cloistered nuns when this building was a convent. Look at the arches that prop up the houses downhill on the left; all over town, arches support earthquake-damaged structures.

At the corner, **Sr. González Oca's tiny barbershop** has some exciting posters of bulls running Pamplona-style through the streets of Arcos during Holy Week—an American from the nearby Navy base at Rota was killed here by a bull in 1994. (Sr. González Oca is now semi-retired, but if he's in, he's happy to show off his posters; drop in and say, "Hola." Need a haircut, guys? €9.) Downstairs in his son's bar, you can see a framed collection of euro coins from each of the 12 original participating nations (under the TV in the corner). Continuing along under the buttresses, notice the scratches of innumerable car mirrors on each wall (and be glad you're walking).

• *Now make your way...*

From the Church to the Market: Completing your circle around the church, turn left under more arches built to repair earthquake damage and walk east down the bright, white Calle Escribanos. From now to the end of this walk, you'll basically go straight until you come to the town's second big church (St. Peter's). After a block, you hit **Plaza Boticas.**

On your right is the last remaining **convent** in Arcos. Notice the no-nunsense window grilles high above, with tiny peepholes in the latticework for the cloistered nuns to see through. Step into the lobby under the fine portico to find their one-way mirror and a spinning cupboard that hides the nuns from view. Push the buzzer, and one of the eight sisters (several are from Kenya and speak English well) will spin out some €5 boxes of excellent, freshly baked pine-nut cookies for you to consider buying (open daily but not reliably 8:30–14:30 & 17:00–19:00; be careful—if you stand big and tall to block out the light, you can actually see the sister through the glass). If you ask for *magdalenas,* bags of cupcakes will swing around (€1.50). These are traditional goodies made from natural ingredients. Buy some cupcakes to support their church work, and give them to kids as you complete your walk.

The **covered market** *(mercado)* at the bottom of the plaza (down from the convent) resides in an unfinished church. At the entry, notice what is half of a church wall. The church was being built for the Jesuits, but construction stopped in 1767 when King Charles III, tired of the Jesuit appetite for politics, expelled the order from Spain. The market is closed on Sunday and Monday—since they rest on Sunday, there's no produce, fish, or meat ready for Monday. Poke inside. It's tiny but has everything you need. Pop into the *servicio público* (public WC)—no gender bias here.

• *Continue straight down Calle Boticas...*

From the Market to the Church of St. Peter: As you walk, peek discreetly into private patios. These wonderful, cool-tiled courtyards filled with plants, pools, furniture, and happy family activities are typical of Arcos. Except in the mansions, these patios are generally shared by several families. Originally, each courtyard served as a catchment system, funneling rainwater to a drain in the middle, which filled the well. You can still see tiny wells in wall niches with now-decorative pulleys for the bucket.

Look for **Las Doce Campañas bakery,** where Juan Miguel or Encarni sells traditional and delicious sultana cookies (€1.20 each). These big, dry macaroons (named for the wives of sultans) go back to Moorish times. At the next corner, squint back above the bakery to the corner of the tiled rooftop. The tiny stone—where the corner hits the sky—is a very eroded mask, placed here to scare evil spirits from the house. This is Arcos' last surviving mask from a tradition that lasted until the mid-19th century.

Also notice the ancient columns on each corner. All over town, these columns—many actually Roman, appropriated from their original ancient settlement at the foot of the hill—were put up to protect buildings from reckless donkey carts and tourists in rental cars.

As you continue straight, notice that the walls are scooped out on either side of the windows. These are a reminder of the days when women stayed inside but wanted the best possible view of any people action in the streets. These "window ears" also enabled boys in a more modest age to lean inconspicuously against the wall to chat up eligible young ladies.

Across from the old facade ahead, find the **Association of San Miguel.** Duck right, past a bar, into the oldest courtyards in town—you can still see the graceful Neo-Gothic lines of this noble home from 1850. The bar is a club for retired men—always busy when a bullfight's on TV or during card games. The guys are friendly, and drinks are cheap (a stiff Cuba Libre costs €1.50). You're welcome to flip on the light and explore the old-town photos in the back room.

Just beyond, facing the elegant front door of that noble house,

is Arcos' second church, **St. Peter's** (€1 donation, Mon–Fri 10:30–14:00 & 17:00–19:00, Sat 10:30–14:00, closed Sun). You know it's St. Peter's because St. Peter, mother of God, is the centerpiece of the facade. Let me explain. It really is the second church, having had an extended battle with Santa María for papal recognition as the leading church in Arcos. When the pope finally favored Santa María, St. Peter's parishioners changed their prayers. Rather than honoring "María," they wouldn't even say her name. They prayed "St. Peter, mother of God." Like Santa María, it's a Gothic structure, filled with Baroque decor, many Holy Week procession statues, humble English descriptions, and relic skeletons in glass caskets (two from the third century A.D.).

In the cool of the evening, the tiny square in front of the church—about the only flat piece of pavement around—serves as the old-town soccer field for neighborhood kids. Until a few years ago, this church also had a resident bellman—notice the cozy balcony halfway up. He was a basket-maker and a colorful character, famous for bringing a donkey into his quarters, which grew too big to get back out. Finally, he had no choice but to kill and eat the donkey.

Twenty yards beyond the church, step into the fine **Galería de Arte San Pedro,** featuring artisans in action and their reasonably priced paintings and pottery. Walk inside. Find the water drain and the well.

Across the street, a sign directs you to **Mirador**—a tiny square 100 yards away that affords a commanding view of Arcos. The reservoir you see to the east of town is used for water sports in the summertime, and forms part of a power plant that local residents protested—to no avail—based on environmental issues.

From the Church of St. Peter, circle down and around back to the main square, wandering the tiny neighborhood lanes. Just below St. Peter's is a delightful little Andalusian garden (formal Arabic style, with aromatic plants such as jasmine, rose, and lavender, and water in the center). The lane, called Higinio Capote—below Santa María—is particularly picturesque with its many geraniums. Peek into patios, kick a few soccer balls, and savor the views.

Nightlife in Arcos

Evening Action in the New Town—The newer part of Arcos has a modern charm. In the cool of the evening, all generations enjoy life out around Plaza de España (10-min walk from the old town). Several fine tapas bars border the square or are nearby.

The big park (Recinto Ferial) below Plaza de España is the late-night fun zone in the summer (June–Aug) when *carpas* (restaurant tents) fill with merrymakers, especially on weekends. The scene includes open-air tapas bars, disco music, and dancing. Throughout the summer, there are free evening events here, including live concerts on Fridays and open-air cinema on Sundays.

Flamenco—The Flamenco en Escena festival takes place during June in Arcos (www.flamencoenescena.es). Flamenco action normally takes place around the old town especially on the Plaza de Cabildo (check with the TI).

Sleeping in Arcos

Hotels in Arcos consider April, May, August, September, and October to be high season. Note that some hotels double their rates during the motorbike races in nearby Jerez (usually April or May, varies yearly, call TI or ask your hotel) and during Holy Week (March 28–April 4 in 2010); these spikes are not reflected in the prices below. However, the IVA tax is included.

In the Old Town

$$$ Parador de Arcos de la Frontera is royally located, with 24 elegant, recently refurbished and reasonably priced rooms (8 have balconies). If you're going to

experience a parador, this is a good one (Sb-€115–124, Db-€144–155, Db with terrace-€173–186, cheaper rates are from Nov–Feb, breakfast-€15, air-con, elevator, minibar, free parking, Plaza del Cabildo, tel. 956-700-500, fax 956-701-116, www.parador.es, arcos@parador.es).

$$ Hotel El Convento, deep in the old town just beyond the parador, is the best value in town. Run by a hardworking family and their wonderful staff, this cozy hotel offers 13 fine rooms—all with great views, most with balconies. In 1998, I enjoyed a big party with most of Arcos' big shots as they dedicated a fine room with a grand-view balcony to "Rick Steves, Periodista Turístico." Guess where I sleep when in Arcos... (Sb with balcony-€55, Sb

Sleep Code

(€1 = about $1.40, country code: 34)
S = Single, **D** = Double/Twin, **T** = Triple, **Q** = Quad, **b** = bathroom, **s** = shower only. Unless otherwise noted, you can assume credit cards are accepted, English is spoken, and breakfast and the 7 percent IVA tax are not included.

To help you easily sort through these listings, I've divided the rooms into three categories, based on the price for a standard double room with bath during high season.

$$$ Higher Priced—Most rooms €100 or more.
  $$ Moderately Priced—Most rooms between €50-100.
   $ Lower Priced—Most rooms €50 or less.

ANDALUCÍA'S HILL TOWNS

with terrace-€68, Db with balcony-€70, Db with terrace-€85, extra person-€18; 10 percent discount in 2010 when you book direct, pay in cash, and show this year's book; cheaper Nov–Feb; parking on Plaza del Cabildo-€3.50, Maldonado 2, tel. 956-702-333, fax 956-704-128, www.hotelelconvento.es, reservas@hotelelconvento.es). Over an à la carte breakfast, bird-watch on their view terrace, with all of Andalucía spreading beyond your *café con leche*.

$$ La Casa Grande is a lovingly appointed *Better Homes and Moroccan Tiles* kind of place that rents eight rooms with big-view windows. Like in a lavish bed-and-breakfast, you're free to enjoy its fine view terrace, homey library, and classy courtyard, where you'll be served a traditional breakfast (Db-€70–84, Db suite-€82–118, Tb-€110–115, Qb suite-€122–138, breakfast-€9, air-con, free Internet access and Wi-Fi, Maldonado 10, tel. 956-703-930, fax 956-717-095, www.lacasagrande.net, info@lacasagrande.net, Elena).

$$ Rincón de las Nieves, with simple Andalusian style, has a cool inner courtyard and a handful of rooms. Some rooms have their own outdoor terraces with obstructed views, and all have access to the rooftop terrace. An apartment is also available for up to seven people (Db-€50–72, higher for Holy Week and Aug, apartment €20–24 per person, air-con, Boticas 10, tel. 956-701-528, mobile 656-886-256, rincondelasnieves@gmail.com).

$ Hostal San Marcos, run from a bar in the heart of the old town, offers four air-conditioned rooms and a great sun terrace with views of the reservoir above a neat little bar (Sb-€25, Db-€35, Tb-€45, includes tax, Marqués de Torresoto 6, tel. 956-700-721, mobile 615-375-077, sanmarcosarcos@mixmail.com). Loli speaks no English.

$ Hostal Callejón de las Monjas is open sporadically, but offers the best cheap beds in the old town. With a tangled floor plan and nine simple rooms, it's on a sometimes-noisy street behind the Church of Santa María (Sb-€20, D-€27, Db-€33, Db with terrace-€39, Tb-€44, Qb apartments-€66, includes tax, air-con, Calle Deán Espinosa 4, tel. & fax 956-702-302, padua @mesonelpatio.com, staff speak no English). Sr. González Oca, a ladies' man, runs a tiny barbershop in the foyer and a restaurant in the cellar.

$ At **Bar-Hostal Zindicato,** the bar comes first, but they also rent four tidy air-conditioned rooms really cheap out back on the ground floor (Db-€30, just below the old town gate at Calle Corredera 2, tel. 956-701-841, mobile 657-911-851).

In the New Town
$$ **Hotel Los Olivos** is a bright, cool, and airy place with 19 rooms, an impressive courtyard, roof garden, generous public spaces, bar, view, friendly folks, and easy parking. The seven view rooms can be a bit noisy in the afternoon, but—with double-paned windows—are usually fine at night (Sb-€40–45, Db-€60–75, Tb-€72–87, extra bed-€12, breakfast-€8, 10 percent discount with cash and this year's book, free Internet access and Wi-Fi, Paseo de los Boliches 30, tel. 956-700-811, fax 956-702-018, www.hotel-losolivos.es, reservas @hotel-losolivos.es, Raquel and Miguel Ángel).

$ **Hostal Málaga** is surprisingly nice, if for some reason you want to stay on the big, noisy road at the Jerez edge of town. Nestled on a quiet lane between truck stops on A-382, it offers 18 clean, attractive rooms and a breezy two-level roof garden (Sb-€20–25, Db-€35–38, Qb apartment-€50, air-con, easy parking, Ponce de León 5, tel. & fax 956-702-010, saturno1004@hotmal .com, Josefa speaks German if that helps).

Eating in Arcos

Restaurants generally serve lunch from 13:00 to 16:00 and dinner from 20:00 until very late (Spaniards don't start dinner until about 21:00).

Dining
The **Parador** (described earlier under "Sleeping") has an expensive restaurant with a cliff-edge setting. Its €36 11-course sampler menu is an interesting option. A costly drink on the million-dollar-view terrace can be worth the price (€25–30 fixed-price meal at lunch, open for lunch and dinner daily, on main square).

Tapas in Arcos' Old Town
There are four decent rustic bar-restaurants in the old town within a block or two of the main square and church. Most serve tapas at the bar and *raciones* at their tables. Prices are fairly consistent (€2

tapas, €5 *media-raciones*, €8 *raciones*).

Bar La Carcel ("The Prison") is run by a hardworking family that brags about its exquisite tapas and *montaditos* (small open-faced sandwiches). I agree. The menu is accessible; prices are the same at the bar or at the tables; and the place has a winning energy, giving the traveler a fun peek at this community (Tue–Sun 12:00–16:00 & 20:00–24:00, closed Mon; during July–Aug it's open Mon and closed Sun; Calle Deán Espinosa 18, tel. 956-700-410).

Alcaraván tries to be a bit trendier yet *típico*, with a hibachi hard at work out front. A flamenco ambience fills its medieval vault in the castle's former dungeon. This place attracts French and German tourists who give it a cool vibe. Francisco and his wife cook from 13:00 and from 21:00 (closed Mon, Calle Nueva 1).

Restaurante San Marcos is a tiny, homey bar with five tables, an easy-to-understand menu offering hearty, simple home-cooking, and cheap €5 plates and €7 fixed-price meals (14:00–16:00 & after 20:00, kitchen sometimes open during siesta hours, Marqués de Torresoto 6).

Restaurante Don Fernando gives rustic a feminine twist with an inviting bar, and both indoor and great outdoor seating on the square just across from the little market (13:30–16:00 & 20:15–23:00 for food, closed Mon, longer hours for drinks on the square, on Plaza Boticas).

Mama Ttina gives you a break from Andalucía, with its Italian pop music and international Italian/Andaluz/Moroccan/British staff. This Italian restaurant fires up the wood-burning oven, and serves up pizzas and pastas for around €9. On weekdays, they also offer a €9 three-course meal (daily 14:00–16:00 & 20:00–24:00, possibly closed Tue–Wed lunch hour, Dean Espinosa 10, tel. 956-703-937).

Tapas in the New Town

Plaza de España, in the lower new town, is lined with tapas bars and restaurants. There's even an Egyptian restaurant if you're in the mood for a change. For a great perch while enjoying the local family scene, consider the busy **Restaurante Bar Terraza** (€12 plates) at the end of Plaza de España. Just beyond that is **Casa Juan Bernal,** a little bar that's enthusiastic about its "prize-winning" tapas (the local gang injects energy after 21:00, Calle Munoz Vazquez 11).

Connections

By Bus

Leaving Arcos by bus can be frustrating (especially if you're going to Ronda)—buses generally leave late, the schedule information boards are often inaccurate, and the ticket window usually isn't open (luckily, you can buy your tickets on the bus). But local buses do give you a glimpse at *España profunda* ("deep Spain"), where everyone seems to know each other, no one's in a hurry, and despite any language barriers, people are quite helpful when approached.

Two bus companies (Los Amarillos and Comes) share the Arcos bus station. Call the Jerez offices for departure times, or ask your hotelier for help. If you want to find out about the Arcos–Jerez schedule, make it clear you're coming from Arcos (Los Amarillos tel. 956-341-063; Comes tel. 902-199-208, www.tgcomes.es). Also try the privately run www.movelia.es for bus schedules and routes.

From Arcos by Bus to: Jerez (hourly, 30 min), **Ronda** (2–3/day, 2 hrs, 4 hrs with transfer in Villamartín—when transferring, confirm with driver what the final destination is—bus could be headed to Ronda or Sevilla, and dashboard destination signs are often inaccurate), **Cádiz** (4–5/day, 1.25 hrs), **Sevilla** (2/day, 2 hrs, more departures with transfer in Jerez). Buses run less frequently on weekends. The closest train station to Arcos is Jerez.

Route Tips for Drivers

The trip to **Sevilla** takes just over an hour if you pay €5 for the toll road. To reach **southern Portugal,** follow the freeway to Sevilla, skirt the city by turning west on C-30 in the direction of Huelva, and it's a straight shot from there.

For more driving tips for the region, see the end of this chapter.

Ronda

With nearly 40,000 people, Ronda is one of the largest white hill towns. It's also one of the most spectacular, thanks to its gorge-

straddling setting. While day-trippers from the touristy Costa del Sol clog Ronda's streets during the day, locals retake the town in the early evening, making nights peaceful. If you liked Toledo at night, you'll love the local feeling of evenings in Ronda. Since it's served by train and bus, Ronda makes a relaxing break for non-drivers traveling between Granada, Sevilla, and Córdoba. Drivers can use Ronda as a convenient base from which to explore many of the other *pueblos blancos*.

Ronda's main attractions are its gorge-spanning bridges, the oldest bullring in

Spain, and an intriguing old town. The cliffside setting, dramatic today, was practical back in its day. For the Moors, it provided a tough bastion, taken by the Spaniards only in 1485, seven years before Granada fell. Spaniards know Ronda as the cradle of modern bullfighting and the romantic home of 19th-century *banditos*. The real joy of Ronda these days lies in exploring its back streets and taking in its beautiful balconies, exuberant flowerpots, and panoramic views. Walking the streets, you feel a strong local pride and a community where everyone seems to know everyone.

Orientation to Ronda

Ronda's breathtaking ravine divides the town's labyrinthine Moorish quarter and its new, noisier, and more sprawling Mercadillo quarter. A massive-yet-graceful 18th-century bridge connects these two neighborhoods. Most things of touristic importance (TI, post office, hotels, bullring) are clustered within a few blocks of the bridge. The paseo (early evening stroll) happens in the new town, on Ronda's major pedestrian and shopping street, Carrera Espinel.

Tourist Information

The central TI is on the main square, Plaza de España, opposite the bridge (Mon–Fri 9:00–19:30, Sat–Sun 10:00–14:00, longer hours in summer, tel. 952-871-272). Get the free Ronda map, the excellent Andalusian road map, and a listing of the latest museum hours. Consider picking up free maps of Granada, Sevilla, or the Route of the White Towns. Another TI is located opposite the bullring at Paseo Blas Infante (Mon–Fri 10:00–19:15, Sat–Sun 10:15–14:00 & 15:30–18:30, tel. 952-187-119, www.turismo deronda.es).

Local Guide: Energetic and knowledgeable **Antonio Jesús Naranjo** will take you on a two-hour walking tour of the city's sights (from €90 Mon–Fri, from €110 Sat–Sun and holidays, reserve early, tel. 952-879-215, mobile 639-073-763, guiajesus @yahoo.es). The TI has a list of other local guides.

Arrival in Ronda

By Train: The station is a 15-minute walk from the center: Turn right out of the station on Avenida de Andalucía, and go through the roundabout (you'll see the bus station on your right). Continue straight down the street (now called San José) until it dead-ends. Turn left and walk downhill past a church and the Alameda del Tajo park. Keep going down this street, passing the bullring, to get to the TI and the famous bridge. A **taxi** to the center costs about €5.

Ronda

TO PILETA CAVE, ARCOS, SEVILLA ① ❶
TO TRAIN STATION ❶

200 YARDS
200 METERS

Ⓣ TAXI STAND
👁 VIEW
Ⓟ PARKING

BUS STATION
PLAZA MERCED
WC
ALAMEDA
PLAZA DEL SOCORRO
MERCADILLO QUARTER
Post
BULLRING
PLAZA DE ESPAÑA
PARADOR
PLAZA C. ABELA
NUEVA
ROSARIO
LOS REMEDIOS
GUADALEVÍN RIVER
PUENTE NUEVO
OLD BRIDGE
CANTOS
REAL
PEÑAS
TRAIL TO PUERTA DE LOS MOLINOS
S. DOMINGO
MOORISH QUARTER
PLAZA DE MARÍA AUXILIADORA
ARAB BRIDGE
ARAB BATHS MUSEUM
MONDRAGÓN PALACE
SANTA MARÍA LA MAYOR
BANDOLERO MUSEUM
CITY WALL
TO COSTA DEL SOL, ⓭ & ㉒
CALLE JEREZ
SAN JOSÉ
SOLIO
POZO
MADRID
ANDALUCÍA
MONTERO
LAURIA
ALMENDRA
CRUZ VERDE
SOUBIRON
NARANJA
ESPINEL
M. CABRERA
CORTES
VIRGEN DE LA

❶ To Hotel Reina Victoria
❷ Hotel Don Miguel
❸ Hotel San Gabriel
❹ Hotel & Rest. Alavera de los Baños
❺ Hotel Enfrente Arte Ronda
❻ Hotel El Tajo & Spar Market
❼ Hotel San Francisco
❽ Hotel Ronda
❾ Hotel Royal
❿ Hostals Ronda Sol & Biarritz
⓫ To Hostal Andalucía
⓬ Hostal Dona Carmen
⓭ To Los Pastores
⓮ Confitería Daver
⓯ Restaurante del Escudero
⓰ Restaurante Pedro Romero
⓱ Rest. Casa Santa Pola
⓲ Bar Lechuguita
⓳ Café & Bar Faustino
⓴ El Porton
㉑ Tragatapas
㉒ To Almocábar Gate, Casa Maria & Bodega Bar Rest. San Francisco
㉓ Casa del Rey Moro Garden
㉔ Palacio del Marqués de Salvatierra
㉕ Lara Museum
㉖ Museo Joaquín Peinado

ANDALUCÍA'S HILL TOWNS

By Bus: To get to the center from the bus station (lockers inside, buy token at kiosk by exit), leave the station walking to the right of the roundabout, then follow the directions for train travelers (above), heading down San José.

By Car: Street parking away from the center is often free. The handiest place to park in the center of Ronda is the underground lot at Plaza del Socorro (1 block from bullring, €18/24 hrs).

Sights in Ronda

Ronda's New Town

▲▲▲**The Gorge and New Bridge (Puente Nuevo)**—The ravine, called El Tajo—360 feet down and 200 feet wide—divides Ronda into the whitewashed old Moorish town (La Ciudad) and the new town (El Mercadillo) that was built after the Christian reconquest in 1485. The New Bridge mightily spans the gorge. A different bridge was built here in 1735, but fell after six years. This one was built from 1751 to 1793. Look down...carefully.

You can see the foundations of the original bridge (and a super view of the New Bridge) from the Jardines de Cuenca park (daily in summer 9:30–21:30, winter 9:30–18:30): From Plaza de España, walk down Calle Rosario, turn right on Calle Los Remedios, and then take another right at the sign for the park. There are good views from the parador, which overlooks the gorge and bridge from the new-town side.

▲▲▲**Bullring**—Ronda is the birthplace of modern bullfighting, and this was the first great Spanish bullring. Philip II initiated bullfighting as war training for knights in the 16th century. Back then, there were two kinds of bullfighting: the type with noble knights on horseback, and the coarser, man-versus-beast entertainment for the commoners (with no rules...much like when the WWF wrestlers bring out the folding chairs). Ronda practically worships Francisco Romero, who melded the noble and chaotic kinds of bullfighting with rules to establish modern bullfighting right here in the early 1700s. He introduced the scarlet cape, held unfurled with a stick. His son Juan further developed the ritual (or art—local aficionados would never call it a "sport"—you'll read newspaper coverage of fights not on the sports pages but in the culture section), and his grandson Pedro was one of the first great matadors (killing nearly 6,000 bulls in his career).

Ronda's bullring and museum are Spain's most interesting to

tour (even better than Sevilla's). To tour the ring, stables, chapel, and museum, buy a ticket at the back of the bullring, the farthest point from the main drag (€6, daily April–Sept 10:00–20:00, March and Oct 10:00–19:00, Nov–Feb 10:00–18:00, tel. 952-874-132). The excellent €2 audioguide describes everything and is essential to fully enjoy your visit. I'd visit in the order listed below:

Chapel: The bullfighters' **chapel** greets you at the entrance. Before going into the ring, every matador would stop here to pray to Mary for safety—and hope to see her again.

Museum: The museum is split in two separate sections (horse gear and weapons on the left; the story of bullfighting on the right, with English translations).

The **horse gear and guns exhibit,** a recent acquisition, makes the connection with bullfighting and the equestrian upper class. And, of course, nobles are into hunting and dueling, hence the fancy guns. Don't miss the well-described dueling section with gun cases for two, as charming as a picnic basket with matching wine glasses.

Backtrack past the chapel to see Spain's best **bullfighting exhibit.** With plenty of stuffed bull heads, photos, artwork (original Goya engravings celebrating the art of bullfighting), posters (all original except the Picasso), and costumes, it's a shrine to bullfighting and the historic Romero family. Displays cover dynasties of fighters, costumes, and capes (bulls are actually colorblind, but the traditional red cape was designed to disguise all the blood). Historically, there were only two arenas built solely as bull arenas: in Ronda and Sevilla. Elsewhere, bullfights were held in town squares—you'll see examples in the museum. (For this reason, to this day, arenas are generally called Plazas de Toros).

Arena: From the museum, take advantage of the opportunity to walk in the actual two-tiered arena, with plenty of time to play *toro,* surrounded by 5,000 empty seats. The arena was built in 1785—on the 300th anniversary of the defeat of the Moors in Ronda. Notice the 136 classy Tuscan columns, creating a kind of 18th-century Italian theater. Lovers of the "art" of bullfighting will explain that the event is much more than the actual killing of the bull. It celebrates the noble heritage and the Andalusian horse culture. With your back to the entry, look left to see the ornamental columns and painted doorway where the dignitaries sit (over the gate where the bull enters). On the right is the place for the band (marked "*música*"), which in the case of a small town like Ronda, is most likely a high school band.

Stables and Equestrian School: The bull thundered out into the arena directly under the dignitaries' box. Walk from the arena through the bulls' entry into the bullpen. There are six bulls per fight (and three matadors). Nine bulls were penned up here, and ropes and pulleys safely opened the right door at the right time. Climb upstairs and find the indoor arena (Picadero) and see Spanish thoroughbred horses training from the Equestrian School of the Real Maestranza (Mon–Fri).

Bullfights are scheduled only for the first weekend of September during the *feria* (fair) and occur rarely in the spring. While every other *feria* in Andalucía celebrates a patron saint, the Ronda fair glorifies legendary bullfighter Pedro Romero. For September bullfights, tickets go on sale the preceding July. (As these sell out immediately, Sevilla and Madrid are more practical places for a tourist to see a bullfight).

Alameda del Tajo—One block away from the bullring, the town's main park is a fine place for people-watching, a snooze in the shade, or practicing your Spanish with seniors from the old folks' home.

Ronda's Old Town

Santa María la Mayor Collegiate Church—This 15th-century church with a fine Mudejar bell tower shares a park-like square with orange trees and the City Hall. It was built on and around the remains of Moorish Ronda's main mosque (which was itself built on the site of a temple to Julius Caesar). In the room where you purchase your ticket, look for the only surviving mosque prayer niche (that's a mirror; look back at the actual mihrab, which faces not Mecca, but Gibraltar—where you'd travel to get to Mecca). Partially destroyed by an earthquake, the reconstruction of the church resulted in the Moorish/Gothic/Renaissance/Baroque fusion (or confusion) you see today.

The front of the church interior is dominated by a magnificent 18th-century Baroque high altar with the standard statue of the Immaculate Conception in the center. The even more ornate chapel to the right is a fine example of Churrigueresque architecture, a kind of Spanish Rococo in which decoration obliterates the architecture—notice that you can hardly make out the souped-up columns. This chapel's fancy decor provides a frame for an artistic highlight of the town, the "Virgin of the Ultimate Sorrow." The big fresco of St. Christopher with baby Jesus on his shoulders (on the left, where you entered) shows the patron saint both of Ronda and of travelers.

An elaborately carved choir with a wall of modern bronze reliefs depicting scenes from the life of the Virgin Mary faces the altar. Similar to the Via Crucis (Way of the Cross), this is the Via Lucis (Way of the Light) with 14 stations (such as #13—the Immaculate Conception, and #14—Mary's assumption into heaven) that serve as a worship aid to devout Catholics. The centerpiece is Mary as the light of the world (with the moon, stars, and sun around her). Don't miss the bright paintings around the choir by a French artist who gave sacred scenes a fresh twist—like the Last Supper attended by women or at least men with women's bodies). The treasury displays vestments that look curiously like matadors' brocaded outfits (€4, daily April–Sept 10:00–20:00, March and Oct 10:00–19:00, Nov–Feb 10:00–18:00, Plaza Duquesa de Parcent in old town).

Mondragón Palace (Palacio de Mondragón)—This beautiful Moorish building was erected in the 14th century, possibly as the residence of Moorish kings, and was carefully restored in the 16th century. Wander through its many rooms to find the kid-friendly prehistory museum, with exhibits on Neolithic toolmaking and early metallurgy (described in English). If you plan to visit the Pileta Cave, find the panels that describe the cave's formation and shape. Even if you have no interest in your ancestors or speleology, the palace is worth a visit for the architecture alone. Don't miss the topographic model of Ronda at the entrance, which helps you envision the fortified old town apart from the grid-like new one (€3, May–Sept Mon–Fri 10:00–19:00, Sat–Sun 10:00–15:00, Oct–April closes an hour earlier, on Plaza Mondragón in old town, tel. 952-878-450). Linger in the two small gardens, especially the shady one.

Leaving the palace, wander left to the nearby Plaza de María Auxiliadora for more views and a look at the two rare *pinsapos* (resembling extra-large Christmas trees) in the middle of the park; this part of Andalucia is the only region in Europe where these ancient trees still grow. For an intense workout but a picture-perfect view, find the *Puerta de los Molinos* sign and head down, down, down. (Just remember you have to walk back up, up, up.) Not for the faint of heart or in the heat of the afternoon sun, this pathway leads down to the viewpoint where windmills once stood. Photographers go crazy reproducing the most famous postcard view of Ronda—the entirety of the New Bridge. Wait until just before sunset for the best light and cooler temperatures.

Lara Museum—This discombobulated collection of Ronda's history in dusty glass cases displays everything from sewing machines to fans to matador outfits (with decent English explanations). The highlight for many is the juvenile displays showing torture devices from the Inquisition and local witchcraft (€4, daily 11:00–20:00, until 19:00 in winter, Calle Arminan 29). The museum hosts flamenco shows three nights a week (€23 includes a drink, April–Nov Wed–Fri at 22:00, tel. 952-871-263).

Museo del Bandolero—This tiny museum, while not as intriguing as it sounds, is an interesting assembly of *bandito* photos, guns, clothing, and knickknacks. The Jesse Jameses and Billy el Niños of Andalucía called this remote area home, and brief but helpful English descriptions make this a fun detour. One brand of romantic bandits fought Napoleon's army—often more effectively than the regular Spanish troops (€3, daily May–Sept 10:00–20:00, Oct–April 10:00–18:00, across main street below Church of Santa María la Mayor at Calle Armiñán 65, tel. 952-877-785, www.museobandolero.com).

▲**Museo Joaquín Peinado**—Housed in an old palace, this fresh museum features a professional overview of the life's work of

Joaquín Peinado, a Ronda native and pal of Picasso. His style evolved through the big "isms" of the 20th century, ranging from Expressionist to Cubist, and even to erotic. Because Franco killed creativity in Spain for much of the last century, nearly all of Peinado's creative work was done in Paris. You'll have an interesting mod-

ern-art experience here without the crowds of Madrid's museums (€4; summer Mon–Fri 10:00–19:00, Sat–Sun 10:00–15:00, closes an hour earlier in winter; Plaza del Gigante, tel. 952-871-585).

Walk Through Old Town to Bottom of Gorge—From the New Bridge, you can descend down Cuesta de Santo Domingo (take the first left at the former Dominican Church, once the headquarters of the Inquisition in Ronda) into a world of whitewashed houses, tiny grilled balconies, and winding lanes—the old town.

The **Casa del Rey Moro** was never the home of any king (it was given its fictitious name by the grandson of President McKinley who once lived here). It offers visitors entry to the fine "Moorish-Hispanic" belle époque garden, designed in 1912 by a French landscape architect (the house interior is not open to visitors). Follow signs to "the Mine," an exhausting series of 280 slick, dark, and narrow stairs (like climbing down and then up a 20-story building) leading to the floor of the gorge. The Moors cut this zigzag staircase into the wall of the gorge in the 14th century to access water when under siege, then used Spanish slaves to haul water up to the thirsty town (€4, generally daily 10:00–19:00).

Fifty yards downhill from the garden is **Palacio del Marqués de Salvatierra** (closed to public). As part of the "distribution" following the Reconquista here in 1485, the Spanish king gave this fine house to the Salvatierra family (who live here to this day). The facade is rich in colonial symbolism from Spanish America—note the pre-Columbian-looking characters (four Peruvian Indians) flanking the balcony above the door and below the family coat of arms.

Just below the palace, stop to enjoy the view terrace. Look

below. A series of square vats are all that remains of the old tanneries. There are two old bridges, with the Arab Baths just to the right, and at the edge of town is a rectangular horse-training area.

Twenty steps farther down, you'll pass through the Philip V gate, for centuries the main gate to the fortified city of Ronda. Continuing downhill, you come to the **Puente Viejo** (Old Bridge), rebuilt in 1616 upon the ruins of an Arabic bridge. Enjoy the views from the bridge (but don't cross it yet), then continue down the old stairs. From the base of the staircase, look back up to glimpse some of the surviving highly fortified Moorish city walls. You've now reached the oldest bridge in Ronda, the Arab Bridge (also called the San Miguel Bridge). Sometimes given the misnomer of Puente Romano (Roman Bridge), it was more likely built long after the Romans left. For centuries, this was the main gate to the fortified city. In Moorish times, you'd purify both your body and your soul here before entering the city, so just outside the gate was a little mosque (now the ruined chapel) and the Arab Baths.

The **Arab Baths**, worth ▲, are evocative ruins worth a quick look. They were located half underground to maintain the temperature and served by a horse-powered water tower. You can still see the top of the shaft (30 yards beyond the bath rooftops, near a cyprus tree, connected to the baths by an aqueduct). Water was hoisted from the river below to the aqueduct by ceramic containers that were attached to a belt powered by a horse walking in circles. Inside, two of the original eight columns scavenged from the Roman ruins still support brick vaulting. A delightful 10-minute video brings the entire complex to life—Spanish and English versions run alternately (€3, Mon–Fri 10:00–19:00, Sat–Sun 10:00–15:00, Nov–April closes Mon–Fri at 18:00).

From here, hike back to the new town along the other side of the gorge: Return to the bridge just uphill. Cross it and take the stairs immediately on the left, which lead scenically along the gorge up to the New Bridge.

Near Ronda: Pileta Cave

The Pileta Cave (Cueva de la Pileta) is the best and probably the most intimate look a tourist can get at prehistoric cave paintings in Spain. Because the famous caves at Altamira in northern Spain are closed (only a nearby replica cave is open), this is your only way to see real Neolithic and Paleolithic paintings that are up to 25,000 years old. Set in a dramatic, rocky limestone ridge at the eastern edge of Sierra de Grazalema Natural Park, Pileta Cave is 14 miles from Ronda, past the town of Benaoján, at the end of an access road.

Farmer José Bullón and his family live down the hill from the cave, and because they strictly limit the number of visitors, Pileta's rare paintings are among the best-preserved in the world. Sr. Bullón and his son lead up to 25 people at a time through the cave, which was discovered by Sr. Bullón's grandfather in 1905. Call the night before to make sure no groups are scheduled for the time you want to visit—otherwise you'll have to wait. Note that if the 13:00 tour is full, it'll be another three hours before the next one starts (€8, 60-min tours on the hour, daily 10:00–13:00 & 16:00–18:00, closes Nov–mid-April at 17:00, closing times indicate last tour, no reservations taken—just join the line, €10 guidebook, no photos, tel. 952-167-343, www.cuevadelapileta.org). Bring a flashlight, sweater, and good shoes. You need a good sense of balance to take the tour. The 10-minute hike, from the parking lot up a trail with stone steps to the cave entrance, is moderately steep. Inside the cave, there are no handrails, and it can be difficult to keep your footing on the slippery, uneven floor while being led single-file, with only a lantern light illuminating the way.

Sr. Bullón is a master at hurdling the language barrier. As you walk the cool half-mile, he'll spend an hour pointing out lots of black, ochre, and red drawings, which are five times as old as the Egyptian pyramids. Mostly it's just lines or patterns, but there are also horses, goats, cattle, and a rare giant fish, made from a mixture of clay and fat by finger-painting prehistoric *hombres*. The 200-foot main cavern is impressive, as are some weirdly recognizable natural formations such as the Michelin man and a Christmas tree.

Getting There: It's possible to get here without wheels, but I wouldn't bother (you'd have to take the Ronda–Benaoján bus—2/day, departs at 8:30 and 13:00, 30 min—and then it's a 2-hour, 3-mile uphill hike). You can get from Ronda to the cave by taxi—it's about a half-hour drive on twisty roads—and have the driver wait (€55 round-trip). If you're driving, it's easy: Leave Ronda through the new part of town, and take A-376. After a few miles, passing Cueva del Gato, exit left toward Benaoján on MA-555. Go through Benaoján and follow the numerous signs to the cave. Leave nothing of value in your car.

Eating near the Cave: Nearby Montejaque has a great outdoor restaurant, **La Casita** (tel. 952-167-120).

Sleeping near the Cave: A good base for visiting Ronda and the Pileta Cave (as well as Grazalema) is **$$ El Cortijo de las Piletas.** Nestled at the edge of Sierra de Grazalema Natural

Park, this spacious family-run country estate has opportunities for swimming, hiking, horseback riding, and exploring the surrounding area. Access is easy from the main highway (Sb-€68–74, Db-€84–90, extra bed-€15–18, includes breakfast, tel. 605-080-295, www.cortijolaspiletas.com, info@cortijolaspiletas.com, Pablo and Elisenda). Another countryside option is **$$ Finca La Guzmana,** run by expat Brits Peter and Claire. Five beautifully appointed pastel rooms surround an open patio at this renovated estate house. Bird-watching, swimming, and trekking are possible (Db-€80, includes tax and breakfast, dinner on request, tel. 600-006-305, www.laguzmana.com, info@laguzmana.com).

Sleeping in Ronda

(€1 = about $1.40, country code: 34)
Ronda has plenty of reasonably priced, decent-value accommodations. It's crowded only during Holy Week (the week leading up to Easter) and the first week of September. Most of my recommendations are in the new town, a short stroll from the New Bridge and about a 10-minute walk from the train station. In the cheaper places, ask for a room with a *ventana* (window) to avoid the few interior rooms. Breakfast is usually not included.

$$$ Hotel Reina Victoria, with its 89 rooms, hangs royally over the gorge at the edge of town and has a marvelous view—Hemingway loved it. I'd choose this, with all its romantic Old World elegance, over the more central parador (Sb-€97–117, Db-€112–156, breakfast-€13, air-con, elevator, pool, free parking, 10-min walk from city center; easy to miss—look for intersection of Avenida Victoria and Calle Jerez, Jerez 25; tel. 952-871-240, fax 952-871-075, www.hotelhusareinavictoriaronda.com, reinavictoria-ronda@husa.es). *206 Great view recheck*

$$$ Hotel Don Miguel, facing the gorge, is just left of the bridge and has all the charm of a tour-group hotel. Of its 30 sparse but comfortable rooms, 20 have balconies and/or gorgeous views at no extra cost, but street rooms come with a little noise (Sb-€58–70, Db-€91–107, includes buffet breakfast, air-con, elevator, parking garage a block away-€10/day, Plaza de España 4, tel. 952-877-722, fax 952-878-377, www.dmiguel.com, reservas@dmiguel.com).

$$ Hotel San Gabriel has 21 pleasant rooms, a kind staff, public rooms filled with art books, a cozy wine cellar, and a fine garden terrace. If you're a cinephile, kick back in the charming TV room—with seats from Ronda's old theater and a collection of DVD classics—then head to the breakfast room to check out photos of big movie stars who have stayed here (Sb-€69, Db-€85–95, Db suite-€106, breakfast-€6.50, air-con, double-park in front and they'll direct you to a free parking place, follow signs on the main street of old town to Calle Marqués de Moctezuma 19, tel. 952-190-392, fax 952-190-117, www.hotelsangabriel.com, info@hotel sangabriel.com, family-run by José Manuel and Ana).

$$ Alavera de los Baños, located next to ancient Moorish baths at the bottom of the hill, has nine small rooms and big inviting public places, with an appropriately Moorish decor. This hotel offers a swimming pool, a peaceful Arabic garden, and a restaurant for guests. You're literally in the countryside, a 10-minute hike below town with sheep and horses outside near the garden (Sb-€60, Db-€80–95, Db with terrace-€90–105, includes tax and breakfast, closed Dec–Jan, free and easy parking, Calle San Miguel, tel. & fax 952-879-143, www.alaveradelosbanos.com, alavera@telefonica .net, personable Christian and Imma).

$$ Hotel Enfrente Arte Ronda is relaxed, funky, and friendly. The 14 rooms are spacious and exotically decorated, but dimly lit. There's also a peaceful bamboo garden, game room, small swimming pool, sauna, views, and terraces. Guests can enjoy themed dinners on certain nights (€15, confirm with reception). It's in all the guidebooks, so reserve in advance (Sb-€70, Db-€80–100, extra bed-€35, includes buffet breakfast and drinks from their bar, air-con, elevator, free Internet access, Real 40, tel. 952-879-088, fax 952-877-217, www.enfrentearte.com, reservations@enfrente arte.com).

$$ Hotel El Tajo has 33 decent, quiet rooms—once you get past the tacky faux-stone Moorish decoration in the foyer (Sb-€45, Db-€65, air-con, parking-€10/day, Calle Cruz Verde 7, a half-block off the pedestrian street, tel. 952-874-040, fax 952-875-099, www .hoteleltajo.com, reservas@hoteleltajo.com).

$$ Hotel San Francisco offers 27 small, nicely decorated rooms a block off the main pedestrian street in the town center (Sb-€40, Db-€60–70, Tb-€80, includes breakfast, air-con, 6 parking spaces-€15, María Cabrera 20, tel. 952-873-299, fax 952-874-688, hotelronda@terra.es).

$$ Hotel Ronda provides an interesting mix of minimalist and traditional Spanish decor, with five rooms located in the old town. Although there are no views, the refurbished mansion is quiet and homey (Sb-€50, Db-€65, additional bed-€20, includes tax, air-con, free Internet access, Ruedo Doña Elvira 12, tel. 952-872-232, www.hotelronda.net, laraln@telefonica.net, no English spoken).

$$ Hotel Royal has 29 clean, spacious, simple rooms—many on the main street that runs between the bullring and bridge. Thick glass keeps out most of the noise, while the tree-lined Alameda del Tajo park across the street is a treat (Sb-€38, Db-€57, Tb-€66, air-con, includes self-serve breakfast, Calle Virgen de la Paz 42, 3 blocks off Plaza de España, tel. 952-871-141, fax 952-878-132, www.ronda.net/usuar/hotelroyal, hroyal@ronda.net, some English spoken).

$ Hostal Ronda Sol has a homey atmosphere with 15 cheap but monkish rooms (S-€15, D-€25, cash only, parking-€10/day, Almendra 11, tel. 952-874-497, friendly María or Rafael). The same owner runs **Hostal Biarritz** next door, which offers 21 similar rooms, some with private bathrooms (S-€15, D-€25, Db-€35, cash only, parking-€10/day, Almendra 7, tel. 952-872-910, no English spoken).

$ Hostal Andalucía has 11 clean, comfortable, and recently renovated rooms immediately across the street from the train station (Sb-€25, Db-€40, includes tax, air-con, easy street parking, Martínez Astein 19, tel. 952-875-450, www.hostalandalucia.net, info@hostalandalucia.net).

$ Hostal Dona Carmen, another basic cheapie, rents 32 rooms in two sections. The rooms sharing a shower down the hall are especially reasonable (S-€15, Sb-€25, D-€25, Db-€45, air-con, Calle Naranja 28, tel. 952-871-994).

Near Ronda

$$ Los Pastores, 2.5 miles southwest of Ronda on A-369, is a pleasant renovated farmhouse in the countryside (Db-€60–75, four-person apartments-€60–95, one-night stay-€10 extra, breakfast-€6–10, four-course lunch or dinner-€15, Apartado de Correos 167, on A-369, tel. 952-798-305 or 952-114-464, www.fincalos pastores.com, info@lospastores.com, Martin).

Eating in Ronda

Plaza del Socorro, a block in front of the bullring, is an energetic scene, bustling with tourists and local families enjoying the square and its restaurants. The pedestrian-only Calle Nueva is lined with hardworking eateries. To enjoy a drink or a light meal with the best view in town, consider the terraces of Hotel Don Miguel just under the bridge. For coffee and pastries, locals like the elegant little **Confiteria Daver** (daily until 20:30, Calle Los Remedios 6). Picnic shoppers find the **Spar** supermarket convenient, opposite Hotel El Tajo (Mon–Sat 9:00–21:30, closed Sun, Calle Cruz Verde 18). The Alameda del Tajo park (with WC) near the bullring is a good picnic spot.

In the City Center

Restaurante del Escudero serves tasty and lovingly presented Spanish food with a posh modern touch in a crystal- and cream-colored dining room or on a terrace overlooking the gorge (€14 fixed-price meals, €33 gourmet tasting meals, closed Sun, behind bullring at Paseo Blas Infante 1, tel. 952-871-367).

Restaurante Pedro Romero, while touristy and overpriced, is a venerable institution in Ronda. Assuming a shrine to bullfighting draped in _el toro_ memorabilia doesn't ruin your appetite, it gets good reviews. Rub elbows with the local bullfighters or dine with the likes (well, photographic likenesses) of Orson Welles, Ernest Hemingway, and Francisco Franco (€17 fixed-price meals, or €30 à la carte, daily, air-con, across the street from bullring at Calle Virgen de la Paz 18, tel. 952-871-110).

Restaurante Casa Santa Pola offers gourmet versions of traditional food with friendly, professional service, with several small dining rooms and a delightful terrace perched on the side of the gorge (€17 fixed-price meal, €20 plates; good oxtail stew, roasted lamb, and honey-tempura eggplant; after crossing New Bridge from the bullring, take the first left downhill and you'll see the sign, Calle Santo Domingo 3; tel. 952-879-208).

Great TAPAS Entre Unos Rondr

Tapas in the City Center

Ronda has a fine tapas scene. You won't get a free tapa with your drink as in some other Spanish towns, but these bars have accessible tapas lists, and they serve bigger plates. While each of the following places could make a fine solo destination for a meal, I'd make a tapa pub crawl in the order listed.

Bar Lechuguita, a hit with older locals early and younger ones later, serves a long and tasty list of tapas for a good price. Rip off a tapas inventory sheet and mark which ones you want. Be adventurous and don't miss the bar's namesake, #14, _Lechuguita_ (a wedge of lettuce with vinegar, garlic, and a secret ingredient). The order form routine makes it easy to communicate and get exactly what you like, plus you know the exact price (closed Sun, no chairs or tables, just a bar and tiny stand-up ledges, Calle los Remedios 35).

Café & Bar Faustino is a place Brueghel would paint—a festival of eating with a fun and accessible menu that works both at the bar and at tables (lots of €1 tapas). The atmosphere makes you want to stay and the selection makes you wish your appetite was even bigger (closed Mon, just off Plaza Carmen Abela at Santa Cecilia 4, tel. 952-190-307).

El Porton is a classy little bar with Ronda ambience a block in front of the bullring. Their €10 mixed plates (choose meat or fish, served at a table) makes a light meal for two. But I'd just belly up to the bar for a drink and their signature tapa—a tiny piece of oily toast with a slice of ham and a fried quail egg (€1, _huevo de codorniz_) that you eat in one delightful pop (Calle Pedro Romero 7, closed Sat–Sun, tel. 952-877-420).

Tragatapas, the accessible little brother of the acclaimed gourmet Restaurante Tragabuches, serves super-creative and always tasty tapas in a stainless-steel minimalist bar. There's just a handful of tall tiny tables and stools, and an enticing blackboard of the day's specials. If you want to sample Andalusian gourmet (e.g., a variety of €2 tapas such as asparagus on a stick sprinkled with manchego cheese grated coconut-style) without going broke, this is the place to do it (closed Mon, Calle Nueva 4, tel. 952-877-209).

Outside the Almocábar Gate

To entirely leave the quaint old town and hustling city center with all of its tourists and grand gorge views, hike 10 minutes out to the far end of the old town, past the Church of the Holy Ghost, to a big workaday square that goes about life as if the world didn't exist outside Andalucía. Among the numerous eateries here are two of special note: The tiny, quirky Casa Maria is the ultimate in an intimate home-cooking experience, and Bodega San Francisco is a cheap tapas bar and a more normal little restaurant.

Casa Maria is like eating in the home of Elias and Isabel and their daughter Maria. There's little English spoken and no menu, so this is the adventure—you trust Elias to cook up whatever's seasonal for a four-course rustic fiesta for €28 to €30, including drinks (Elias loves red meat). Show Elias this book and you'll get more than the standard glass of house wine, although wine-lovers will want to pay a bit more for a finer bottle (facing Plaza Ruedo Alameda at #27, tel. 952-876-212).

Bodega Bar Restaurante San Francisco is a rustic bar with tables upstairs and a homey restaurant across the street. The bar is your budget option with an accessible list of *raciones* and tapas; the restaurant, while also rustic, comes with serious plates and big splittable portions. This place is understandably a neighborhood favorite (closed Thu, Ruedo de Alameda 32, tel. 952-878-162).

Connections

Note that some destinations are linked with Ronda by both bus and train. Direct bus service to other hill towns can be sparse (as few as one per day), and train service usually involves a transfer in Bobadilla. It's worth spending a few minutes in the bus or train station on arrival to plan your departure. Your options improve from major transportation hubs such as Málaga.

From Ronda by Bus to: Algeciras (6/day, 2 hrs), **La Línea/ Gibraltar** (no direct bus, transfer in Algeciras; Algeciras to Gibraltar—2/hr, 45 min, can buy ticket on bus), **Arcos** (2–3/day, 2 hrs), **Benaoján** (2/day, 30 min), **Jerez** (4/day, 2.5–3 hrs), **Grazalema** (2/day, 45 min), **Zahara** (1/day, Mon–Fri only, 1 hr), **Sevilla** (5/day, 2.5 hrs, fewer on weekends; also see trains below), **Málaga** (10/ day, 1.75 hrs *directo*, 3 hrs *ruta*; access other Costa del Sol points

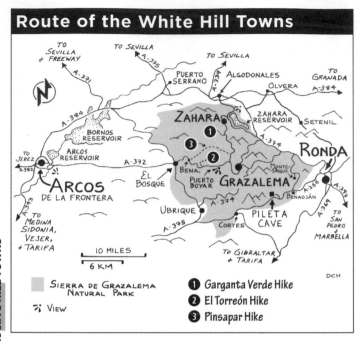

Route of the White Hill Towns

TO SEVILLA & FREEWAY
TO SEVILLA
TO SEVILLA
A-375
A-371
A-339
PUERTO SERRANO
ALGODONALES
OLVERA
TO GRANADA
A-384
A-384
BORNOS RESERVOIR
ZAHARA
ZAHARA RESERVOIR
SETENIL
A-374
TO JEREZ
A-382
ARCOS RESERVOIR
A-372
RONDA
ARCOS DE LA FRONTERA
EL BOSQUE
BENA.
PUERTO BOYAR
GRAZALEMA
MONTE-JAQUE
A-366
A-369
A-397
TO MEDINA SIDONIA, VEJER, & TARIFA
UBRIQUE
A-374
BENAOJÁN
A-375
CORTES
PILETA CAVE
TO SAN PEDRO & MARBELLA
TO GIBRALTAR & TARIFA

10 MILES
6 KM

SIERRA DE GRAZALEMA NATURAL PARK
VIEW

DCH

1 Garganta Verde Hike
2 El Torreón Hike
3 Pinsapar Hike

from Málaga), **Marbella** (6/day, 75 min), **Fuengirola** (5/day, 2 hrs), **Nerja** (4 hrs, transfer in Málaga; can take train or bus from Ronda to Málaga). If traveling to **Córdoba**, it's easiest to take the train since there are no direct buses (see below). There's no efficient way to call "the bus company" because four share the same station; one of them is at tel. 952-187-061. It's best to just drop by and compare schedules (on Plaza Concepción García Redondo, several blocks from train station).

By Train to: Algeciras (6/day, 1.5–2 hrs), **Bobadilla** (4/day, 1 hr), **Málaga** (2/day, 2 hrs—morning train direct, evening train with transfer in Bobadilla), **Sevilla** (2/day, 4 hrs, transfer in Bobadilla), **Granada** (3/day, 2.5 hrs), **Córdoba** (2/day direct, 1.75 hrs; more with transfer in Bobadilla, 3.5 hrs), **Madrid** (2/day, 4 hrs). Transfers are a snap and time-coordinated in Bobadilla; with four trains arriving and departing simultaneously, double-check that you're jumping on the right one. Train info: tel. 902-240-202.

More Hill Towns: Zahara and Grazalema

There are plenty of undiscovered and interesting hill towns to explore. About half of the towns I visited were memorable. Unfortunately, public transportation is frustrating, so I'd do these towns only by car. Or you could consider a tour—Andalusian Minibus Tours stops at Zahara and Grazalema on their all-day trip from Sevilla. Useful information on the area is rare. Fortunately, a good map, the tourist brochure (pick it up in Sevilla or Ronda), and a spirit of adventure work fine. Along with Arcos, Zahara and Grazalema are my favorite white villages.

Zahara

This tiny town in a tingly setting under a Moorish castle (worth the climb) has a spectacular view. While the big church facing the town square is considered one of the richest in the area, the smaller church has the most-loved statue. The Virgin of Dolores is Zahara's answer to Sevilla's Virgin of Macarena (and is similarly paraded through town during Holy Week). While Grazalema is a better overnight stop, Zahara is a delight for those who want to hear only the sounds of the wind, birds, and elderly footsteps on ancient cobbles.

Orientation to Zahara

Tourist Information

The TI is located in the main plaza (daily 9:00–13:30, gift shop, Plaza del Rey 3, tel. 956-123-114). It has a single computer with Internet access (€1.50, one-hour limit). Upstairs from the TI are Spanish-only displays about the flora and fauna of nearby Sierra de Grazalema Natural Park. Drivers can park for free in the main plaza, or continue up the hill to the parking lot at the base of the castle, just past the cliffside Hotel Arco de la Villa, the town's only real hotel (16 small modern rooms, Db-€63, tel. 956-123-230, www.tugasa.com).

Sights in Zahara

▲**Zahara Castle**—During Moorish times, Zahara lay within the fortified castle walls above today's town. It was considered the gateway to Granada and a strategic stronghold for the Moors by the Christian forces of the Reconquista. Locals tell of the Spanish conquest of the Moors' castle (in 1482) as if it happened yesterday:

After the Spanish failed several times to seize the castle, a clever Spanish soldier noticed that the Moorish sentinel would check if any attackers were hiding behind a particular section of the wall by tossing a rock and setting the pigeons in flight. If they flew, the sentinel figured there was no danger. One night a Spaniard hid there with a bag of pigeons and let them fly when the sentinel tossed his rock. Upon seeing the birds, the guard assumed he was clear to enjoy a snooze. The clever Spaniard then scaled the wall and opened the door to let in his troops, who conquered the castle. Ten years later Granada fell, the Muslims were back in Africa, and the Reconquista was complete.

It's a fun climb up to the remains of the castle (free, tower always open). Start at the paved path across from the town's upper parking lot. It's a moderately easy 15-minute hike past newly discovered Roman ruins and along a cactus-rimmed ridge to the top, where you can enter the tower. Use your penlight or feel along the stairway to reach the roof, and enjoy spectacular views from this almost impossibly high perch far above the town. As you pretend you're defending the tower, realize that what you see is quite different from what the Moors saw: The huge lake dominating the valley is a reservoir—before 1991, the valley had only a tiny stream.

Molino El Vínculo—This family-run olive mill welcomes visitors for a look at its traditional factory, as well as a taste of some homemade sherry and olive oil, produced on this site for centuries by the Urruti family. Juan will treat you to a glass of sherry if you show this book (€6 for a formal tour and tasting, daily 9:30–14:00 & 16:00–18:00, on CA-531 a half-mile beyond the castle side of Zahara, tel. 956-123-002, mobile 696-404-368, www.molinoel vinculo.com, molinoelvinculo@telefonica.net). A short visit is often free—they hope you'll buy something.

Grazalema

A beautiful postcard-pretty hill town, Grazalema offers a royal balcony for a memorable picnic, a square where you can watch old-

timers playing cards, and plenty of quiet whitewashed streets and shops to explore. Grazalema, situated within Sierra de Grazalema Natural Park, is graced with lots of scenery and greenery. Driving here from Ronda on A-372, you pass through a beautiful park-like grove of cork trees. While the park is known as the rainiest place in Spain, the clouds seem to wring themselves out before they reach the town—I've only ever had blue skies. If you want to sleep in a small Andalusian hill town, this is a good choice.

The **TI** is located at the car park at the cliffside viewpoint, Plaza de los Asomaderos (tel. 956-132-073). Enjoy the view, then wander into the town. A tiny lane leads a block from the center rear of the plaza to Plaza de Andalucía (filled by the tables of a commotion of tapas bars). Shops sell the town's beautiful and famous handmade wool blankets and good-quality leather items from nearby Ubrique. A block farther uphill takes you to the main square with the church, Plaza de España. A coffee on the square here is a joy. Small lanes stretch from here into the rest of the town.

Popular with Spaniards, the town makes a good home base for exploring Sierra de Grazalema Natural Park—famous for its spectacularly rugged limestone landscape of cliffs, caves, and gorges (see sidebar). For outdoor gear and adventures, including hiking, caving, and canoeing, contact **Horizon** (summer Tue–Sat 9:00–14:00 & 17:00–19:00, rest of year Tue–Sat 9:00–14:00 & 16:00–19:00, closed Sun–Mon year-round, off Plaza de España at Corrales Terceros 29, tel. & fax 956-132-363, mobile 655-934-565, www.horizonaventura.com, grazalema@horizonaventura.com).

Sleeping in Grazalema

$$ La Mejorana Guest House is the best bet in town—if you can manage to get one of its six rooms. You won't want to leave this beautifully perched garden villa, with its royal public rooms overlooking the valley from the upper part of town. Helpful Ana and Andres will call to get you a hiking permit in the park (Db-€55, includes breakfast and tax, Wi-Fi, pool, located at top of town on tiny lane below Guardia Civil headquarters at Santa Clara 6,

Sierra de Grazalema Natural Park

Sierra de Grazalema Natural Park is unique for its rugged mountain landscape and its relatively rainy climate, which support a wide variety of animals and plant life.  One-third of Spain's flowers bloom here, wild ibex (mountain goats) climb the steep slopes, and Europe's largest colony of griffon vultures soars high above. The park's plant poster child is the *pinsapo,* a type of fir tree left over from the last Ice Age (the park is one of the few places in Europe where these trees still grow). About a fifth of the 200-square-mile park is a special reserve area, where access is limited, largely to protect these rare trees from forest fires. Hikers need to get (free) permits for most trails in the reserve.

Zahara, Grazalema, and the Pileta Cave all fall within the park boundaries. Drivers will get an eyeful of scenery just passing through the park on their way to these sights.

If you want to more fully experience the park—by hiking, caving, canoeing, kayaking, or horseback riding—the easiest way is to take a tour from Zahara Catur (in Zahara, www.zaharacatur.com) or Horizon (in Grazalema, www.horizonaventura.com). They also handle the permit procedure for you.

If you want to hike in the park on your own, you'll need a park map, a permit for most hikes within the reserve area (see permit procedure on next page), and a car to get to the trailhead. And from July through September, you may have to go with a guided group anyway, if you want to hike in the reserve (about

tel. 956-132-327, mobile 649-613-272, www.lamejorana.net, info @lamejorana.net).

$$ Villa Turística de Grazalema is a big, popular national-park-lodge kind of place. It's good for kids, and has a huge lobby and fireplace. Its 38 apartments and 24 regular hotel rooms open onto either the swimming-pool garden from the ground floor, or balconies on the first floor (Sb-€37, Db-€60, extra person-€15, apartments-€70–123, extra bed-€23, includes breakfast, restaurant, turn right just before crossing the bridge into town, tel. 956-132-136, fax 956-132-213, www.tugasa.com).

$$ Hotel Peñón Grande, named for a nearby mountain, is just off the main square and rents 16 comfortable business-class rooms (Sb-€38, Db-€55, extra bed-€14, includes tax, air-con, Plaza Pequeña 7, tel. 956-132-434, fax 956-132-435, www.hotel grazalema.es, hotel@hotelgrazalema.es).

€12–16/person for a half-day hike, offered by Zahara Catur and Horizon).

Popular hikes in the reserve (all requiring permits) include:

Garganta Verde: Explore a canyon with a huge open cave near vulture breeding grounds (1.5 miles each way, initially gentle hike then very steep descent, allow 4–5 hours).

El Torreón: Climb the park's highest mountain, at 5,427 feet (1.75 miles each way, steep incline to summit, allow 4–5 hours).

Pinsapar: Hike on mountain slopes forested with *pinsapo* trees (8.5 miles each way, steep climb for first third of trail then downhill, allow 6 hours).

Information: The TIs in Grazalema and Zahara sell a Spanish-only park guide with descriptions and trail maps (€15).

Getting a Hiking Permit: A permit is free but required; a ranger will fine you if you don't have one. To get a permit, call or visit the park office in the town of El Bosque, a gateway to the park. You can request a permit for a specific hike up to 15 days in advance. Pick up the permit in El Bosque, or have them fax it to the TI in Grazalema or Zahara (El Bosque park office hours generally Mon–Sat 10:00–14:00 & 16:00–18:00, Sun 9:00–14:00, tel. 956-727-029, passport number required, Avenida de la Diputación, allow plenty of time for this process as it's hard to get through on the phone). If you're staying at the recommended La Mejorana Guest House in Grazalema, your host will call for you.

Hikes from Grazalema (No Permit Required): If you'd rather not hassle with getting a permit, or if you don't have a car to reach the trailheads, try one of several hikes that start from the town of Grazalema. You'll find descriptions in pamphlets available at the Grazalema TI or Horizon (€1).

$ Casa de Las Piedras, just a block from the main square, has 16 comfortable rooms with private baths and 14 super-cheap basic rooms with shared bathrooms. The beds feature the town's locally made wool blankets (Sb-€35, D-€25, Db-€48, 10 percent discount with this book and two-night minimum stay, buffet breakfast-€6, Calle Las Piedras 32, tel. & fax 956-132-014, www.casadelas piedras.org, info@casadelaspiedras.org, Katy and Rafi).

Eating in Grazalema

Grazalema offers many restaurants and bars. Tiny Plaza de Andalucía has several good bars for tapas with umbrella-flecked tables spilling across the square, including **Zulema** (big salads, tel. 956-132-402) and **La Posadilla** (tel. 956-132-051).

El Torreón specializes in local lamb and game dishes, and also has many vegetarian options (closed Wed, Calle Agua 44, tel. 956-132-313).

El Pinsapar, up the hill from the main plaza, is appreciated for its good prices and local specialties, including fresh trout (closed Wed, air-con, Dr. Mateos Gago 22, tel. 956-132-202).

Meson el Simancon serves well-presented cuisine typical of the region in a romantic setting. While a bit more expensive, it's considered the best restaurant in town (closed Tue, facing Plaza de los Asomaderos and the car park, tel. 956-132-421).

Connections

Bus service to Grazalema is provided by Los Amarillos (www.touristbus.es).

From Grazalema by Bus to: Ronda (2/day, 45 min), **El Bosque** (2/day, 45 min).

Jerez

With nearly 200,000 people, Jerez is your typical big-city mix of industry and dusty concrete suburbs, but it has a lively old center and two claims to touristic fame: horses and sherry.

Jerez is ideal for a noontime visit on a weekday. See the famous horses, sip some sherry, wander through the old quarter, and swagger out.

Orientation to Jerez

There is no easy way to feel oriented in Jerez due to the complicated, medieval street plan, so ask for directions liberally.

Tourist Information

The helpful TI, on Plaza Alameda Cristina, gives out free maps and info on the sights (June–mid-Sept Mon–Fri 9:00–15:00 & 17:00–19:00, Sat–Sun 9:30–14:30, mid-Sept–May Mon–Fri 8:00–15:00 & 16:30–18:30, Sat–Sun 9:30–14:30, tel. 956-338-874, www.turismojerez.com).

Arrival in Jerez

By Bus or Train: Both the bus and train stations are by the enormous headless statue at Glorieta del Minotauro. Unfortunately, you can't store luggage at either one. However, you can stow bags for free in the Royal Andalusian School's *guardaropa*, or coat room, if you attend their Horse Symphony show (see "Sights").

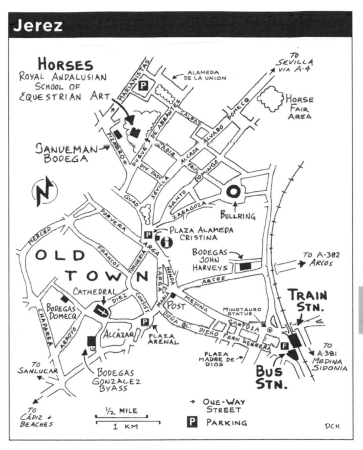

Jerez

HORSES
ROYAL ANDALUSIAN
SCHOOL OF
EQUESTRIAN ART

SANUEMAN
BODEGA

ALAMEDA
DE LA UNION

TO
SEVILLA
VIA A-4

HORSE
FAIR
AREA

BULLRING

OLD

TOWN

PLAZA ALAMEDA
CRISTINA

BODEGAS
JOHN
HARVEYS

TO A-382
ARCOS

CATHEDRAL

BODEGAS
DOMECQ

POST

MEDINA

TRAIN
STN.

MINOTAURO
STATUE

ALCÁZAR

PLAZA
ARENAL

PLAZA
MADRE DE
DIOS

TO
SANLUCAR

BODEGAS
GONZALEZ
BYASS

BUS
STN.

TO
A-381
MEDINA
SIDONIA

TO
CÁDIZ &
BEACHES

½ MILE

1 KM

→ ONE-WAY
STREET

P PARKING

DCH

The center of town and the TI are a 20-minute walk from both stations. When exiting either station, keep the large parking lot on your left. You'll soon be greeted by the gigantic Glorieta del Minotauro statue at a traffic circle. Take the crosswalk straight over to Calle Medina and follow it faithfully. At the confusing five-way intersection, angle right on Honda, continue past a small roundabout decorated with empty sherry barrels, and go straight until you reach Plaza Alameda Cristina—the TI is tucked away on your right.

By Car from Arcos: Driving in Jerez can be frustrating. The outskirts are filled with an almost endless series of roundabouts. Continuing straight through each one will eventually bring a rail bridge into sight, with Bodegas Harvey on the right side. Continue to follow traffic and signs to *centro ciudad.* The route may seem circuitous (it is) but will eventually take you past the main TI on Plaza Alameda Cristina.

If you're going straight to see the horses, follow the directions in the listing on next page; otherwise it's best to park in one of the many underground garages and catch a cab or walk. Plaza Arenal (€1.30/hr) is the most centrally located lot, or there's the handy underground parking lot at Plaza Alameda Cristina. For street parking, blue-line zones require prepaid parking tickets on your dashboard (Mon–Fri 9:00–13:30 & 17:00–20:00, Sat 9:00–14:00, Sun and July–Aug afternoons free).

Sights in Jerez

▲▲**Royal Andalusian School of Equestrian Art**—If you're into horses, this is a must. Even if you're not, this is art like you've never seen. The school does its Horse Symphony show Tuesday and Thursday at 12:00 during most of the year (also on Fri in Aug, Nov–Feb Thu only; €18 general seating, €24 "preference" seating, 90 min with 15-min intermission; no photos in show, stables, or museum; tel. 956-318-008, fax 956-318-015, tickets available online at www.realescuela .org). General seating is fine; some "preference" seats are too close for good overall views. The show explanations are in Spanish.

This is an equestrian ballet with choreography, purely Spanish music, and costumes from the 19th century. The stern riders and their talented, obedient steeds prance, jump, hop on their hind legs, and do-si-do in time to the music, all to the delight of an arena filled with mostly tourists and local horse aficionados.

The riders, trained in dressage (dreh-SAZH), cue the horses with the slightest of commands, whether verbal or with body movements. You'll see both purebred Spanish horses (of various colors, with long tails, calm personalities, and good jumping ability) and the larger mixed breeds (with short tails and a walking—not prancing—gait). The horses must be three years old before their three-year training begins, and most performing horses are male (stallions or geldings), since mixing the sexes brings problems.

The equestrian school is a university, open to all students in the EU, and with all coursework in Spanish. Although still a male-dominated activity, there have recently been a few female graduates. Tight-fitted mushroom hats are decorated with different stripes to show each rider's level. Professors often team with students and evaluate their performance during the show.

Training sessions on non-performance days offer the public a sneak preview (€10; Mon, Wed, and Fri—except no Fri in Aug,

Sherry

Spanish sherry is not the sweet dessert wine sold in the States as sherry. In Spain, sherry is (most commonly) a chilled white

very dry fortified wine, often served with appetizers such as tapas, seafood, and cured meats.

British traders invented the sherry-making process as a way of transporting wines that wouldn't go bad on a long sea voyage. Some of the most popular brands (such as Sandeman and Osbourne) were begun by Brits, and for years it was a foreigners' drink. But today, sherry is typically Spanish.

Sherry is made by blending wines from different grapes and vintages, all aged together. Start with a strong, acidic wine (from grapes that grow well in the hot, chalky soil around Jerez). Mature it in large vats until a yeast crust *(flor)* forms on the surface, protecting the wine from the air. Then fortify it with distilled alcohol.

Next comes sherry-making's distinct *solera* process. Pour the young fortified wine into the top barrel of a unique contraption—a stack of oak barrels called a *criadera*. Every year, one-third of the oldest sherry (in the barrels on the ground level) is bottled. To replace it, one-third of the sherry in the barrel above is poured in, and so on. This continues until the top barrel is one-third empty, waiting to be filled with the new year's vintage.

Fino is the most popular type of sherry (and the most different from Americans' expectations)—white, dry, and chilled. The best-selling commercial brand of *fino* is Tío Pepe; *manzanilla* is a regional variation of *fino*—best from Córdoba. Darker-colored and sometimes sweeter varieties of sherry include *amontillado* and *oloroso*. And yes, Spain also produces the thick, sweet cream sherries served as dessert wines. A good raisin-y, syrupy-sweet variety is Pedro Ximénez, made from sun-dried grapes of the same name.

also on Tue in Nov–Feb; arrive anytime between 11:00–13:00). Big tour groups crowd in at 11:00 and schedules may vary, so it's wise to call ahead. Sessions can be exciting or dull, depending on what the trainers are working on. After the training session, you can take a 90-minute guided tour of the stables, horses, multimedia and carriage museums, tack room, gardens, and horse health center. Sip sherry in the arena's bar to complete this Jerez experience.

Getting There: After passing the TI on Plaza Alameda Cristina, follow pink signs with arrows pointing to the *Real Escuela* *de Arte Ecuestre*. Parking is located behind the horse school, and one-way streets mean there is only one way to arrive. Expect to make at least one wrong turn, so give yourself a little extra time.

From the bus or train stations to the horses, it's about a €5 taxi ride or a 40-minute walk.

▲▲**Sherry Bodega Tours**—Spain produces more than 10 million gallons per year of this fortified wine. The name "sherry" comes from English attempts to pronounce Jerez. While traditionally the drink of England's aristocracy, today it's more popular with Germans. Your tourist map of Jerez is speckled with *venencia* symbols, each representing a sherry bodega that offers tours and tasting. *Venencias* are specially designed ladles for dipping inside the sherry barrel, breaking through the yeast layer, and getting to the good stuff.

Sandeman Sherry: Just around the corner from the horse school is the venerable Sandeman winery, which has been pro-ducing sherry since 1790 and is the longtime choice of English royalty. This tour is the aficionado's choice for its knowledgeable guides and their quality explanations of the process. Each stage is explained in detail, with visual examples of *flor* (the yeast crust) in backlit barrels, graphs of how different blends are made, and a quick walk-through of the bottling plant. The finale is a chance to taste three varieties (€6.50 for regular sherries, €10.50 for rare sherries, light tapas lunch with tour—€12.50, English tours on the half-hour Mon, Wed, and Fri 10:30–15:00, Sat 11:00–15:00, on the hour Tue and Thu 10:00–16:00, closed Sun, tour times adjust with the horse show, call to confirm, reservations not required, tel. 956-151-700, www.sandeman.com). It's efficient to see the Horse Symphony, which ends at 13:30, and then walk to Sandeman's for the next English tour.

Harveys Bodega: Their English-language tours aren't substantial, but they do include a 15-minute video, a visit to the winery, and all the sherry you like in the tasting room (€8.50, Mon–Fri at 12:00, 90-min tour, reservations recommended one day in advance, Calle Pintor Muñoz Cebrian, tel. 956-151-551, fax 956-349-427, www.bodegasharveys.es, bodegasharveys@beamglobal.com).

González Byass: The makers of the famous Tío Pepe offer a tourist-friendly tour, with more pretense and less actual sherry-making on display (it's done in a new, enormous plant outside of town). The tourist train through fake vineyards and a video presentation are forgettable, but the grand circle of sherry casks signed by a *Who's Who* of sherry-drinkers is worthwhile. Taste two sherries at the end of the 90-minute tour (€10, light tapas lunch with tour-€15, tours run hourly at :30 past the hour, Mon–Sat 11:30–17:30, extra tour at 14:00; July–Sept no tours at 14:00 and 15:30, extra tour at 18:30; Sun 11:30–14:00; Manuel María González 12, tel. 956-357-000, fax 956-357-046).

Alcázar—This gutted castle looks tempting, but don't bother. The €3 entry fee doesn't even include the Camera Obscura (€6.30 combo-ticket covers both, Mon–Sat 10:00–18:00, Sun 10:00–15:00). Its underground parking is convenient for those touring González Byass (€1.30/hr).

Connections

Jerez's bus station is shared by six bus companies, each with its own schedule. Some specialize in certain destinations, while others share popular destinations such as Sevilla and Algeciras. The big ones serving most southern Spain destinations are Los Amarillos (tel. 902-210-317, www.losamarillos.es), Comes (tel. 902-199-208, www.tgcomes.es), and Linesur (tel. 956-341-063, www.linesur .com). Shop around for the best departure time and most direct route. While here, clarify routes for any further bus travel you may be doing in Andalucía—especially if you're going through Arcos de la Frontera, where the ticket office is often closed. Also try the privately run www.movelia.es for bus schedules and routes.

From Jerez by Bus to: Tarifa (2/day on Algeciras route with Comes, 2 hrs, more frequent with transfer in Cádiz), **Algeciras** (2/day with Comes, 9/day with Linesur, 2.5 hrs), **Arcos** (hourly, 30 min), **Ronda** (4/day, 2.5–3 hrs), **La Línea/Gibraltar** (2/day, 3 hrs), **Sevilla** (7/day, 1.5 hrs), **Málaga** (3/day, 4.5–5 hrs), **Granada** (1/day, 4.5 hrs), **Madrid** (3/day, more service on weekends, 7 hrs).

By Train to: Sevilla (12/day, 1.25 hrs), **Madrid** (2/day, 4.5 hrs), **Barcelona** (one overnight, 12 hrs). Train info: tel. 902-240-202.

By Car: It's a zippy 30 minutes from Jerez to Arcos.

Stops for Drivers

If you're driving between Arcos and Tarifa, here are several sights to explore.

Yeguada de la Cartuja

This breeding farm, which raises Hispanic Arab horses according to traditions dating back to the 15th century, offers shows on Saturday at 11:00 (€18.50 for best seats in *tribuna* section, Finca Fuente del Suero, Carretera Medina–El Portal, km 6.5, Jerez de la Frontera, tel. 956-162-809, www.yeguadacartuja.com). From Jerez, take the road to Medina Sidonia, then turn right in the direction of El Portal—you'll see a cement factory on your right. Drive for five minutes until you see the farm. A taxi from Jerez will cost about €14 one-way.

Medina Sidonia

This town is as whitewashed as can be, surrounding its church and hill, which is topped with castle ruins. I never drive through here without a coffee break and a quick stroll. Signs to *centro urbano* route you through the middle to Plaza de España (lazy cafés, bakery, plenty of free parking just beyond the square out the gate). If it's lunchtime, consider buying a picnic, as all the necessary shops are nearby and the plaza benches afford a fine workaday view of a perfectly untouristy Andalusian town. According to its own TI, the town is "much appreciated for its vast gastronomy." Small lanes lead from the main square up to Plaza Iglesia Mayor (church and TI open in summer daily 10:00–14:00 & 17:00–19:00; in winter Tue–Sun 10:00–14:00 & 16:00–18:00, closed Mon; tel. 956-412-404). At the church, a man will show you around for a tip. Even without giving a tip, you can climb yet another belfry for yet another vast Andalusian view. The castle ruins just aren't worth the trouble.

Vejer de la Frontera

Vejer, south of Jerez and just 30 miles north of Tarifa, will lure all but the very jaded off the highway. Vejer's strong Moorish roots give it a distinct Moroccan (or Greek Island) flavor—you know, black-clad women whitewashing their homes, and lanes that can't decide if they're roads or stairways. Only a generation ago, women here wore veils. The town has no real sights—other than its women's faces—and very little tourism, making it a pleasant stop. The TI is at Marqués de Tamarón 10 (tel. 956-451-736).

The coast near Vejer has a lonely feel, but its fine, windswept beaches are popular with windsurfers and sand flies. The Battle of Trafalgar was fought just off Cabo de Trafalgar (a nondescript lighthouse today). I drove the circle so you don't have to.

Sleeping in Vejer: A newcomer on Andalucía's tourist map, the old town of Vejer has just a few hotels.

$$ Hotel La Botica, a boutique place high in the old town, provides 13 comfortable rooms in what was once a local apothecary. Homey decor and view patios—tailor-made for an afternoon beer—add to the charm (interior Db-€60, exterior Db-€70, €20 more in June–Aug, extra bed-€15–20, includes taxes and breakfast, mention this book to see if there are any deals, air-con, Wi-Fi, 200 yards above Plaza de España—go through the gate and left to Canalejas 13, tel. 956-450-225, mobile 617-477-636, www.labotica devejer.com, info@laboticadevejer.com). If Josip isn't home, call his mobile number and he will be.

$$ Convento de San Francisco is a poor man's parador in a refurbished convent with pristine, spacious rooms and elegant public lounges (Sb-€50, Db-€71, breakfast-€4, air-con, free Wi-Fi in lobby, La Plazuela, tel. 956-451-001, fax 956-451-004, convento -san-francisco@tugasa.com).

$$ Hotel Bandolero is for nature-lovers. Settle into the rustic rooms, go hiking and bird-watching, or take a dip in their pool (Sb-€45–50, standard Db-€64–101, superior Db-€73–111, Db suite-€90–128, restaurant, Avenida Havaral 43, tel. 952-183-660, www.hotelbandolero.com, reservas@hotelbandolero.com).

$ Hostal La Posada's 10 clean and charming rooms, in a modern apartment flat, are cheap and funky. This family-run place has no reception (S-€20, Db-€35–45, Los Remedios 21, tel. & fax 956-450-258, no English spoken).

Route Tips for Drivers

Sevilla to Arcos (55 miles): The remote hill towns of Andalucía are a joy to tour by car with Michelin map 578 or any other good map. Drivers can zip south on N-IV from Sevilla along the river, following signs to *Cádiz*. Take the fast toll expressway (blue signs, E-5, A-4); the toll-free N-IV is curvy and dangerous. About halfway to Jerez, at Las Cabezas, take CA-403 to Villamartín. From there, circle scenically (and clockwise) through the thick of the Pueblos Blancos—Zahara and Grazalema—to Arcos.

It's about two hours from Sevilla to Zahara. You'll find decent but winding roads and sparse traffic. It gets worse (but very scenic) if you take the tortuous series of switchbacks over the 4,500-foot summit of Puerto de Las Palomas (Pass of the Pigeons, climb to the viewpoint) on the direct but difficult road from Zahara to Grazalema (you'll see several hiking trailheads into Sierra de Grazalema Natural Park, though most require free permits).

Another scenic option through the park from Grazalema to Arcos is the road that goes up over Puerto del Boyar (Pass of the

174   Rick Steves' Snapshot Sevilla, Granada & Southern Spain

Boyar), past the pretty little valley town of Benamahoma, and down to El Bosque. The road from Ronda to El Gastor, Setenil (cave houses and great olive oil), and Olvera is another picturesque alternative.

Arcos to Tarifa (80 miles): You can drive from Arcos to Jerez in 30 minutes. If you're going to Tarifa, take the tiny C-343 road at the Jerez edge of Arcos toward Paterna and Vejer. Later, you'll pick up signs to *Medina Sidonia,* and then to *Vejer* and *Tarifa.*

Costa del Sol to Ronda and Beyond: Drivers coming up from the coast catch A-397 at San Pedro de Alcántara and climb about 20 miles into the mountains. A-369 offers a much longer, winding, but scenic alternative that takes you through a series of whitewashed villages.

Beware if you have old maps. The road numbering system from the coast into Sevilla was changed a couple of years ago: From Marbella to Ronda, take A-397 (formerly A-376). From Ronda to Jerez, start on A-374 (formerly A-376) then get on A-384 (which at Arcos may still be labeled with its old number, A-382). To head to Seville, branch off from A-384 onto A-375.

ANDALUCÍA'S HILL TOWNS

SPAIN'S SOUTH COAST

Nerja • Gibraltar • Tarifa

Spain's famous Costa del Sol is so bad, it's interesting. To northern Europeans, the sun is a drug, and this is their needle. Anything resembling a quaint fishing village has been bikini-strangled and Nivea-creamed. Oblivious to the concrete, pollution, ridiculous prices, and traffic jams, tourists lie on the beach like game hens on skewers—cooking, rolling, and sweating under the sun.

Where Europe's most popular beach isn't crowded by high-rise hotels, most of it's in a freeway choke hold. Wonderfully undeveloped beaches between Tarifa and Cádiz, and east of Almería, are ignored, while human lemmings make the scene where the coastal waters are so polluted that hotels are required to provide swimming pools. It's a fascinating study in human nature.

Laugh with Ronald McDonald at the car-jammed resorts. But if you want a place to stay and play in the sun, unroll your beach

towel at **Nerja.** And don't forget that you're surprisingly close to jolly olde England: The land of tea and scones, fish-and-chips, pubs and bobbies awaits you—in **Gibraltar.** Beyond "The Rock," the whitewashed port of **Tarifa**—the least-developed piece of Spain's generally over-developed southern coast—provides an enjoyable springboard for a quick trip to Morocco (see next chapter). These three places alone—Nerja, Gibraltar, and Tarifa—make the Costa del Sol worth a trip.

Costa del Sol

Planning Your Time

My negative opinions on the "Costa del Turismo" are valid for peak season (mid-July–mid-Sept). If you're there during a quieter time and you like the ambience of a beach resort, it can be a pleasant stop. Off-season it can be neutron-bomb quiet.

The whole 150 miles of coastline takes six hours by bus or three hours to drive with no traffic jams. You can resort-hop by bus across the entire Costa del Sol and reach Nerja for dinner. If you want to party on the beach, it can take as much time as Mazatlán.

To day-trip to Tangier, Morocco, take a tour from Tarifa.

Nerja

While cashing in on the fun-in-the-sun culture, Nerja (NEHR-hah) has actually kept much of its quiet Old World charm. It has good beaches, a fun evening paseo (strolling scene) that culminates in the proud Balcony of Europe terrace, enough pastry shops and nightlife, and locals who get more excited about their many festivals than the tourists do.

Thanks to cheap airfares and the completion of the expressway, real estate boomed here in the last decade (property values doubled in six years). But when the recent financial crisis hit, the bubble collapsed. All along the Costa del Sol, real estate, construction, and tourism had powered the economy, and the effects of its decline are apparent. On the upside, restaurants have cut prices, and hotel rates are soft (but that could change by the time you're using this book). Meanwhile, however, crime and racial tension have risen, as many once-busy immigrants are now without work.

Because of "residential tourism," Nerja's population swells from about 22,000 in winter to about 90,000 in the summer. Most of the foreign visitors are British—you'll find beans on your breakfast plate and Tom Jones for Muzak. Spanish visitors complain that some restaurants have only English menus, and indeed, the typical expats here actually try *not* to integrate. I've heard locals say of the British, "If they could, they'd take the sun back home with them—but they can't, so they stay here." They enjoy English TV and radio, and many barely learn a word of Spanish. (Special school buses take British children to private English-language schools that connect with Britain's higher-education system.) For an insight into this British community, read the free local expat magazines.

There's a long tradition of Spanish people retiring and vacationing here as well. Pensioners from northern Spain retire here—enjoying long life spans, thanks in part to the low blood pressure that comes from a diet of fish and wine. While they could afford to travel elsewhere, an inertia remains from Franco's day, when people generally vacationed within the country. In summer, to escape the brutal heat of inland Spain and the exhaustion that comes with having kids at home from school all day, many Spanish moms take the kids to condos on the south coast, while dads stay home to work. This is a time when many husbands get to "be Rodriguez" (i.e., anonymous and free), and enjoy (at a minimum) a break from the rigors of family life.

Orientation to Nerja

The tourist center of Nerja is right along the water and crowds close to its famous bluff, the "Balcony of Europe" (Balcón de Europa). Two fine beaches flank the bluff. The old town is just inland from the Balcony, while the more modern section slopes up and away from the water.

Tourist Information

The helpful, English-speaking TI has bus schedules, tips on beaches and side-trips, and brochures for nearby destinations, such

Nerja

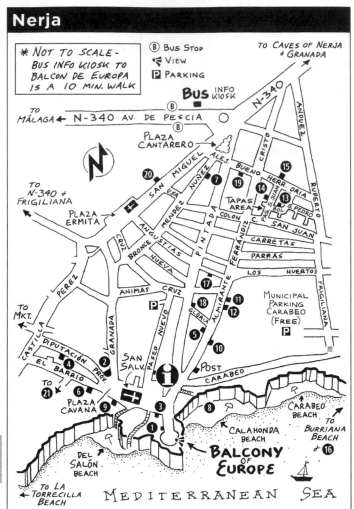

* NOT TO SCALE -
BUS INFO KIOSK TO
BALCON DE EUROPA
IS A 10 MIN. WALK

Ⓑ BUS STOP
📢 VIEW
Ⓟ PARKING

TO CAVES OF NERJA
& GRANADA

BUS INFO KIOSK

N-340

ANDUEZ

TO MÁLAGA ← N-340 AV. DE PESCIA

PLAZA CANTARERO

CRISTO

SAN MIGUEL

ALEJ.

NÚÑEZ

BUENO

HERR. ORIA

RUPERTO

Ⓟ 20 MERCADONA

USA

Ⓟ 7

Ⓟ 19

Ⓟ 15

Ⓟ 14

Ⓟ 13

S. PEDRO

TO N-340 & FRIGILIANA

MÉNDEZ

PINTADA

TAPAS AREA

C. PTO. S. JUAN

BOL.

PLAZA ERMITA

ANGUSTIAS

COLÓN

SAN JUAN

CRUZ

BRONCE

FERRÁNDIZ

CARRETAS

PÉREZ

NUEVA

PARRAS

TO MKT.

ANIMAS

CRUZ

LOS HUERTOS

Ⓟ 17

Ⓟ 18

Ⓟ 11

MUNICIPAL PARKING CARABEO (FREE)

CASTILLA

DIPUTACIÓN

GRANADA

PASEO NUEVO

GLORIA

ALMIRANTE

Ⓟ 12

FRIGILIANA

EL BARRIO

Ⓟ 4

Ⓟ 2

PROV.

SAN SALV.

Ⓟ 5

Ⓟ 10

TO 21

Ⓟ 6

PLAZA CAVANA

Ⓟ 9

POST

CARABEO

PLAZA CAVANA

Ⓟ 3

Ⓟ 1

Ⓟ 8

CALAHONDA BEACH

CARABEO BEACH

TO BURRIANA BEACH

Ⓟ 16

DEL SALÓN BEACH

BALCONY OF EUROPE

TO LA TORRECILLA BEACH

M E D I T E R R A N E A N   S E A

SPAIN'S SOUTH COAST

❶ Hotel Balcón de Europa
❷ Hotel Plaza Cavana
❸ Hostal Marissal & Cochran's Terrace
❹ Hostal Don Peque
❺ Hostal Miguel
❻ Pensión Mena
❼ Hostal Lorca
❽ Papagayo Beach Rest.
❾ Casa Luque Restaurante
❿ Pepe Rico & El Pulguilla Rest.

⓫ Pinocchio Restaurante
⓬ Haveli Restaurante
⓭ El Chispa
⓮ La Puntilla Bar Restaurante
⓯ Los Cuñaos
⓰ To Ayo's Café
⓱ Bar El Molino
⓲ El Burro Blanco
⓳ Bodega Los Bilbainos
⓴ Mercadona Supermarket
㉑ To Internet Cafés (2)

as Málaga and Gibraltar (daily 10:00–14:00; 100 yards from the Balcony of Europe and half a block inland from the big church, tel. 952-521-531, www.nerja.org, turismo@nerja.org). Ask for a free city map and the *Leisure Guide,* which has a comprehensive listing of activities. Their *Hiking the Sierra of Nerja and Cliffs of Maro* booklet describes good local walks.

Arrival in Nerja

By Bus: The Nerja bus station is actually just a bus stop with an info booth on Avenida de Pescia (daily 6:00–20:15, schedules posted, tel. 952-521-504). To travel from Nerja, buy tickets at the info kiosk—don't assume they're available on the bus. Since many buses leave at the same times, arrive at least 15 minutes before departure to avoid having to elbow other tourists.

By Car: Follow *Balcón de Europa* signs, and then into the big €1/hr underground parking lot (which deposits you 200 yards from the Balcony of Europe). Or park for free at the circus grounds, which doubles as the enormous Municipal Parking Carabeo (except in October, when circus is in town; follow *parador* signs, at last roundabout follow signs to parking lot, entrance off Calle Frigiliana). While this is free and very handy, many fall prey to a bogus "parking attendant" (even in a yellow vest) soliciting a euro coin for his "service."

Helpful Hints

Internet Access: Nerja's scenically situated Internet café is on a square overlooking Playa Torrecilla, where Calle Castilla Pérez meets Calle Málaga: **Europ@Web** (daily 10:00–22:00, until 24:00 in summer, 24 computers, tel. 952-526-147).

Radio: For a taste of the British expat scene, pick up the monthly *Street Wise* magazine or tune in to Coastline Radio at 97.6 FM.

Local Guide: Carmen Fernandez is good, with knowledge of the entire region (standard rate €125/5-hour day, mobile 610-038-437, mfeyus@yahoo.es).

Massage: Tiny yet muscular Marie, who moved here from France, runs a massage parlor out of her apartment. She does an excellent one-hour massage for €40—just give her a call (**Amarilys Masaje,** Calle Castilla Perez 10, mobile 667-825-828).

Getting Around Nerja

You can easily walk anywhere you need to go. A goofy little **tourist train**—nicknamed the "Wally Trolley" by Brits here—does a half-hour loop through town every 45 minutes (€4, daily 10:30–22:30, until 24:00 July–Aug, until 18:30 or earlier in winter, departs from Plaza de Cavana). You can get on and off at will (use the same ticket to catch another train). Unfortunately, it doesn't go to the popular Burriana Beach (route is posted on door of train). Nerja's **taxis** charge set fees (e.g., €5 to Burriana Beach, tel. 952-524-519). To clip-clop in a **horse and buggy** through town, it's €30 for about 25 minutes (hop on at Balcony of Europe).

Sights in Nerja

In Nerja

▲▲**Balcony of Europe (Balcón de Europa)**—The bluff, jutting happily into the sea, is the center of Nerja's paseo and a magnet for street performers. The mimes, music, and puppets can draw bigger crowds than the Balcony itself, which overlooks the Mediterranean, miles of coastline, and little coves and caves below. A castle, and later a fort, occupied this spot from the ninth century until the earthquake of 1884. Now it's a people-friendly view terrace.

Built in the early 1800s to defend against Napoleon, the English-Spanish fort here protected the harbor with the help of seven cannons. When the 1884 earthquake destroyed the castle and fort, it sent the cannons into the sea. A century later, two were salvaged, cleaned up, and placed here. Study the beautifully aged metal work.

The cute statue of King Alfonso XII reminds locals of how this popular sovereign (the great-grandfather of today's King Juan Carlos) came here after the devastating earthquake (a huge number of locals had died). He mobilized the local rich to dig out the community and put things back together. Standing on this promontory amid the ruins of the earthquake-devastated castle, he marveled at the view and coined its now-famous name, "Balcón de Europa."

The Nerja castle was part of a 16th-century lookout system. After the Christian Reconquista in 1492 drove Muslim Moors into exile, pirate action from Muslim countries in North Africa picked up. Lookout towers were stationed within sight of each other all along the coast. Warnings were sent whenever pirates threatened (smoke by day, flames by night). Look to the east—you can see three towers crowning bluffs in the distance.

Also to the east you can just see the tip of Burriana Beach. Spaniards love their *chiringuitos*, as local beach restaurants are called. The *chiringuito* immediately below you, Papagayo, is understandably popular.

Scan the horizon. Until recently, this was a favored landing spot (just beyond the tighter security zone near Gibraltar) for ille-

Costa del Sol History

Many Costa del Sol towns come in pairs: the famous beach town with little history, and its smaller yet much more historic partner established a few miles inland—safely out of reach of the Barbary pirate raids that plagued this coastline for centuries. Nerja is a good example of this pattern. While it has almost no history and was just an insignificant fishing village until tourism hit, its more historic sister, Frigiliana, hides out in the nearby hills. The Barbary pirate raids were a constant threat. In fact, the Spanish slang for "the coast is clear" is *"no hay moros en la costa"* (there are no Moors on the coast).

Nerja was overlooked by the tourism scene until about 1980, when the phenomenal Spanish TV show *Verano Azul (Blue Summer)* was set here. This post-Franco program featured the until-then off-limits topics of sexual intimacy, marital problems, adolescence, and so on in a beach-town scene (imagine combining *All in the Family, Baywatch,* and *The Hills*). To this day when Spaniards hear the word "Nerja," they think of this TV hit.

Despite the fame, development didn't really hit until about 2000, when the expressway finally and conveniently connected Nerja with the rest of Spain. Thankfully, a building code prohibits any new buildings higher than three stories in the old town.

gal immigrants and drug runners coming in from Africa. Many Moroccan teens try to sneak into Europe here, as local laws prohibit turning away undocumented children (the police use DNA tests to determine the age of recent arrivals—if they're under 18, they stay). Laws also grant automatic EU citizenship to anyone born in Europe, so many pregnant women try to slip in (once the baby's born, the mother's legal, too). However, illegal immigration is down: With the help of a new high-tech satellite-scanning system, the Guardia Civil can now detect floating objects as small as makeshift rafts and intercept them before they reach land.

Walk below the Balcony for views of the scant remains (bricks and stones) of the ninth-century Moorish castle. Locals claim an underground passage connected the Moorish fortress with the mosque that stood where the San Sebastián church stands today.

Church of San Salvador—Just a block inland from the balcony, this church was likely built upon the ruins of a mosque (c. 1600). Its wooden ceiling is *mudéjar*—made by Moorish artisans working in Christian times. The woodworking technique is similar to that featured in the Alhambra in Granada. The modern fresco of the Annunciation (in the rear of the nave) is by Paco Hernandez, the top local artist of this generation. In front, on the right, is a niche featuring Jesus with San Isidoro (as a little boy). Isidoro is the patron saint of Madrid, Nerja, and farmers (sugar-cane farming was the leading industry here before tourism hit). From the porch of the church, look inland to see City Hall, marked by four flags (Andalucía's is green for olive trees and white for the color of the houses in this part of Spain).

Town Strolls—As Nerja was essentially destroyed after the 1884 earthquake—and at the time there was little more here beyond the castle anyway—there's not much to see in the town itself. However, a few of its main streets are worth a quick look. From the Balcony of Europe head inland, across the street from the horses. Consider first grabbing some ice cream at El Valenciano Helados, a local favorite run by a Valencia family (Spaniards think of Valencia as the city with the best ice cream). Try the refreshing tiger-nut specialty called *horchata*.

A block farther inland, the old town's three main streets come together. The oldest street, Calle Carabeo, heads off to your right (notice how buildings around here are wired on the outside). On the left, Calle Pintada heads inland. Its name means "the painted street," as it was spiffed up in 1885 for the king's visit. Today it's the town's best shopping street. And between those streets runs Calle Almirante Ferrandiz, Nerja's restaurant row, which is particularly lively in the evenings.

Seaside Promenades—Pleasant seaview promenades lead in opposite directions from the Balcony of Europe, going east to Burriana Beach and west to Torrecilla Beach. Start your day with an early-morning walk along the delightful Paseo de los Carabineros, which stretches from the Balcony of Europe to Burriana Beach past several coves (10-min walk, farther to get to Ayo's for breakfast—see "Eating in Nerja").

Spanish law requires that all beaches are open to the public (except the one in Rota, which is reserved for American soldiers). The Paseo de los Carabineros is technically closed for liability reasons, as a few places along the promenade are in disrepair, and high tide can make passing tricky. It still makes a nice hike, if you don't mind doing it at your own risk (you'll need to slip around two barriers and climb a six-foot brick wall).

Beaches (Playas)—Nerja has several good beaches. They are well-equipped, with bars and restaurants, free showers, and rentable lounges and umbrellas (about €4 per couple for chairs and umbrella, same cost for 10 min or all day). Nearby restaurants rent umbrellas, and you're welcome to take drinks and snacks out to

your spot. During the summer, Spanish sun-worshippers pack the beach from about 11:00 until around 13:30, when they move into the beach restaurants for relief from the brutal sun. Watch out for red flags on the beach, which indicate when the seas are too rough for safe swimming (blue = safe, orange = caution, red = swimming prohibited). Don't take valuables to the beach, as thieves have fast fingers.

The pebbly **Calahonda Beach** (Playa Calahonda) is full of fun pathways, crags, and crannies (head down through the arch behind the horses). The humble Papagayo restaurant is open all day. Antonio can be seen each morning working with his nets and sorting through his fish. His little pre-tourism beach hut is wonderfully photogenic.

The sandiest—and most crowded—is **Del Salón Beach** (Playa del Salón), down the walkway to the right of Restaurante Marissal, just west of the Balcony of Europe. For great drinks-with-a-view, stop by either Cochran's Terrace or Casa Luque on the way down (see "Eating in Nerja"). Continuing farther west, you'll reach another sandy beach, **Playa La Torrecilla,** at the end of Calle Málaga.

El Playazo ("Big Beach") is a short hike west of Playa La Torrecilla. Locals prefer this beach, as it's less developed than the more central ones, offering a couple of miles of wide-open spaces that allow for fine walks and a chance to "breathe in the beach."

Burriana Beach (Playa de Burriana) is Nerja's leading beach (a 10-min walk east from the Balcony of Europe along the Paseo de los Carabineros—technically closed but easy to scale barriers if you like). It's fun for families, with paddleboats and entertainment options. It's also a destination for those visiting Ayo's paella-feast restaurant (see "Eating in Nerja").

Cantarriján Beach, a 15-minute drive east of Nerja (4.5 miles), is the nudists' choice (see next page).

Near Nerja

▲Caves of Nerja (Cuevas de Nerja)—These caves (2.5 miles east of Nerja, exit 295), with an impressive array of stalactites and stalagmites, are a classic roadside attraction. The huge caverns are filled with backlit formations and a big hit with cruise-ship groups and Spanish families. The visit involves a 30-minute unguided ramble deep into the mountain, up and down 400 dark stairs. At the end, you reach the Hall of the Cataclysm, where you'll circle

SPAIN'S SOUTH COAST

the world's largest stalactite column (certified by *Guinness Book of World Records*). Someone figured out that it took one trillion drops to make the column (€8.50, daily 10:00–14:00 & 16:00–18:30, July–Aug until 19:30, easy parking–€1, tel. 952-529-520).

The free exhibit in the Centro de Interpretación explains the cave's history and geology (house next to bus parking; exhibit in Spanish, but includes free English brochure).

To get to the caves, catch a bus from the Nerja bus stop on Avenida de Pescia (€1, 13/day, 10 min). During the festival held here the third week of July, the caves provide a cool venue for hot flamenco and classical concerts (tickets sold out long in advance). The restaurant offers a view and three-course fixed-price meals for €8, and the picnic spot (behind the ticket office) offers pine trees, benches, and a kids' play area.

Frigiliana—This picture-perfect whitewashed village, only four miles inland from Nerja, is easy to reach by car or bus (€1, 9/day, 15 min, none on Sun). It's a worthwhile detour from the beach, particularly if you don't have time for the Pueblos Blancos hill towns. To bring the town to life, consider hiring David Riordan, an American who settled here nearly 20 years ago. He offers an entertaining 90-minute town walk for €7.50 per person, and will schedule a tour for as few as two people (reserve by phone or email, mobile 625-986-065, davidwriordan@gmail.com). He does Nerja and regional tours in his car as well.

Cantarriján Beach—If you're craving a more desolate beach—and have a car—drive 12 miles east (toward Herradura) to the Cerro Gordo exit, and follow *Playa Cantarriján* signs (paved road, just before the tunnel). Park at the viewpoint and hike 30 minutes down to the beach, where rocks and two restaurants separate two pristine beaches—one for people with bathing suits, the other for nudists. As this beach is in a natural park and requires a long hike, it provides a fine—and rare—chance to experience the Costa del Sol in some isolation.

Hiking—Europeans visiting the region for a longer stay generally use Nerja as a base from which to hike. The TI can describe a variety of hikes. One of the most popular includes a refreshing and delightful two- to three-hour walk up a river (up to your shins in water). Another, more demanding hike takes you to the 5,000-foot summit of El Cielo for the best memorable king-of-the-mountain feeling this region offers.

Nightlife in Nerja

Bar El Molino offers live Spanish folk singing nightly in a rustic cavern that's actually an old mill—the musicians perform where the mule once tread. It's touristy but fun (starts at 22:00 but pretty dead before 23:00, no cover—just buy a drink, Calle San José 4). The local sweet white wine, *vino del terreno*—made up the hill in Frigiliana—is popular here (€2.50 per glass).

El Burro Blanco is a touristy flamenco bar with shows nightly from 22:30. Keeping expectations pretty low, they advertise "The Best Flamenco Bar in Nerja" (no cover—just buy a drink, on corner of Calle Pintada and Calle de la Gloria).

Bodega Los Bilbainos is a classic old dreary dive—a favorite with local men and communists (tapas and drinks, Calle Alejandro Bueno 8).

For more trendy and noisy nightlife, check out the karaoke bar on Pintada (near El Burro Blanco) and the bars and dance clubs on Antonio Millón and Plaza Tutti Frutti.

Sleeping in Nerja

The entire Costa del Sol is crowded during August and Holy Week (March 28–April 4 in 2010), when prices are at their highest. Reserve in advance for peak season—basically mid-July through mid-September—which is prime time for Spanish workers to hit the beaches. Any other time of year, you'll find that Nerja has plenty of comfy, easy-going low-rise resort-type hotels and rooms. Room rates are generally three-tiered: low season (Nov–March), middle season (April–June and Oct), and high season (July–Sept).

Compared to the pricier hotels, the better *hostales* are an excellent value. Hostal Don Peque and Pensión Mena are each within three blocks of the Balcony of Europe.

Breakfast: Some hotels here overcharge for breakfast. Don't hesitate to go elsewhere, as many places serve breakfast for more reasonable prices. If you don't mind a short beach hike before

SPAIN'S SOUTH COAST

Sleep Code

(€1 = about $1.40, country code: 34)
S = Single, **D** = Double/Twin, **T** = Triple, **Q** = Quad, **b** = bathroom, **s** = shower only. Unless otherwise noted, credit cards are accepted and English is spoken. Breakfast is not included (unless noted).

To help you easily sort through these listings, I've divided the rooms into three categories, based on the price for a standard double room with bath during high season:

$$$ **Higher Priced**—Most rooms €100 or more.
$$ **Moderately Priced**—Most rooms between €50–100.
$ **Lower Priced**—Most rooms €50 or less.

breakfast, consider **Ayo's** on Burriana Beach (see "Eating in Nerja"). For a cheap breakfast with a front-row view of the promenade action on the Balcony of Europe, head to **Hostal Marissal** and grab a wicker seat under the palm trees (€5 standard or English breakfasts). **Papagayo** serves breakfast on the beach, just below the Balcony of Europe, to those who like a little sand in their coffee (from 10:00).

Close to the Balcony of Europe

$$$ Hotel Balcón de Europa is the most central place in town. It's right on the water and the square, with the prestigious address Balcón de Europa 1. It has 110 rooms with all the modern comforts, including a pool and an elevator down to the beach. It's popular with groups. All the suites have seaview balconies, and most regular rooms also come with views (Sb-€71/82/107, standard Db-€98/115/148, about €40 extra for sea view and balcony, breakfast-€12, air-con, elevator, parking-€10/day, tel. 952-520-800, fax 952-524-490, www.hotelbalconeuropa.com, reservas@hotelbalcon europa.com).

$$$ Hotel Plaza Cavana, with 39 rooms, overlooks a plaza lily-padded with cafés. It feels institutional, but if you like a central location, marble floors, modern furnishings, an elevator, and a small rooftop swimming pool, dive in (Sb-€50–80, Db-€75–125, extra bed-€20, 10 percent discount and free breakfast for those booking direct with this guidebook in 2010, some view rooms, air-con, second small pool in basement, parking-€12/day, 2 blocks from Balcony of Europe at Plaza de Cavana 10, tel. 952-524-000, fax 952-524-008, www.hotelplazacavana.com, info@hotelplaza cavana.com).

$$ Hostal Marissal has an unbeatable location next door to the fancy Balcón de Europa hotel, and 23 modern, spacious rooms—some with small view balconies overlooking the action on the Balcony of Europe. Their cafeteria and bar, run by helpful staff, make the Marissal even more welcoming (Sb-€30/35/45, Db-€40/50/60, apartment for up to 4 people-€80–150, breakfast with beans-€5, double-paned windows, air-con, elevator, Internet access, Balcón de Europa 3, reception at Marissal café, tel. 952-520-199, fax 952-526-654, www.hostalmarissal.com, reserva @hostalmarissal.com, Carlos and María).

$$ Hostal Don Peque has 10 bright and cheery rooms, 8 with balconies. Owners Roberto and Clara moved here from France and have infused the place with their personality. They rent beach equipment at reasonable prices, but their bar-terrace with fantastic views may be more enticing (Sun–Thu: Db-€40/50/60, Tb-€55/75/90; Fri–Sat: Db-€50/60/75, Tb-€60/75/90; breakfast-€6, air-con, free Wi-Fi, Diputación 13, tel. 952-521-318, www.hostaldonpeque.com, info@hostaldonpeque.com).

$ Hostal Miguel offers nine sunny and airy rooms in the heart of "Restaurant Row." Top-floor rooms have mountain views, and breakfast is served on the pretty green terrace. The owners—British expats Ian, Jane, and Hannah—are long-time Nerja devotees (Sb-€28–38, Db-€35–52, book direct for these prices, 4 percent more if paying with credit card, family suite, beach equipment available on request, Almirante Ferrándiz 31, tel. 952-521-523, mobile 696-799-218, www.hostalmiguel.com, hostalmiguel @gmail.com).

$ Pensión Mena rents 11 fine rooms—four with seaview terraces (€5 extra and worth it)—and offers a quiet, breezy garden (Sb-€18–25, Db-€27–40, some street noise, El Barrio 15, tel. & fax 952-520-541, hostalmena@hotmail.com, María). During the off-season, check–in is only available when reception is open (Nov–March daily 9:30–13:30 & 17:00–20:30).

In a Residential Neighborhood

$ Hostal Lorca is located in a quiet residential area five minutes from the center, three blocks from the bus stop, and close to a small, handy grocery store and free parking lot. Run by a friendly young Dutch couple, Femma and Rick, this *hostal* has nine modern, comfortable rooms and an inviting compact backyard with a terrace, palm tree, and small pool. You can use the microwave and take drinks (on the honor system) from the well-stocked fridge. This quiet, homey place is a winner (Sb-€25–33, Db-€29–50, extra bed-€12, cash only, look for yellow house at Mendez Nuñez 20, tel. 952-523-426, www.hostallorca.com, info@hostallorca.com).

Eating in Nerja

There are three Nerjas: the private domain of the giant beachside hotels; the central zone, packed with fun-loving (and often tipsy) expats and tourists eating and drinking from trilingual menus; and the back streets, where local life goes on as if there were no tourists. The whole old town (around the Balcony of Europe) is busy with lively restaurants. Wander around and see who's eating best.

To pick up picnic supplies, head to the **Mercadona** supermarket (Mon–Sat 9:15–21:15, closed Sun, inland from Plaza Ermita on Calle San Miguel).

Near the Balcony of Europe

Papagayo, a classic *chiringuito* (beach restaurant), lounges in the sand a few steps below the Balcony of Europe. While you'll pay for the location, it's quite a location. They serve drinks and snacks to those enjoying their beach umbrellas (open with demand, daily breakfast from 10:00, lunch 12:00–17:00, tel. 952-523-816, "moon beach parties" on summer evenings).

Cochran's Terrace serves mediocre meals in a wonderful seaview setting, overlooking Del Salón Beach (daily, open all day for drinks, 12:00–15:00 & 19:00–23:00 for meals, just behind Hostal Marissal).

Casa Luque, between the El Salvador Church and the cliff-side, is a worthwhile splurge, featuring a terrace in back with wicker furniture, sea views, and enough ambience to justify the price. Its dining room, despite its lack of view, is the most high-end and romantic I've seen in town (€22 for 7-tapas tasting meal, wines can be purchased by the glass, closed Sun lunch and all day Wed, tel. 952-521-004).

Along Restaurant Row

Strolling up Calle Almirante Ferrándiz (which changes its name farther uphill to "Cristo"), you'll find a good variety of eateries, albeit filled with Brits and possessing all the elegance of Blackpool. On the upside, the presence of expats means you'll find places serving food earlier in the evening than the Spanish norm. Here are my choices in four categories: Romantic, Italian, Indian, and Spanish seafood and tapas.

Pepe Rico is the most romantic along this street, with a big terrace and a cozy dining room (€25 4-course meals, closed Sun, Calle Almirante Ferrándiz 28).

Pinocchio seems to be the local favorite for Italian (€8 pizzas and pastas, daily, Calle Almirante Ferrándiz 51).

Haveli, run by Amit and his Swedish wife Eva, serves good Indian food. It's been a hit with Brits, who know their Indian food, for two decades (€10–12 plates, daily 19:00–24:00 in summer, closed Mon off-season, Cristo 42, tel. 952-524-297).

El Pulguilla is a great, high-energy place for Spanish cuisine, fish, and tapas. Its two distinct zones (tapas bar up front and more formal restaurant out back) are both jammed with enthusiastic locals and tourists. The lively no-nonsense stainless-steel tapas bar doubles as a local pick-up joint later in the evening. Drinks come with a free small plate of clams, mussels, shrimp, chorizo sausage, or seafood salad. For a sit-down meal, head back to the terrace. Though not listed on the menu, half-portions *(media-raciones)* are available for many items, allowing you to easily sample different dishes (€10–15 dinners, closed Mon, Almirante Ferrándiz 26, tel. 952-521-384).

Tapas Bars near Herrera Oria

A 10-minute uphill hike from the water takes you into the residential thick of things, where the sea views come thumbtacked to the walls, prices are lower, and locals fill the tables. These three eateries are within a block of each other. Each is a colorful local hangout with different energy levels on different nights. Survey all three before choosing one, or have a drink and tapa at each. These places are generally open all day for tapas and drinks, and serve table-service meals during normal dining hours. Remember—tapas are snack-size portions generally not for sale but free with each drink. To turn them into more of a meal, ask for the menu and order a full-size *ración*, or half-size *media-ración*. The half-portions are generally bigger than you'd expect.

El Chispa is big on seafood, which locals enjoy on an informal terrace. Their *tomate ajo* (garlic tomato) is tasty, and their *berenjenas* (fried and salted eggplant) comes piping hot and is also worth considering. They'll want you to try the molasses-like sugar-cane syrup on the eggplant. They serve huge portions—*media-raciones* are enough for two (closed Mon, San Pedro 12, tel. 952-523-697).

La Puntilla Bar Restaurante is a boisterous little place, with its rickety plastic furniture spilling out onto the cobbles on hot summer nights (generous splittable salads, daily 12:00–24:00, a block in front of Los Cuñaos at Calle Bolivia 1, tel. 952-528-951).

Los Cuñaos hangs the banners of the entire soccer league on the walls. Local women hang out to chat, and kids wander around like it's home. While it has the least interesting menu, it has the most interesting business card (closed Sat, Herrera Oria 19, tel. 650-359-226).

Paella Feast on Burriana Beach

Ayo's is famous for its character of an owner and its €6 beachside all-you-can-eat paella feast at lunchtime. For 30 years, Ayo—a lovable ponytailed bohemian who promises to be here until he dies—has been feeding locals. Ayo is a very big personality—one of the five kids who discovered the Caves of Nerja, formerly a well-known athlete, and now someone who makes it a point to hire hard-to-employ people as a community service.

The paella fires get stoked up at about noon. Grab one of a hundred tables under the canopy next to the rustic open-fire cooking zone, and enjoy the beach setting in the shade with a jug of sangria. Fill your plate as many times as you like for €6. It's a 20-minute walk from the Balcony of Europe to the east end of Burriana Beach—look for Ayo's orange rooftop pyramid (daily "sun to sun," breakfast from 9:00—see below, paella served only at lunch, Playa de Burriana, tel. 952-522-289).

Breakfast at Ayo's: Consider hiking the deserted beach early and arriving at Ayo's at 9:00 for breakfast. Locals order the *tostada con aceite de oliva* (toast with olive oil and salt-€0.50); Ayo also serves toasted ham-and-cheese sandwiches and good coffee.

Connections

Nerja

From Nerja by Bus to: Nerja Caves (13/day, 10 min), **Frigiliana** (9/day, 15 min, none on Sun), **Granada** (6/day, 2.5 hrs, more with transfer in Motril—but check the departure time from Motril to Granada to make sure you're really saving time; Nerja to Motril, 1 hr, Motril to Granada, 1.75 hrs), **Córdoba** (1/day, 4.5 hrs), **Sevilla** (3/day, 4 hrs). Remember to double-check the codes on bus schedule—for example, 12:00*S* means 12:00 daily except Saturday.

To the Málaga Airport (about 40 miles west): Catch the bus to Málaga (€4, 18/day, 1.25–1.5 hrs), then take a local bus to the airport (€1, about 2/hr, 30 min); or pay €55 for a taxi from Nerja (airport tel. 952-048-804).

Málaga

This seaside city's busy airport is the gateway to the Costa del Sol. The closest train station to Nerja is in Málaga.

Málaga's train and bus stations—a block apart—both have pickpockets and lockers (train station lockers are more modern; both cost €3/day). You can rent a car at the train station from Atesa or Europcar. If you have time to kill, the train station is connected to a modern shopping mall, and another mall is located across from the bus station roundabout. Both have decent food courts.

From Málaga by Train to: Ronda (1/day direct in evening, 2 hrs; 4/day with transfer in Bobadilla), **Algeciras** (3/day, 4 hrs, transfer in Bobadilla), **Madrid** (12/day, 2.25–3 hrs on AVE), **Córdoba** (15/day, 1 hr on fast AVE or AVANT trains; 2/day, 2.25–3 hrs on slower trains), **Granada** (3/day, 2.5–3.25 hrs on AVE, transfer in Bobadilla or Antequera), **Sevilla** (11/day, 2 hrs on AVE or AVANT, 2.5 hrs on other trains), **Barcelona** (3/day, fast AVE train leaves at 16:50, 5.5 hrs, 13 hrs on slow trains). Train info: tel. 902-240-202, www.renfe.es.

Buses: Málaga's bus station, a block from the train station, has a helpful information office with bus schedules (daily 7:00–22:00, tel. 952-350-061) and a TI (daily 11:00–19:00, Internet access, ATM, and lockers, on Paseo de los Tilos).

By Bus to: Algeciras (17/day, 1.75 hrs *directo*, 3 hrs *ruta*), **Nerja** (18/day, 1.25–1.5 hrs), **Ronda** (14/day, 1.75 hrs *directo*, 3 hrs *ruta*), **La Línea/Gibraltar** (4/day, 3 hrs), **Tarifa** (2/day, 3.5 hours), **Sevilla** (9/day, 7 direct, 2.5–3.5 hrs), **Jerez** (3/day, 4.5–5 hrs), **Granada** (hourly, 1.5–2 hrs), **Córdoba** (5/day, 3–3.5 hrs), **Madrid** (11/day, 6 hrs), **Marbella** (5/day, 50 min). Bus info: www.estabus.emtsam.es.

Between Nerja and Gibraltar

Buses take five hours to make the Nerja–Gibraltar trip, including a transfer in Málaga, where you may have to change bus companies (they leave nearly hourly from Nerja to Málaga). Along the way, buses stop at each of the following towns.

Fuengirola and Torremolinos— The most built-up part of the region, where those most determined to be envied settle down, is a bizarre world of Scandinavian package tours, flashing lights, pink flamenco, multilingual menus, and all-night happiness. Fuengirola is like a Spanish Mazatlán with a few older, less-pretentious budget hotels between the main drag and the beach. The water here is clean and the nightlife fun and easy. James Michener's idyllic Torremolinos has been strip-malled and parking-metered.

Marbella—This is the most polished and posh town on the Costa del Sol. High-priced boutiques, immaculate streets set with intricate pebble designs, and beautifully landscaped squares testify to Marbella's arrival on the world-class-resort scene. Have a *café con leche* on the beautiful Plaza de Naranjos in the old city's pedestrian section. Wander down to new Marbella and the high-rise beachfront apartment buildings to walk along the wide promenade lined with restaurants. Check out the beach scene. Marbella is an easy stop on the Algeciras–Málaga bus route (as you exit the bus station, take a left to reach the center of town). You can also catch a handy direct bus here from the Málaga airport (20/day, fewer off-season, 45 min, www.ctsa-portillo.com).

San Pedro de Alcántara—This town's relatively undeveloped sandy beach is popular with young travelers. San Pedro's neighbor, Puerto Banús, is "where the world casts anchor." This luxurious, Monaco-esque jet-set port, complete with casino, is a strange mix of Rolls-Royces, yuppies, boutiques, rich Arabs, and budget browsers.

Gibraltar

One of the last bits of the empire upon which the sun never set, Gibraltar is a quirky mix of Anglican propriety, "God Save the Queen" tattoos, English bookstores, military memories, and tourist shops. In 20 years the economy has gone from one dominated by the military to one based on tourism (as, it seems, happens to many empires). On summer days and  weekends, the tiny colony is inundated by holiday-goers, primarily the Spanish (who come here for tax-free cigarettes and booze) and British (who want a change in weather but not in culture).

While it's hard to imagine a community of 30,000 that feels like its own nation, real Gibraltarians, as you'll learn when you visit, are a proud bunch. They were evacuated during World War II, and it's said that after their return, a national spirit was forged. If you doubt that, be here on Gibraltar's national holiday, September 10, when everyone's decked out in red and white, the national colors.

Gibraltarians have a mixed and interesting heritage. Spaniards call them Llanitos (yah-NEE-tohs), meaning "flat" in Spanish, though the residents live on a rock. The locals—a fun-loving and tolerant mix of British, Spanish, and Moroccan—call their place "Gib."

A passport is required to cross the border (you'll only get a stamp if you need a visa—otherwise, you'll just get a wave-through).

Planning Your Time

Make Gibraltar a day trip (or just one overnight); rooms are expensive compared to Spain.

For the best day trip to Gibraltar, consider this plan: Walk across the border, catch bus #3, and ride it to the end, following my self-guided tour (described later in this chapter). Ride bus #3 back to the cable-car station, then catch the cable car to the peak for Gibraltar's ultimate top-of-the-rock view. From there, either walk down or take the cable car back into town. From the cable-car station, follow my self-guided town walk all the way to Casemates Square. Spend your remaining free time in town before returning to Spain.

Tourists who stay overnight find Gibraltar a peaceful place in

Gibraltar

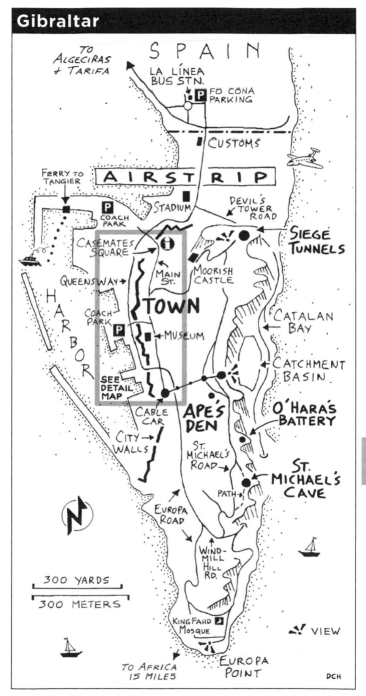

the evening, when the town can just be itself. No one's in a hurry. Families stroll, kids play, seniors window-shop, and everyone chats...but the food is still pretty bad.

There's no reason to side-trip into Morocco from Gibraltar—for many reasons, it's better from Tarifa (specifics covered in next chapter).

Orientation to Gibraltar

(tel. code: 350-200)
Gibraltar is a narrow peninsula (three miles by one mile) jut-ting into the Mediterranean.  Virtually the entire peninsula is dominated by the steep-faced Rock itself. The locals live down below in the long, skinny town at the western base of the mountain (much of it on reclaimed land).

For information on all the little differences between Gibraltar and Spain—from area codes to electricity—see "Helpful Hints," later in this chapter.

Tourist Information

Gibraltar's main TI is at Casemates Square, the grand square at the Spain end of town (Mon–Fri 9:00–17:30, Sat 10:00–15:00, Sun 10:00–13:00, tel. 74982, www.gibraltar.gi). Another TI is in the Duke of Kent House (off Cathedral Square in the town center, Mon–Fri 9:00–17:30, closed Sat–Sun, bus #3 stops here, tel. 74950).

Arrival in Gibraltar

By Bus: Spain's La Línea bus station is a five-minute walk from the Gibraltar border (baggage storage-€3/day, Mon–Fri 9:00–12:30 & 13:30–18:00, closed Sat–Sun, longer hours in summer, purchase token—*ficha*—from Portillo ticket counter). You'll need your passport to cross the border.

From the Border into Town: To get into town from the "fron-tier" (as the border is called), you can walk (30 min), take a taxi to the cable-car station (pricey at €9/£6), or hop on a bus (€1/£0.60, runs every 15 min). Catch either the #3 bus to the TI at Cathedral Square (you can also stay on to continue my self-guided tour, later) or the London-style double-decker bus to Casemates Square, which also has a TI. To get into town by foot, walk straight across the runway (look left, right, and up), then head down Winston Churchill Avenue, angling right at the Shell station on Smith Dorrien Avenue.

Spain vs. Gibraltar

Spain has been annoyed about Gibraltar ever since Great Britain snagged this prime 2.5-square-mile territory through the Treaty of Utrecht in 1713, at the end of the War of the Spanish Succession. Although Spain long ago abandoned efforts to reassert its sovereignty by force, it still tries to make Gibraltarians see the error of their British ways. Over the years, Spain has limited Gibraltar's air and sea connections, choked traffic at the three-quarter-mile border, and even messed with the local phone system in efforts to convince Britain to give back the Rock. Still, given the choice—which they got in referenda in 1967 and 2002—Gibraltar's residents steadfastly remain Queen Elizabeth's loyal subjects, voting overwhelmingly (99 percent in the last election) to continue as a self-governing British dependency. Gibraltar's governor, who is serving his third four-year term, is popular for dealing forcefully and effectively with Spain on these issues.

By Car: Customs checks at the border create a bit of a bottleneck for drivers getting in and out. But at worst, there's a 15-minute wait during the morning rush hour into Gibraltar and the evening rush hour back out. Parking is free and easy except for weekday working hours, when it's tight and frustrating. It's simpler to park in La Línea (explained below) and just walk across the border.

Freeway signs in Spain say *Algeciras* and *La Línea,* pretending that Gibraltar doesn't exist until you're very close. After taking the La Línea–Gibraltar exit off the main Costa del Sol road, continue as the road curves left (with the Rock to your right). Enter the left-hand lane at the traffic circle before the border and you'll end up in La Línea. The Fo Cona underground parking lot is handy (€1/hr, €6/day, on "20th of April" street). You'll also find blue-lined parking spots in this area (€1/hr from meter, 6-hr limit 9:00–20:00, free before and after that, bring coins, leave ticket on dashboard). From La Línea, it's a five-minute stroll to the border, where you can catch a bus or taxi into town (see "From the Border into Town," on previous page).

If driving into Gibraltar, drive along the sea side of the ramparts (on Queensway—but you'll see no street name). There are big parking lots here and at the cable-car terminal. Parking is generally free—if you can find a spot. By the way, while you'll still find the English-style roundabouts, cars here stopped driving on the British side of the road in the 1920s.

Helpful Hints

Gibraltar Isn't Spain: Gibraltar, a British colony, uses different coins, currency (see below), stamps, and phone cards than those used in Spain. Note that British holidays such as the Queen's (official) Birthday (June 15 in 2010) and Bank Holidays (May 3, May 31, and Aug 30 in 2010) are observed, along with local holidays such as Gibraltar's National Day (Sept 10).

Use Pounds, not Euros: Gibraltar uses the British pound sterling (£1 = about $1.60). They also accept euros...but for about a 20 percent extra cost to you. Gibraltar is expensive even at fair pound sterling rates. You'll save money by hitting up an ATM and taking out what you'll need. But before you leave, stop at an exchange desk and change back what you don't spend (at about a 5 percent loss), since Gibraltar currency is hard to change in Spain. (If you'll be making only a few purchases, you can try to avoid this problem by skipping the ATM and buying things with your credit card.) Be aware that if you pay for anything in euros, you may get pounds back in change.

Hours: This may be the United Kingdom, but Gibraltar follows a siesta schedule, with some businesses closing 13:00–15:00 on weekdays, and shutting down at 14:00 on Saturdays until Monday morning.

Electricity: If you have electrical gadgets, note that Gibraltar uses the British three-pronged plugs (not the European two-pronged ones). Your hotel may be able to loan you an adapter.

Telephone: To telephone Gibraltar from anywhere in Europe, dial 00-350-200 and the five-digit local number. To call Gibraltar from the US or Canada, dial 011-350-200-local number.

Internet Access: Café Cyberworld has pricey Internet access (daily 12:00–24:00, Queensway 14, in Ocean Heights Gallery, an arcade 100 yards toward the water from Casemates Square, tel. 51416). **Western Union** has an Internet center on Main Street (£0.75/hr; at #269, right before Convent Square). Another cheap place for Internet access is the cultural center listed next.

John Mackintosh Cultural Centre: This is your classic British effort to provide a cozy community center. The upstairs library, without a hint of tourism, welcomes drop-ins to enjoy all the local newspapers and publications, and to check their email cheaply and easily (£0.85/30 min, Mon–Fri 9:30–19:30, closed Sat–Sun).

Side-Trip to Tangier, Morocco: Travel agencies in Gibraltar sell trips to Tangier. Ferries cross the strait only a few days a week, leaving Gibraltar at 23:00 and departing Tangier at 19:00 Morocco time (£32 one-way, £57 round-trip). Because Gibraltar is expensive compared to Spain, it makes sense to use your time here to see the Rock, but to day-trip to Morocco from Tarifa instead.

Self-Guided Bus Tour

Gibraltar Town Bus #3 Orientation Tour

Upon arrival at the "frontier," pick up a map at the TI window. Then walk straight ahead for 200 yards to the bus stop on the right. Catch bus #3 and enjoy this three-mile orientation ride that takes you from one end of the colony to the other (Mon–Fri 4/hr, Sat–Sun 2–3/hr, buy ticket from driver, ride 20 min to the end of the line: Europa Point). A single ticket gives you on-and-off privileges for an hour (€1/£0.60). To save money, ask the driver for an all-day ticket (€1.90/£1).

Here's the tour. It goes quickly. Read fast...

Airstrip: You enter Gibraltar by crossing an airstrip. Three or four times a day, the entry road into Gibraltar is closed to allow planes to land or take off. Originally a horse-racing stadium, this area was later filled in with stones excavated from the 30 miles of military tunnels carved into the Rock. This airstrip was a vital lifeline in the days when Spain and Britain were quarreling over Gibraltar (especially 1970–1985) and the border was closed. If you look at the face of the Rock, you can see the tiny windows that were once perches from where big cannons could fire. Behind them lie siege tunnels, open as a tourist attraction (described later in this chapter).

Moorish Castle: Just after the airstrip, at the first round-about, the bus passes a road leading left (which heads clockwise around the Rock to the town of Catalan Bay, peaceful beaches, and the huge mountainside rainwater-catchment wall). The Moorish Castle above dates back over a thousand years. On the right is land reclaimed in 1989, filled mostly with government-subsidized apartments.

Ramparts: You'll cross the bridge and drive onto the ramparts. Water once came all the way up to the ramparts—50 percent of the city is on reclaimed land. Gibraltar's heritage shows in the architecture: tiles (Portuguese), shutters (Genoese Italian), and wrought iron (Georgian English).

On the right after the next stop, you'll see World War memorials. The first is the American War Memorial (the building-like structure with a gold plaque and arch), built in 1932 to commemorate American sailors based here in World War I. Farther along you'll see 18th-century cannons and a memorial to Gibraltarians who died in World War II.

Downtown: The following sights come up quickly: Passing the NatWest House office tower on the left, you'll immediately see a **synagogue** (only the top peeks out above a wall; the wooden doors in the wall bear the Star of David). In the 19th century, half of Gibraltar was Jewish. The Jewish community now numbers 600. Just after the synagogue is little **Cathedral Square,** with a playground, TI, and the Moorish-looking Anglican cathedral (behind the playground). Gibraltar is the European headquarters of the Anglican Church. Now you'll pass a long wall; most of it is the back of the Governor's Residence (a.k.a. The Convent).

Charles V Wall: The next bus stop is at the old Charles V wall, built in response to a 1552 raid in which the pirate Barbarossa captured 70 Gibraltarians into slavery. Immediately after you pass under the wall, you'll see a green park on your left that contains the **Trafalgar cemetery.** Buried here are some British sailors who died defeating the French off the coast of Spain's Cape Trafalgar in 1805.

Botanical Gardens: The next stop is at the big parking lot for the **cable car** to the top of the Rock, as well as for the **botanical gardens** (free, daily 8:00–sunset), located at the base of the lift. You can get off to do this now—or finish the tour and come back here later, on the way back into town.

Out of Town: Heading uphill out of town, your best views are on the right. It's believed that the body of Admiral Nelson was pickled in a barrel of spirits in a harbor just below you after his victorious (yet fatal) Battle of Trafalgar. You pass the big former naval hospital and barracks. Reaching the end of the Rock, you pass modern apartments and the mosque.

King Fahd Mosque: This $20 million gift from the Saudi sultan was completed in 1997, and Gibraltar's 900 Muslims worship here each Friday. Five times a day—as across the strait in Morocco—an imam sings the call to prayer.

Europa Point: The lighthouse marks windy Europa Point—the end of the line. Buses retrace the route you just traveled, departing about every 15 minutes (every 20–30 min on weekends). Europa Point, up the mound from the bus stop and tourist shop (on right), is an observation post. A plaque here identifies the mountains of Morocco 15 miles across the strait. The glow of the lighthouse (150 feet tall, from 1841, closed to visitors) can be seen from Morocco.

Your tour is finished. Enjoy the views before catching a bus back into town. Get off at the cable-car station to ride to the top of the Rock, tour the botanical gardens, or begin the town walk described next.

Self-Guided Walk

Welcome to Gibraltar

Gibraltar town is long and skinny, with one main street (called Main Street). Stroll the length of it from the cable-car station to Casemates Square, following this little tour. A good British pub and a room-temperature pint of beer await you at the end.

Just past the cable-car terminal is the **Trafalgar cemetery,** a reminder of the colony's English military heritage. Next you come to the **Charles V wall**—a reminder of its Spanish military heritage—built in 1552 by the Spanish to defend against marauding pirates. Gibraltar was controlled by Moors (711–1462), Spain (1462–1704), and then the British (since 1704). Passing through the Southport Gates, you'll see one of the many red history plaques posted about town.

Heading into town, you pass the tax office, then the **John Mackintosh Cultural Centre,** which has cheap Internet access and a copy of today's *Gibraltar Chronicle* upstairs in its library. The *Chronicle* comes out Monday through Friday and has covered the local news since 1801. The Methodist church sponsors the cheap and cheery **Carpenter's Arms** tearoom just above one of several fish-and-chips joints (rare in Iberia).

The pedestrian portion of Main Street begins near the **Governor's Residence.** The British governor of Gibraltar took over a Franciscan convent, hence the name of the local white house: The Convent. The **Convent Guard Room,** facing the Governor's Residence, is good for photos.

Gibraltar's courthouse stands behind a **small tropical garden,** where John and Yoko got married back in 1969 (as the ballad goes, they "got married in Gibraltar near Spain"). Sean Connery did, too. Actually, many Brits like to get married here because weddings are cheap, fast (only 48 hours' notice required), and legally recognized as British.

Main Street now becomes a **shopping drag.** You'll notice lots of colorful price tags advertising tax-free booze, cigarettes, and sugar (highly taxed in Spain). Lladró porcelain, while made in Valencia, is popular here (because it's sold without the 16 percent Spanish VAT—Value-Added Tax). The big **Marks & Spencer department store** helps vacationing Brits feel at home, while the Catholic cathedral retains a whiff of Arabia (as it was built upon the remains of a mosque).

The town (and this walk) ends at **Casemates Square.** While a lowbrow food circus today, it originated as a barracks and place for ammunition storage. When Franco closed the border with Spain in 1969, Gibraltar suffered a labor shortage, as Spanish guest workers could no longer commute into Gibraltar. The colony countered by inviting Moroccan workers to take their place—ending a nearly 500-year Moroccan absence, which began when the Moors fled in 1462. As a result, today's Moroccan community dates only from the 1970s. While the previous Spanish labor force had simply commuted into work, the Moroccans needed apartments, so Gibraltar converted the Casemates barracks for that purpose. Cheap Spanish labor has crept back in, causing many locals to resent store clerks who can't speak proper English.

On Casemates Square, there's a crystal shop that makes its own crystal right there (you can watch). They claim it's the only thing actually "made in Gibraltar." But just upstairs, on the upper floor of the barracks, you'll find a string of local crafts shops. Beyond the square (behind the TI) is the covered **produce market.**

Sights in Gibraltar

In Gibraltar Town

▲**Gibraltar Museum**—Built atop a Moorish bath, this museum tells the story of a chunk of land that has been fought over for centuries. Start with the fine 15-minute video overview of the story of the Rock—a worthwhile prep for the artifacts (such as ancient Roman anchors made of lead) you'll see in the museum. Then, wander through the scant remains of the 14th-century Moorish baths. Upstairs you'll see military memorabilia, a 15-foot-long model of the Rock, wonderful century-old photos of old Gibraltar, paintings by local artists, and, in a cave-like room off the art gallery, a collection of prehistoric remains and artifacts. The famous skull of a Neanderthal woman found in Forbes' Quarry is a copy (the original is in the British Museum in London). Found in Gibraltar in 1848, this was the first Neanderthal skull ever discovered. No one realized its significance until a similar skull found years later in Germany's Neanderthal Valley was correctly identified—stealing the name, claim, and fame from Gibraltar (£2, Mon–Fri 10:00–18:00, Sat 10:00–14:00, last entry 30 min before closing, closed Sun, no photos, on Bomb House Lane near the cathedral).

Up on the Rock

The actual Rock of Gibraltar is the colony's best sight. Its attractions: the stupendous view from the very top, quirky apes, a hokey cave (St. Michael's), and the impressive Siege Tunnels drilled through the rock face for military purposes. The Rock, which is technically called the "Upper Rock Nature Reserve," is open daily 9:30–19:00.

You have two £8 options for touring the Rock: Ride the cable car or take a 90-minute taxi tour. The taxi tour includes a couple of extra stops and the running commentary of your licensed cabbie/guide. Hikers can ride the lift up and walk down, connecting the various sights (you'll walk on paved military lanes, not trails).

In either case, to tour St. Michael's Cave or the Siege Tunnels, you'll need to pay £8 extra for a combo-ticket. Because the cable car doesn't get you very close to the cave and tunnels, take the taxi tour if you'll be visiting these sights. On the other hand, the cable car takes you to the very top of the Rock (which the taxi tours don't). Frankly, the sights are not much; the Rock's best attractions—enjoying views from the top and playing with the monkeys—are free.

There's certainly no reason to take a big bus tour (advertised and sold all over town) considering how fun, cheap, and easy the taxi tours are. Private cars are not allowed high on the Rock.

Taxi Tours: Minibuses driven by cabbies trained and licensed to lead these little trips are standing by at the border and on Cathedral Square in town. They charge £32 per carload

or £8 per person, whichever is more. (Remember, you'll pay an additional £8 for admission to the cave and the tunnels; if you opt out, you'll have to sit in the car while the other passengers make these little visits.) Taxi tours and big buses do the same 90-minute loop tour with four stops: a Mediterranean viewpoint (called the Pillar of Hercules), St. Michael's Cave (15-min visit), a viewpoint near the top of the Rock where you can get up close to the monkeys, and the Siege Tunnels (20-min visit). Buddy up with other travelers and share the cost.

Cable Car to the Summit: The ride costs £8 (6/hr, daily 9:30–17:15, last ride down at 17:45, closed Sun in winter and when windy or rainy—ask at TI if cable car is running when weather is questionable, pick up map with ticket). Your cable-car ride includes a multimedia device that explains what you're seeing from the spectacular viewpoints (pick it up at the well-marked booth when you disembark at the top). The cable car stops halfway down for those who want to get out, see the monkeys, and take a later car down. From there, many hike to St. Michael's Cave (skippable and described below).

To see all the sights, you'll end up hiking down, rather than taking the cable car back. Approximate hiking times: from the top of the cable car to St. Michael's Cave—25 minutes; from the cave to the Apes' Den—20 minutes; from the Apes' Den to the Siege Tunnels—30 minutes; from the tunnels back into town, passing the Moorish Castle—20 minutes. Total from top to bottom: about 90 minutes (on paved roads with almost no traffic), not including sightseeing.

▲▲▲**The Summit of the Rock**—The cable car takes you to the real highlight of Gibraltar: the summit of the spectacular Rock

itself. (Taxi tours do not go here—they stop on a ridge below the summit, where you enjoy a commanding view—but one that's nowhere near as good.) The limestone massif, or large rock mass, is nearly a mile long, rising 1,400 feet high with very sheer faces. According to legend, this was one of the Pillars of Hercules (paired with Djebel Musa, another mountain across the strait in Morocco), marking the edge of the known world in ancient times. Local guides say that these pillars are the only places on the planet where you can see two seas and two continents at the same time.

In A.D. 711, the Muslim chieftain Tarik ibn Ziyad crossed over from Africa and landed on the Rock, beginning the Moorish conquest of Spain and naming the Rock after himself—Djebel-Tarik ("Rock of Tarik"), which became "Gibraltar."

At the top of the Rock (the cable-car terminal) there's a view terrace and a restaurant. From here, you can explore old ramparts and drool at the 360-degree view of Morocco (including the Rif Mountains and Djebel Musa), the Strait of Gibraltar, the bay stretching west toward Algeciras, and the twinkling Costa del Sol arcing eastward. The views are especially crisp on brisk off-season days. Below you (to the east) stretches the giant catchment system that the British built to collect rainwater in the not-so-distant past, when Spain allowed neither water nor tourists to cross its disputed border. Broad sheets catch the rain, sending it through channels to reservoirs located inside the rock.

O'Hara's Battery—While it's closed to visitors, some travelers still hike up here (20 min from the top of the cable-car lift). At 1,400 feet, this is the actual highest point on the Rock. A 100-ton nine-inch gun sits on the summit where a Moorish lookout post once stood. It was built after World War I, and the last test shot was fired in 1974. Locals are glad it's been mothballed—during test firings, they had to open their windows, which might otherwise have shattered from the pressurized air blasted from this gun.

The iron rings you see every 30 yards or so along the military lanes around the Rock once anchored pulleys used to haul up guns like the huge one at O'Hara's Battery.

▲**St. Michael's Cave**—Studded with stalagmites and stalactites, eerily lit, and echoing with classical music, this cave is dramatic, corny, and slippery when wet. Considered a one-star sight since Neolithic times, these caves were alluded to in ancient Greek legends—when the caves were believed to be the Gates of Hades (or the entrance of a tunnel to Africa). All taxi tours stop here. This sight requires a long walk for cable-car riders.

▲**Apes of Gibraltar**—The Rock is home to about 200 "apes" (actually, tailless Barbary macaques—a type of monkey). Taxi tours come with great monkey fun. Those riding the cable car can get off halfway down to photograph the apes. The males are bigger, females have beards, and newborns are black. They live about 15–20 years. Legend has it that as long as the apes remain here, so will the Brits. Keep your distance from the

apes. (Guides say that for safety reasons, "They can touch you, but you can't touch them.") Beware of their kleptomaniac tendencies; they'll ignore the peanut in your hand and claw after the full bag in your pocket. If there's no ape action, wait for a banana-toting taxi tour to stop by and stir some up.

▲**Siege Tunnels**—Also called the Upper Galleries, these chilly tunnels were blasted out of the rock by the Brits during the Spanish

and French siege (1779–1783). The clever British, safe inside the Rock, used hammers and gunpowder to carve these tunnels in order to plant four big guns on the north face and drive off the French. During World War II, 30 more miles of tunnels were blasted out. Hokey but fun dioramas help recapture a time when Brits were known more for conquests than for crumpets.

Moorish Castle—Actually more a tower than a castle, this building offers a tiny museum of Moorish remnants and carpets. (In the interest of political correctness, the tourist board is trying to change the name to "Medieval Castle"...but it is Moorish.) It was constructed on top of the original castle built in A.D. 711 by the

Moor Tarik ibn Ziyad, who gave his name to Gibraltar. The tower marks the end of the Upper Rock Nature Reserve. A short hike downhill drops you back in town.

Nightlife in Gibraltar

Gibraltar is quiet at night. You can sip a drink on the waterfront at the Queensway Quay Marina (see next spread). Other than that, it's music in the pubs and lounges. O'Callaghan Eliott Hotel hosts free live jazz on Monday and Thursday evenings, and Casemates Square is everyone's choice for live music in the pubs. The Queen's Cinema (by the cable car) is the colony's only movie theater.

Sleeping in Gibraltar

Gibraltar is not a good value for hotels. Except at the hostel, the beds are either bad or overpriced. Remember, you'll pay a 20 percent premium if paying with euros—pay with local cash or your credit card.

$$$ O'Callaghan Eliott Hotel, with four stars, boasts a rooftop pool with a view, a fine restaurant, bar, terrace, inviting sit-a-bit public spaces, and 120 modern if sterile rooms (sky-high rack rates of Db-£240–270, but often around Db-£100 with Web booking during non-peak days, breakfast-£13, non-smoking floors, air-con, elevator, free parking, centrally located at Governor's Parade up Library Street from main drag, tel. 70500, fax 70243, www.ocallaghanhotels.com, reservations@ocallaghanhotels.com).

$$$ Bristol Hotel offers basic English rooms in the heart of Gibraltar (Sb-£63–68, Db-£81–87, Tb-£93–99, higher prices for exterior rooms, breakfast-£5, air-con, elevator, swimming pool, free parking, Cathedral Square 10, tel. 76800, fax 77613, www.bristolhotel.gi, reservations@bristolhotel.gi).

Sleep Code

(£1 = about $1.60, tel. code: 350-200)
S = Single, **D** = Double/Twin, **T** = Triple, **Q** = Quad, **b** = bathroom, **s** = shower only. All of these places accept credit cards and speak English. To help you easily sort through these listings, I've divided the rooms into three categories, based on the price for a standard double room with bath during high season:

$$$ Higher Priced—Most rooms £75 or more.
$$ Moderately Priced—Most rooms between £35–75.
$ Lower Priced—Go back to Spain.

Gibraltar Town

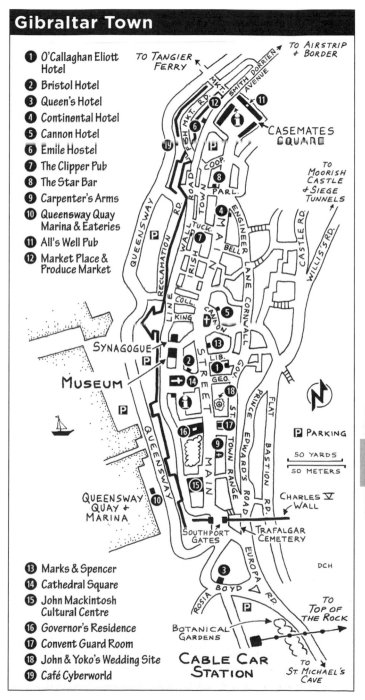

1. O'Callaghan Eliott Hotel
2. Bristol Hotel
3. Queen's Hotel
4. Continental Hotel
5. Cannon Hotel
6. Emile Hostel
7. The Clipper Pub
8. The Star Bar
9. Carpenter's Arms
10. Queensway Quay Marina & Eateries
11. All's Well Pub
12. Market Place & Produce Market

13. Marks & Spencer
14. Cathedral Square
15. John Mackintosh Cultural Centre
16. Governor's Residence
17. Convent Guard Room
18. John & Yoko's Wedding Site
19. Café Cyberworld

TO TANGIER FERRY

TO AIRSTRIP & BORDER

FISH MKT. RD.

SMITH DORRIEN AVENUE

CASEMATES SQUARE

TO MOORISH CASTLE & SIEGE TUNNELS

COOP.

PARL.

TOWN

WALL

IRISH

RECLAMATION

LINE

ROAD

QUEENSWAY

COLL.

KING

CANNON

ENGINEER LANE

CORNWALL

BELL

TUCK.

MAIN

CASTLE RD.

WILLIS'S RD.

SYNAGOGUE

MUSEUM

STREET

LIB.

GEO.

ST.

GOV.

PRINCE EDWARD'S ROAD

FLAT BASTION RD.

P PARKING

50 YARDS
50 METERS

TOWN RANGE

QUEENSWAY

QUEENSWAY QUAY & MARINA

CHARLES V WALL

SOUTHPORT GATES

TRAFALGAR CEMETERY

EUROPA RD.

DCH

ROSIA

BOYD

BOTANICAL GARDENS

CABLE CAR STATION

TO TOP OF THE ROCK

TO ST. MICHAEL'S CAVE

SPAIN'S SOUTH COAST

$$ Queen's Hotel, near the cable-car lift, has 62 comfortable remodeled rooms in a noisy location (Sb-£60, Db-£70, seaview Db-£85–95, Tb-£90, Qb-£110, includes English breakfast, 20 percent discount for students with ISIC cards and paying cash, elevator, free parking, at #3 bus stop, Boyd Street 1, tel. 74000, fax 40030, www.queenshotel.gi, queenshotel@gibtelecom.net).

$$ Continental Hotel isn't fancy, but it has a friendly feel. Its 17 high-ceilinged, air-conditioned rooms border an unusual elliptical atrium (Sb-£52, Db-£70, Tb-£85, Qb-£95, includes continental breakfast, elevator, a couple of blocks south of Casemates TI in Main Street pedestrian area, Engineer Lane, tel. 76900, fax 41702, contiho@gibtelecom.net).

$$ Cannon Hotel is a run-down dive. But it's also well-located and friendly and has the only cheap hotel rooms in town. Its 18 rooms (most with wobbly cots and no private bathrooms) look treacherously down on a little patio (S-£29, D-£40, Db-£50, T-£50, Tb-£66, includes full English breakfast, behind cathedral at Cannon Lane 9, tel. 51711, fax 51789, www.cannonhotel.gi, cannon@gibnet.gi).

$ Emile Hostel, charming and the cheapest place in town, welcomes people of any age (42 beds, dorm bed-£15, S-£20, D-£35, includes breakfast, on Montagu Bastion diagonally across the street from a petrol station, ramped entrance on Line Wall Road, tel. & fax 51106, www.emilehostel.com, emilehostel@yahoo.co.uk).

Eating in Gibraltar

Take a break from *jamón* and sample some English pub grub: fish-and-chips, meat pies, jacket potatoes (baked potatoes with fillings), or a good old greasy English breakfast. English-style beers include chilled lagers and room-temperature ales, bitters, and stouts. In general, the farther you venture away from Main Street, the cheaper and more local the places become.

The Clipper, my favorite pub for dinner, is friendly and offers filling £6 meals and Murphy's stout on tap (English breakfast-£5, Mon–Sat 9:30–22:00, Sun 10:00–22:00, on Irish Town Lane).

The Star Bar, which brags that it's "Gibraltar's Oldest Bar," is on a quiet street with a pubby interior and good £7 plates (daily 7:00–24:00, food served till 22:00, on Parliament Lane off Main Street, across from Corner House Restaurant).

Carpenter's Arms is a fast, cheap-and-cheery café run by the

Methodist church, serving £3 meals with a missionary's smile. It's upstairs in the Methodist church on Main Street (Mon–Fri 9:00–14:00, closed Sat–Sun and Aug, volunteer-run, 100 yards past the Governor's Residence at 297 Main Street).

Queensway Quay Marina: To dine in yacht-club ambience, stroll the marina and choose from a string of restaurants serving the boat-owning crowd. When the sun sets, the quay-side tables at each of these places are prime dining real estate. **Waterfront Restaurant** has a lounge-lizard interior and great marina-side tables outside (£15 plates with daily specials, Indian, and classic British; daily 9:00–24:00, last orders 22:45, tel. 45666). **Claus on the Rock Bistro** has a colorful menu with dishes from around the world (£15 plates, closed Sun, tel. 48686). The marina promenade also has Italian and Indian restaurants.

Casemates Square Food Circus: The big square at the entrance of Gibraltar contains a variety of restaurants, ranging from fast food (fish-and-chips joint, Burger King, and Pizza Hut) to inviting pubs spilling out into the square. The **All's Well** pub serves £8 meals (Moroccan *tajine,* salads, burgers, fish-and-chips, and more) and offers pleasant tables with umbrellas under leafy trees (daily 9:30–19:00). Fruit stands and cheap take-out food stalls bustle just outside the entry to the square at the **Market Place** (Mon–Sat 9:00–15:00, closed Sun).

Groceries: An **In & Out** minimarket is on Main Street, off Cathedral Square (Mon–Fri 8:30–20:00, Sat 8:30–18:00, closed Sun). Nearby, **Marks & Spencer** has an inside take-out window that serves roast chicken and fresh-baked cookies (Mon–Sat 8:30–19:00, Sun 10:00–15:00).

Connections

Gibraltar is expanding its flight schedule. Currently there are daily Iberia Airlines flights to Madrid and about four British Air flights a day between London/Gatwick and Madrid. The discount airline Monarch flies to London's Luton Airport.

Bus travelers walk five minutes from Gibraltar's border into Spain to reach La Línea, the nearest bus station (tel. 902-199-208 or 956-172-396). The nearest train station is at Algeciras, which is the region's main transportation hub (for Algeciras connections, see "Connections" near the end of this chapter).

From La Línea by Bus to: Algeciras (2/hr, 45 min, can buy ticket on bus), **Tarifa** (7–8/day direct, 1 hr; 10/day with change in Algeciras, 1.5 hrs), **Málaga** (4/day, 3 hrs), **Ronda** (no direct bus, transfer in Algeciras; Algeciras to Ronda: 6/day, 2 hrs), **Granada** (2/day, 5 hrs), **Sevilla** (4/day, 4 hrs), **Jerez** (2/day, 3 hrs), **Huelva** (1/day, 6 hrs), **Madrid** (2/day, 8 hrs).

Tarifa

Europe's southernmost town is whitewashed and Arab-looking, with a lovely beach, an old castle, restaurants swimming in fresh seafood, inexpensive places to sleep, enough windsurfers to sink a ship, and best of all, hassle-free boats to Morocco.

As I stood on Tarifa's town promenade under the castle, looking out at almost-touchable Morocco across the Strait of Gibraltar, I regretted only that I didn't have this book to steer me clear of gritty Algeciras on earlier trips. Tarifa, with daily 35-minute boat transfers to Tangier, is the best jumping-off point for a Moroccan side-trip.

Tarifa has no blockbuster sights (and can be quiet off-season), but it's a town where you just feel good to be on vacation. Given its lofty status as a breezy mecca among windsurfers, it's mobbed with young German and French adventure-seekers in July and August.

Orientation to Tarifa

The old town, surrounded by a wall, slopes gently up from the water's edge. The modern section stretches farther inland from Tarifa's fortified gate.

Tourist Information

The TI is on Paseo de la Alameda (June–Sept daily 10:00–13:30 & 18:00–20:00; Oct–May Mon–Fri 10:00–14:00 & 16:00–18:00, Sat–Sun 10:00–14:00; hours may vary slightly on slow or bad-weather days, tel. 956-680-993, turismo@aytotarifa.com).

Arrival in Tarifa

By Bus: The bus station (actually a couple of portable buildings with an outdoor sitting area) is on Batalla del Salado, about a five-minute walk from the old town. (The more-central TI also has bus schedules.) Buy tickets directly from the driver if the ticket booth is closed (Mon–Fri 7:30–9:30 & 10:00–11:00 & 14:30–18:30, Sat–Sun 15:00–19:30, hours vary slightly depending on season, tel. 956-684-038, 902-199-208). To reach the old town, walk away from the wind generators perched on the mountain ridge.

By Car: If you're staying in the center of town, follow signs for *Alameda* or *Puerto,* and continue along Avenida de Andalucía.

Tarifa

1. Hostal Alborada
2. Hotel La Mirada
3. La Sacristía
4. Casa Blan+co
5. Hotel Misiana
6. La Casa Amarilla
7. Hostal La Calzada
8. Hostal Alameda
9. Hostal Africa
10. Pensión Correo
11. Hostal Villanueva
12. Restaurante Morilla
13. Rest. La Pescaderia
14. Pizzeria La Capricciosa
15. Ristorante La Trattoria
16. To Restaurante Souk
17. Café Central & FIRMM
18. Bar El Francés
19. Café Bar Los Mellis & Bar El Pasillo
20. Casino Tarifeno
21. Confitería LaTarifeña
22. Churrería La Palmera
23. Supermarket
24. Mercado (Market)
25. Internet Café
26. Girasol Adventure
27. Whale Watch España & Marruecotur
28. Speedlines Tours

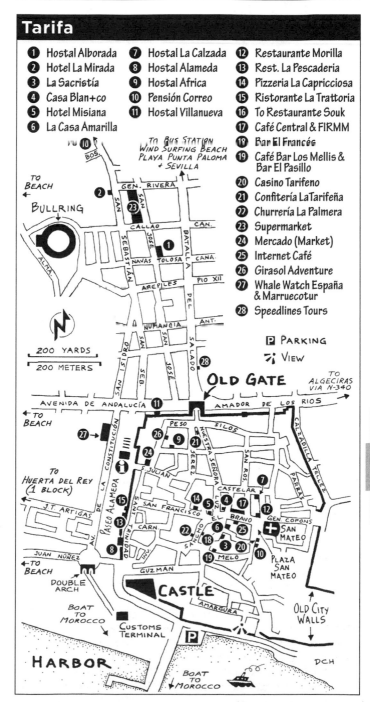

P PARKING
⚞ VIEW

Side-Tripping to Morocco

Tangier, worth ▲▲▲, is the main reason to go to Tarifa. The fast, modern catamaran ride (a huge car ferry that zips over every two hours all year long) takes less than an hour. You walk from the Tangier port into a remarkable city—the fifth-largest in Morocco—which is no longer the Tijuana of Africa, but a booming town enjoying the enthusiastic support and can-do vision of a new and activist king.

Most tourists do the mindless belly-dancing-and-shopping excursion (which costs about €65 including the ferry ride—essentially the same as the round-trip ferry ride sans tour). They're met by a guide, taken on a bus tour and a walk through the old town market, offered a couple of crass Kodak moments with snake charmers and desert dancers, and given lunch with live music and belly-dancing. Then they visit a big shop and are hustled back down to their boat where—five hours after they landed—they return to the First World thankful they don't have diarrhea.

The alternative is to simply take the ferry on your own and leave the tourist track. Things are cheap and relatively safe. Since more than 90 percent of visitors choose the comfort of a tour, independent adventurers rarely see another tourist and avoid all the kitsch. You can catch the first boat (9:00) and spend the entire day, returning that evening; extend with an overnight in Tangier; or even head deeper into Morocco.

If you're planning a day trip or an overnight stay, see the Tangier chapter for all the details. If you're going to stay longer in Morocco, you'll need the help of another guidebook.

Follow signs to make an obligatory loop to the port entrance, and park at Calle Juan Núñez (on the harbor, at the base of the castle, reasonable cost, generally a place available). Note that Avenida de la Constitución is one-way (going away from the port). There's plenty of free parking just outside Tarifa's old town walls. Blue lines indicate paid parking.

Helpful Hints

Internet Access: Pandor@, in the heart of the old town, is across from Café Central and near the church (generally in summer daily 10:00–24:00, in winter daily 10:00–14:30 & 16:30–18:00, 15 computers).

Excursions: Girasol Adventure offers a variety of outdoor excursions, including mountain-bike rentals (€18/day with helmet), guided bike tours, hikes in the national park, beginners' rock-climbing classes, and, when you're all done...a massage (€45/hr). The various activities generally last a half-day and cost around €25. Ask Sabine or Chris for details (Mon–Fri

10:15–14:00 & 18:30–20:30, Sat 11:00–14:00, closed Sun, Calle Colón 12, tel. 956-627-037, www.girasol-adventure.com).

Sights in Tarifa

Church of St. Matthew (Iglesia de San Mateo)—Tarifa's most important church, facing its main drag, is richly decorated for being in such a small town. Most nights, it seems life squirts from the church out the front door and into the fun-loving Calle El Bravo. Wander inside (daily 9:00–13:00 & 17:30–20:30; there may be English-language leaflets inside on the right).

Find the fragment of an ancient tombstone—a tiny square (eye-level, about the size of this book) in the wall just before the transept on the right side. Probably the most important historical item in town, this stone fragment proves there was a functioning church here during Visigothic times, before the Moorish conquest. The tombstone reads, in a kind of Latin Spanish (try reading it), "Flaviano lived as a Christian for 50 years, a little more or less. In death he received forgiveness as a servant of God on March 30, 674. May he rest in peace." If that gets you in the mood to light a candle, switch on an electric "candle" by dropping in a coin. (It works.)

Step into the side chapel around the corner in the right transept. The centerpiece of the **altar** is a boy Jesus. By Andalusian tradition, he used to be naked, but these days he's clothed with outfits that vary with the Church calendar. Cherubs dance around on the pink-and-purple interior above an exquisite chandelier.

A statue of **St. James the Moor-Slayer** (missing his sword) is on the right wall of the main central altar. Since the days of the Reconquista, James has been Spain's patron saint. For more on this important figure—and why he's fighting invaders that came to Spain centuries after his death.

The left side of the nave harbors several **statues**—showing typically over-the-top Baroque emotion—that are paraded through town during Holy Week. The **Captive Christ** (with hands bound, on left wall) evokes a time when Christians were held captive by Moors. The door on the left side of the nave is the **"door of pardons."** For a long time, Tarifa was a dangerous place—on the edge of the Reconquista. To encourage people to live here, the Church offered a second helping of forgiveness to anyone who lived in Tarifa for a year. One year and one day after moving to Tarifa, they would have the privilege of passing through this special "door of pardons," and a Mass of thanksgiving would be held in that person's honor.

Castle of Guzmán el Bueno—This castle is a concrete hulk in a vacant lot, interesting only for the harbor views from its ramparts (closed indefinitely for restoration). It was named after a 13th-century Christian general who gained fame in a sad show of courage while fighting the Moors. Holding Guzmán's son hostage, the Moors demanded he surrender the castle or they'd kill the boy. Guzmán refused, even

throwing his own knife down from the ramparts. It was used on his son's throat. Ultimately, the Moors withdrew to Africa, and Guzmán was a hero. *Bueno* (when open: €2, Tue–Sat 11:00–14:00 & 18:00–20:00, Sun 11:00–14:00, closed Mon).

If you can't get into the castle, you'll get equally good views from the plaza just left of the town hall. Follow *ayto* signs to the ceramic frog fountain in front of the Casa Consistorial and continue left.

Bullfighting—Tarifa has a third-rate bullring where novices botch fights on occasional Saturdays through the summer. Professional bullfights take place the first week of September. The ring is a short walk from town. You'll see posters everywhere.

▲Whale-Watching—Daily whale- and dolphin-watching excursions are offered by several companies in Tarifa. In little more than 40 years, people in this area went from eating whales to protecting them and sharing them with 20,000 visitors a year. Talks are under way between Morocco and Spain to protect the Strait of Gibraltar by declaring it a national park.

For any of the tours, it's wise (but not always necessary) to reserve one to three days in advance. You'll get a multilingual tour and a two-hour boat trip (usually no WC on board). Sightings occur more than 90 percent of the time. Dolphins and pilot whales frolic here any time of year (they like the food), sperm whales visit May through July, and orcas pass through in July and August. In bad weather, boats may leave instead from Algeciras—drivers follow in a convoy, people without cars usually get rides from staff, and you'll stand a lesser chance of seeing whales.

The best company is the Swiss nonprofit **FIRMM** (Foundation for Information and Research on Marine Mammals), which gives a 25-minute educational talk before departure (€30/person, 1–5 trips/day April–Oct, sometimes also Nov, also offers courses, around the corner from Café Central—one door inland at Pedro Cortés 4, tel. 956-627-008, mobile 619-459-441, www.firmm.org, firmm98 @aol.com). If you don't see any whales or dolphins on your tour, you can join another trip for free.

Whale Watch España is another good option (Avenida de la Constitución 6, tel. 956-627-013, mobile 639-476-544, www.whalewatchtarifa.net, run by Lourdes and Flor).

▲▲**Windsurfing**—Tarifa's vast, sandy beach stretches west for about five miles. You can walk the beach from Tarifa or those with

a car can explore farther (following Cadiz Road). On windy summer days, the sea is littered with sprinting windsurfers, while kitesurfers flutter in the sky. It's a fascinating scene: A long string of funky beach resorts is packed with vans and fun-mobiles from northern Europe under mountain ridges lined with modern energy-generating windmills. The various resorts each have a sandy access road, parking, a cabana-type hamlet with rental gear, beachwear shops, a bar, and a hip, healthy restaurant. I like Valdevaqueros beach (five miles from Tarifa), with a wonderful thatched restaurant serving hearty salads, paella, and burgers. Camping Torre de la Peña also has some fun beach eateries.

Camping—In July and August, inexpensive buses do a circuit of nearby campgrounds, all on the waterfront (€2, departures about every 2 hours, confirm times with TI). Trying to get a parking spot in August can take the joy out of this experience.

Sleeping in Tarifa

Room rates vary with the season. For many hotels, I've listed the three seasonal tiers (highest prices—mid-June–Sept; medium prices—spring and fall; and lowest prices—winter).

Outside the City Wall

These hotels are about five blocks from the old town, right off the main drag, Batalla del Salado, in the plain, modern part of town. They are close to the beach and the bus station with free and easy street parking.

$$ Hostal Alborada is a squeaky-clean, family-run 37-room place with two attractive courtyards and modern conveniences. Carlos, Quino, and family offer to help make your Morocco tour or ferry reservation. If they're not too busy, they'll even give you a free lift to the port (Sb-€35/50/60, Db-€46/65/80, Tb-€70/80/99, pay for first night when reserving, upon arrival show this book for a 10 percent discount in 2010—*except* during high season, strict 15-day cancellation policy, breakfast-€2.50–5, air-con, pay Internet access, free Wi-Fi, laundry-€12, Calle San José 40, tel. 956-681-140, fax 956-681-935, www.hotelalborada.com, alborada@cherry tel.com).

Sleep Code

(€1 = about $1.40, country code: 34)

S = Single, **D** = Double/Twin, **T** = Triple, **Q** = Quad, **b** = bathroom, **s** = shower only. Unless otherwise noted, credit cards are accepted and English is spoken. Breakfast is not included (unless noted).

To help you easily sort through these listings, I've divided the rooms into three categories, based on the price for a standard double room with bath during high season:

$$$ Higher Priced—Most rooms €100 or more.
$$ Moderately Priced—Most rooms between €50–100.
$ Lower Priced—Most rooms €50 or less.

$$ Hotel La Mirada has 25 mod and renovated rooms, most with sea views at no extra cost (Sb-€45/50/60, Db-€60/75/90, breakfast-€5, elevator, free Wi-Fi, expansive sea views from large roof terrace with inviting lounge chairs, Calle San Sebastián 41, tel. 956-684-427, fax 956-681-162, www.hotel-lamirada.com, reservas@hotel-lamirada.com, Antonio and Salvador).

On or Inside the City Wall

$$$ La Sacristía, formerly a Moorish stable, now houses travelers who want stylish surroundings. It offers 10 fine rooms, each decorated differently: chic Spanish on the first floor, Asian-style on the second floor. They offer spa treatments, custom tours of the area, and occasional special events—partake in the party since you won't sleep (Db-€115, superior Db-€135, extra bed-€35, same prices all year, includes breakfast, fans, massage room, roof terrace, very central at San Donato 8, tel. 956-681-759, fax 956-685-182, www .lasacristia.net, tarifa@lasacristia.net, helpful Teresa).

$$$ Casa Blan+co, where minimalist meets Moroccan, is the newest reasonably priced designer hotel on the block. Each of its seven rooms (with double beds only—no twins) is decorated (and priced) differently. The place is decked out with practical amenities (mini-fridge and stovetop) as well as romantic touches—loft beds, walk-in showers, and subtle lighting (Db-€52–70 in low season, Db-€91–134 in high season, breakfast, small roof terrace, off main square at Calle Nuestra Señora de la Luz 2, tel. & fax 956-681-515, www.casablan-co.com, info@casablan-co.com).

$$$ Hotel Misiana has 13 comfortable, newly remodeled, spacious rooms. Their designer gave the place a mod, pastel boutique-ish ambience. To avoid street noise, request a room on a higher floor (Sb-€50/60/115, Db-€70/85/135, fancy top-floor Db suite-€110/140/250, low and mid-season rates are €10–20 more on weekends, includes breakfast, double-paned windows, elevator, 100 yards directly in front of the church at Calle Sancho IV El Bravo 18, tel. 956-627-083, fax 956-627-055, www.misiana.com, reservas@misiana.com).

$$ La Casa Amarilla ("The Yellow House") offers 10 posh apartments plus three regular rooms with modern decor and tiny kitchens (three Db-€43/63/80, larger apartment Db-€55/77/102, secure reservation with credit card, across street from Café Central, Calle Sancho IV El Bravo 9, tel. 956-681-993, fax 956-684-029, www.lacasaamarilla.net, info@lacasaamarilla.net).

$$ Hostal La Calzada has eight airy, well-appointed rooms right in the lively old-town thick of things (Db-€50–80, extra bed-€15, closed Nov–March, air-con, 20 yards from church at Calle Justino Pertinez 7, tel. 956-681-492, fax 956-680-366, www.hostallacalzada.com, Diego).

$$ Hostal Alameda, overlooking a square where the local children play, glistens with pristine marble floors and dark red decor. The main building has 11 bright rooms and the annex has 16 more-modern rooms; both face the same delightful square (Db-€60/70/90, extra bed-€20–30, can gouge in Aug, includes tax, air-con, Paseo de la Alameda 4, tel. 956-681-181, fax 956-680-264, www.hostalalameda.com, reservas@hostalalameda.com, Antonio).

$$ Hostal Africa, with 13 bright rooms and an inviting roof garden, is buried on a very quiet street in the center of town. Its dreamy blue-and-white color scheme and stripped-down feel give it a Moorish ambience (S-€20/25/35, Sb-€25/35/50, D-€30/40/50, Db-€35/50/65, Tb-€50/75/100, laundry-€10 (€20 in high season), storage for boards and bikes, Calle María Antonia Toledo 12, tel. 956-680-220, mobile 606-914-294, hostal_africa@hotmail.com, Miguel and Eva keep the reception desk open only from 9:00–24:00).

$$ Pensión Correo rents 12 simple rooms at a fair value—especially Room 8, with its private roof terrace (S-€20–35, D-€35–60, Db-€45–80, extra bed-€15–20, reservations accepted within 24 hours of arrival, roof garden, Coronel Moscardo 8, tel. 956-680-206, www.pensioncorreo.com, welcome@pensioncorreo.com, María José and Luca).

$ Hostal Villanueva offers 12 remodeled rooms at budget prices. It's simple, clean, and friendly, and includes an inviting terrace that overlooks the old town. On a busy street, it's dominated by its restaurant, with no lounge or public area. Pepe asks that you reconfirm your reservation by phone the day before you arrive (Sb-€25–30, Db-€35–45, higher rates in July–Aug, just west of the old-town gate at Avenida de Andalucía 11, access from outside the wall, tel. & fax 956-684-149).

Eating in Tarifa

I've grouped my recommendations below into two categories: Sit down to a real restaurant meal, or enjoy a couple of the many characteristic tapas bars in the old town.

Restaurant Dining

Restaurante Morilla, facing the church and on the town's prime piece of people-watching real estate, serves tasty local-style fish—grilled or baked. This is a real restaurant (no tapas) with good indoor and outdoor seating. A list of the day's available fish is scribbled on a piece of paper that the waiter reviews with you; it's sold by weight, so confirm the price carefully (€12 fish plates, daily 12:00–24:00, Calle Sancho IV El Bravo, tel. 956-681-757).

Restaurant La Pescaderia is a thriving fish place with an inviting menu and great seating, both inside and on delightful Paseo de la Alameda. Their specialty is a paella-style rice and fish stew (€10–15 fish plates, daily 13:00–16:30 & 20:00–23:00, in summer till 23:30, no reservations, tel. 956-627-078).

Pizzeria La Capricciosa, cozy and fun, is one of the numerous pizza-and-pasta joints supported by the large expat Italian community. It serves creative, hearty dinner salads and €8 pizzas and pastas under a wall full of Sergio's bike trophies (daily 20:00–24:00, July–Aug also open 13:00–16:00, at the beginning of Calle San Francisco 6, tel. 956-685-040).

Ristorante La Trattoria, on the Alameda, is another good Italian option, with cloth-napkin class and a friendly staff (€9–12 pizzas and pastas, Thu–Tue 19:30–24:00, closed Wed, Paseo de la Alameda, tel. 956-682-225).

Outside of Town

Restaurante Souk serves a tasty fusion of Moroccan, Indian, and Thai cuisine in a dark, exotic, and romantic ambience. This is a fine place to spend €20—if you don't mind a 10-minute walk out of town. Head up Calle San Sebastian until you see a big staircase on the right, which you'll take to Mar Tirreno 46 (daily 18:00–24:00, closed Tue in Sept–June, also closed Feb–March, good wine list, tel. 956-627-065, friendly Patricia).

Tapas

Café Central is *the* happening place nearly any time of day—it's the perch for all the cool tourists. The tapas are priced at €1.30; just go to the bar and point. They also offer breakfast with eggs; great ingenious €6 salads (study the menu); and impressively therapeutic healthy fruit drinks (daily 9:00–24:00, off Plaza San Mateo, near church, tel. 956-680-560).

Bar El Francés is a thriving hole-in-the-wall where "Frenchies" (as the bar's name implies) Marcial and Alexandra serve tasty little plates of tapas. From Café Central, follow the cars 100 yards to the first corner on the left to reach this simple, untouristy standing-and-stools-only eatery. This spot is popular for its fine *raciones* (€5–9) and tapas (generally €1.30)—especially oxtail *(rabo del toro),* pork with tomato sauce *(carne con tomate),* and pork with spice *(chicharrones).* The outdoor terrace with restaurant-type tables (no tapas served here) is an understandably popular spot to enjoy a casual meal (Mon–Fri open long hours, especially April–Sept; closed Sat–Sun and Jan except open some summer weekends; show this book and Marcial will be happy to bring you a free sherry, Calle Sancho IV El Bravo 21A).

Café Bar Los Mellis is a local favorite for feasts on rickety tables set on cobbles. This family-friendly place offers a good chorizo sandwich and *patatas bravas*—potatoes with a hot tomato sauce served on a wooden board (Thu–Tue 13:00–16:00 & 20:00–24:00, closed Wed, run by brothers José and Ramón; from Bar El Francés, cross parking lot and take Calle del Legionario Ríos Moya up 1 block). **Bar El Pasillo,** next to Los Mellis, also serves tapas (closed Mon).

Casino Tarifeno is just to the sea side of the church. It's an old-boys' social club "for members only," but it offers a musty Andalusian welcome to visiting tourists, including women. Wander through. There's a low-key bar with tapas, a TV room, a card room, and a lounge. There's no menu, but prices are standard. Just point and say the size you want: tapa, *media-ración,* or *ración.*

Pastries, Beach Bars, and Picnics

Breakfast or Dessert: **Confitería La Tarifeña** serves super pastries and flan (closed Mon, at the top of Calle Nuestra Señora de la Luz, near the main old-town gate).

Churrería La Palmera serves breakfast before most hotels and cafés have even turned on the lights—early enough for you to get your coffee fix, and/or bulk up on *churros* and chocolate, before hopping the first ferry to Tangier (Sanchez IV El Bravo 34, across from Bar El Francés).

Windsurfer Bars: If you have a car, head to the string of beaches. Many have bars and thatched fun-loving restaurants that keep the wet-suited gang fed and watered (see "Windsurfing," earlier in the chapter).

Picnics: Stop by the *mercado municipal* (farmers market, Mon–Sat 8:00–14:00, closed Sun, in old town, inside gate nearest TI), any grocery, or the **Eroski Center supermarket** (Mon–Sat 9:15–21:15, closed Sun, has simple cafeteria, near the hotels in the new town at Callao and San José).

Connections

Tarifa

From Tarifa by Bus to: La Línea/Gibraltar (6/day direct, 1 hr, starting around 12:00; 10/day with transfer in Algeciras, 1.5 hrs), **Algeciras** (10/day, 30 min, first departure from Tarifa weekdays at 6:30, on Sat 8:00, on Sun 10:00; return from Algeciras as late as 21:00), **Jerez** (2/day, 2 hrs, more frequent with transfer in Cádiz), **Sevilla** (4/day, 3 hrs), **Huelva** (for those Portugal-bound, 1/day, 5 hrs), and **Málaga** (2/day, 3.5 hrs). All bus service from Tarifa is by Comes (tel. 902-199-208, www.tgcomes.es).

Algeciras

Algeciras is only worth leaving. It's useful to the traveler mainly as a transportation hub, offering ferries to Tangier and trains and buses to destinations in southern and central Spain. The **TI** is on Juan de la Cierva, a block inland from the port. It's on the same street as both the train and bus station, which runs frequent service to Tarifa and La Línea.

Trains: The train station is four blocks inland, opposite Hotel Octavio (tel. 956-630-202). If arriving by train, head down San Bernardo toward the sea to Juan de la Cierva for the TI and port. As an alternative, you can also purchase ferry tickets at the train station branch of Viajes Algemar Travel (open daily, follows train schedules, tel. 956-657-311).

From Algeciras by Train to: Madrid (2/day, 5.5 hrs, arrives at Atocha), **Ronda** (6/day, 1.5–2 hrs), **Granada** (3/day, 4.25–5 hrs), **Sevilla** (3/day, 5 hrs, transfer at either Córdoba, Antequera, or Bobadilla), **Córdoba** (2/day, 3.5 hrs), **Málaga** (4/day, 4 hrs, transfer in Bobadilla). With the exception of the route to Madrid, these are particularly scenic trips; the best is the mountainous journey to Málaga via Bobadilla.

Buses: Algeciras is served by three different bus companies (Comes, Portillo, and Linesur), all located in the same terminal next to Hotel Octavio and directly across from the train station. The companies generally serve different destinations, but there is some overlap. Compare schedules and rates to find the most convenient bus for you. By the ticket counter you'll find an easy red letter board listing departures. Lockers are by the platforms—purchase a token at the machines.

Comes (tel. 902-199-208, www.tgcomes.es) runs buses to **La Línea** (2/hr, 45 min, 7:00–22:30), **Tarifa** (10/day, 30 min), **Sevilla** (4/day, 3.5 hrs), **Jerez** (2/day, 2.5 hrs), **Huelva** (1/day, 6 hrs), and **Madrid** (4/day, 8 hrs).

Portillo (tel. 956-654-304, www.ctsa-portillo.com) offers buses to **Málaga** (17/day, 1.75 hrs *directo*, 3 hrs *ruta*, some buses run by Alsina Graells) and **Granada** (5/day, 4–5.5 hrs).

Linesur (tel. 956-667-649, www.linesur.com) runs the most frequent direct buses to **Sevilla** (11/day, 2 direct, fewer on weekends, 2.25–2.5 hrs) and **Jerez** (9/day, 2.5 hrs).

Ferries from Algeciras to Tangier, Morocco: If you plan to sail from Algeciras, buy your ticket at the port instead of one of the many divey-looking travel agencies littering the town. To find the ticket office, go to the farthest building at the port, which is labeled in large letters: *Estación Marítima Terminal de Pasajeros* (luggage storage available here, easy parking at port-€6). The official offices of the seven boat companies are inside this main port building, directly behind the helpful little English-speaking info kiosk (8–22 ferries/day, port open daily 6:45–21:45, tel. 956-585-463).

Route Tips for Drivers

Tarifa to Gibraltar (45 min): This short drive takes you past a silvery-white forest of windmills, from peaceful Tarifa past Algeciras to La Línea (the Spanish town bordering Gibraltar). Passing Algeciras, continue in the direction of Estepona. At San Roque, take the La Línea–Gibraltar exit.

Gibraltar to Nerja (130 miles): Barring traffic problems, the trip along the Costa del Sol is smooth and easy by car—much of it on a new highway. Just follow the coastal highway east. After Málaga, follow signs to *Almería* and *Motril*.

Nerja to Granada (80 miles, 1.5 hrs, 100 views): Drive along the coast to Motril, catching N-323 north for about 40 miles to Granada. While scenic side-trips may beckon, don't arrive late in Granada without a confirmed hotel reservation.

MOROCCO

MOROCCO

Al-Maghreb

A young country with an old history, Morocco is a photographer's delight and a budget traveler's dream. It's cheap, exotic, and easier and more appealing than ever. Along with a rich culture, Morocco offers plenty of contrast—from beach resorts to bustling desert markets, from jagged mountains to sleepy, mud-brick oasis towns. And there's a distinct new energy as its popular activist king asserts his vision.

Morocco (*Marruecos* in Spanish; *Al-Maghreb* in Arabic) also provides a good dose of culture shock—both bad and good. It makes Spain and Portugal look meek and mild. You'll encounter oppressive friendliness, brutal heat, the Arabic language, the Islamic faith, ancient cities, and aggressive beggars.

While Morocco is clearly a place apart from Mediterranean Europe, it doesn't really seem like Africa either. It's a mix, reflecting its strategic position between the two continents. Situated on the Strait of Gibraltar, Morocco has been flooded by waves of invasions over the centuries. The Berbers, the native population, have had to contend with the Phoenicians, Carthaginians, Romans, Vandals, and more.

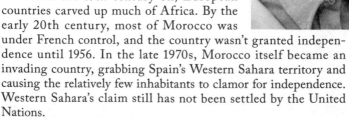

The Arabs brought Islam to Morocco in the seventh century A.D. and stuck around, battling the Berbers in various civil wars. A series of Berber and Arab dynasties rose and fell; the Berbers won out and still run the country today.

From the 15th century on, European countries carved up much of Africa. By the early 20th century, most of Morocco was under French control, and the country wasn't granted independence until 1956. In the late 1970s, Morocco itself became an invading country, grabbing Spain's Western Sahara territory and causing the relatively few inhabitants to clamor for independence. Western Sahara's claim still has not been settled by the United Nations.

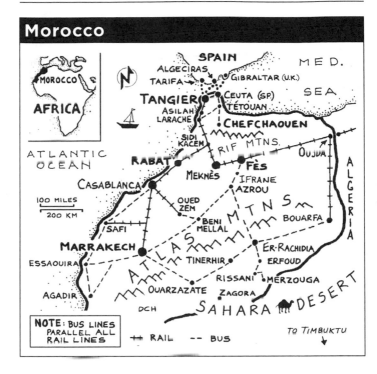

Unfortunately, most of the English-speaking Moroccans whom the typical tourist meets are hustlers. Most visitors develop some intestinal problems by the end of their visit. Most women are harassed on the streets by horny but generally harmless men. Things don't work smoothly. In fact, compared to Morocco, Spain resembles Sweden in terms of efficiency.

When you cruise south across the Strait of Gibraltar, leave your busy itineraries and split-second timing behind. Morocco must be taken on its own terms. In Morocco things go smoothly only *"Inshallah"*—if God so wills.

Helpful Hints

Politics: Americans pondering a visit understandably wonder how they'll be received in this Muslim nation. Al Jazeera blares from televisions in all the bars. Regardless, I saw no angry graffiti or posters and felt no animosity toward American individuals there. Western visitors feel a warm welcome in post-9/11 Morocco. And it's culturally enriching for Westerners to experience Morocco—a Muslim monarchy with women still in traditional dress and roles, succeeding on its own terms without embracing modern "norms."

MOROCCO

Hustler Alert: While Moroccans are some of Africa's wealthiest people, you are still incredibly rich to them. This imbalance causes predictable problems. Wear your money belt. Assume con artists are more clever than you. Haggle when appropriate (prices skyrocket for tourists). You'll attract hustlers like flies at every famous tourist sight. In the worst-case scenario, they'll lie to you, get you lost, blackmail you, and pester the heck out of you. Never leave your car  or baggage where you can't get back to it without someone else's "help." Anything you buy in a guide's company gets him a 20 percent commission. Normally locals, shopkeepers, and police will come to your rescue if the hustlers' heat becomes unbearable. Consider hiring a guide, since it's helpful to have a translator, and once you're "taken," the rest seem to leave you alone.

Marijuana Alert: In Morocco, marijuana *(kif)* is as illegal as it is popular, a fact that many Westerners in local jails would love to remind you of. As a general rule, just walk right by those hand-carved pipes in the marketplace. Some dealers who sell it cheap make their profit after you get arrested. Cars and buses are stopped and checked by police routinely throughout Morocco—especially in the north and in the Chefchaouen region, which is Morocco's *kif* capital.

Health: Morocco is much more hazardous to your health than Spain or Portugal. Eat in clean—not cheap—places. Peel fruit, eat only cooked vegetables, and drink reliably bottled water (Sidi Harazem or Sidi Ali). When you do get diarrhea—and you should plan on it—adjust your diet (small and bland meals, no milk or grease) or fast for a day, but make sure you replenish lost fluids. Relax: Most diarrhea is not serious, just an adjustment that will run its course.

Closed Days: Friday is the Muslim day of rest, when most of the country (except Tangier) closes down.

Ramadan: During this major month-long religious holiday (Aug 11–Sept 10 in 2010), Muslims focus on prayer and reflection. Following Islamic doctrine, they refrain during daylight hours from eating, drinking (including water), smoking, and having sex. On the final day of Ramadan, Muslims celebrate *Eid* (an all-day feast and gift-giving party, similar to Christmas) and travelers may find some less-touristy stores and restaurants closed.

MOROCCO

Money: Euros work here (as do dollars and pounds). If you're on a five-hour tour, bring along lots of €1 and €0.50 coins for tips, small purchases, and camel rides. But if you plan to do anything independently, change some money into Moroccan dirhams upon arrival (8 Moroccan dirhams = about $1). Banks and ATMs have uniform rates. If you use an exchange desk, just be sure you can see the buying and selling rates; they should be within 10 percent of each other with no extra fees. Don't leave the country with Moroccan money unless you want a souvenir, since few places in Spain are willing to change dirhams to euros or dollars.

Information: Travel information, English or otherwise, is rare here. For an extended trip, bring guidebooks from home or Spain. Lonely Planet and Rough Guide both publish good ones, and the green Michelin *Morocco* guidebook is worthwhile (if you read French). Buy the best map you can find locally—names are always changing, and it's helpful to have towns, roads, and place names written in Arabic.

Language: It's unusual to be in a country where a trilingual sign or menu doesn't include English. English ranks fourth here after Arabic, French, and Spanish. The Arabic squiggle-script, its many difficult sounds, and the fact that French is Morocco's second language combine to make communication tricky for English-speaking travelers. A little French goes a long way, but learn a few words in Arabic. Have your first local friend help you with the pronunciation:

English	Arabic	Pronounced
Hello. ("Peace be with you")	*Salaam alaikum.*	sah-LAHM ah-LAY-koom
Hello. (response: "Peace also be with you")	*Wa alaikum salaam.*	wah ah-LAY-koom sah-LAHM
Please.	*Min fadlik.*	meen FAHD-leek
Thank you.	*Shokran.*	SHOH-kron (like "sugar on")
Excuse me.	*Ismahli.*	ees-SMAH-lee
Yes.	*Yeh.*	EE-yeh
No.	*Lah.*	lah
Give me five. (kids enjoy this...not above but straight ahead)	*Ham sah.*	hahm sah
OK.	*Wah hah.*	wah hah
Very good.	*Miz yen biz ef.*	meez EE-yehn beez ehf
Goodbye.	*Maa salama.*	mah sah-LEM-ah

MOROCCO

Moroccans are more touchy-feely than their Spanish neighbors. Expect lots of hugs if you make an effort to communicate. When greeting someone, a handshake is customary, followed by a fist over your heart. Listen carefully and write new words phonetically. Bring an Arabic phrase book. In markets, I sing, "la la la la la" to my opponents. *Lah shokran* means, "No, thank you."

Getting Around Morocco: Moroccan trains are quite good. Second class is cheap and comfortable. Buses connect all smaller towns quite well. By car, Morocco is easy, but drive defensively and never rely on the oncoming driver's skill. Night driving is dangerous. Pay a guard to watch your car overnight.

Keeping Your Bearings: Navigate the labyrinthine *medinas* (old towns) by altitude, gates, and famous mosques or buildings. Write down what gate you came in, so you can enjoy being lost—temporarily. *Souk* is Arabic for a particular market (such as leather, yarn, or metalwork).

TANGIER

Go to Africa. As you step off the boat, you realize that the crossing (less than an hour) has taken you further culturally than did the trip from the US to Spain. Morocco needs no museums; its sights are living in the streets. For decades, its coastal city of Tangier deserved its reputation as the "Tijuana of Africa." But that has changed. The new king is enthusiastic about Tangier, and there's a fresh can-do spirit in the air. The town is as Moroccan as ever...yet more enjoyable and less stressful.

Morocco in a Day?

While Morocco certainly deserves more than a day, many visitors touring Spain see it in a quick side-trip. And, though such a short sprint through Tangier is only a tease, it's far more interesting than another day in Spain. A day in Tangier gives you a good introduction to Morocco, a legitimate taste of North Africa, and a non-threatening slice of Islam. All you need is a passport (no visa or shots required) and €66 for the round-trip ferry crossing. Your big decisions: where to sail from; whether to go on your own or buy a ferry/guided tour day-trip package; and whether to make it a day trip or spend the night.

Time Difference: Morocco is on Greenwich Mean Time (like Great Britain), and does not observe Daylight Saving Time. This means it's two hours behind Spain in summer, and one hour behind in winter.

Terminology: Note that the Spanish refer to Morocco as "Marruecos" (mar-WAY-kohs) and Tangier as "Tanger" (pronounced with a guttural "g" at the back of the throat, sounding like TAHN-hair).

Going on Your Own, by Ferry from Tarifa

While the trip from Spain to Tangier can be made from three different ports (Tarifa, Algeciras, or Gibraltar), it's easiest, fastest, and cheapest from Tarifa. I'll describe the trip assuming you're sailing from Tarifa, which is most logical for the typical traveler.

Ferry Crossing: Just buy a ferry ticket (at the port, through your Tarifa hotel, or from a local travel agency). There is only one ferry company (FRS), and prices should be the same everywhere (€37 one-way, €66 round-trip). In summer, the ferry departs daily from Tarifa to Tangier at 9:00, 11:00, 13:00, 15:00,

17:00, 19:00, 21:00, and 23:00; and from Tangier to Tarifa at 7:00, 9:00, 11:00, 13:00, 15:00, 17:00, 19:00, and 21:00. In winter, boats leave Tangier on the even hours—the first at 8:00, and the last at 22:00 (the winter schedule starts when Daylight Saving Time ends in Spain). Because of its popularity with tours, the 9:00 ferry in July and August is sometimes too full for walk-ons. Boats are most crowded in July (when Moroccans in Spain go home for holiday), and in August (when the Costa del Sol groups come en masse). A few crossings a year are canceled because of storms or wind, mostly in winter.

Procedure: The ferry from Tarifa is a fast Nordic hydrofoil that theoretically takes 35 minutes to cross. It often leaves late. You'll go through Spanish customs at the port and Moroccan customs on the ferry. Whether taking a tour or traveling on your own, you *must* get a stamp (available on board) from the Moroccan immigration officer. After you leave Spain, find the customs desk on the boat, line up, and get your passport and entry paper stamped. If you're coming back the same day and know your return time, the immigration official will also give you an exit stamp (for your return from Morocco)—this prevents delays at the port at departure time. (If your return is open, you will have to go through a passport check and get your exit stamp on the way back to Spain.) The ferry is equipped with WCs, a shop, and a snack bar. Tarifa's modern little terminal has a cafeteria and WCs.

Hiring a Guide: Even if you're visiting Morocco independently, I recommend hiring a local guide to show you around Tangier (for tips, see "Guides," later in this chapter).

Taking a Tour

Taking a tour is easier but less rewarding than doing it on your own. A typical day-trip tour includes a round-trip crossing and a guide who meets you at a prearranged point in Tangier, then hustles you through the hustlers and onto your tour bus. Several guides await the arrival of each ferry in Tangier and assemble their groups. (Tourists wear stickers identifying which tour they're with.) All offer essentially the same five-hour Tangier experience: a city bus tour, possibly a trip to the desolate Atlantic Coast for some rugged African scenery, the famous ride-a-camel stop (five-minute camel ride for a couple of euros), a drive through the ritzy palace neighborhood, a walk through the medina (old town), and a too-thorough look at a sales-starved carpet shop (where prices include a 20 percent commission for your guide and tour company). The tour wraps up with lunch in a palatial Moroccan setting with live music (and non-Moroccan belly dancing), topped off by a final walk back to your boat through a gauntlet of desperate merchants.

Sound cheesy? It is. But no amount of packaging can gloss over this exotic and different culture. This kind of cultural voyeurism is almost embarrassing, but it's nonstop action. The shopping is...Moroccan. Bargain hard!

The day trip is so tightly organized that tourists have hardly any time alone in Tangier. For many people, that's just fine. But frankly, seeing a line of day-trippers clutching their bags nervously like paranoid kangaroos reminded me of the Tehran hostage crisis—the big difference being this one is self-imposed. It was pathetic.

You rarely need to book a tour more than a day in advance, even during peak season. Tours generally cost about €65, roughly the same price as a ferry ticket alone—the tour company makes its money off commissions if you shop, and gets a group rate on the ferry tickets. Prices are roughly the same at the various travel agencies. I wouldn't worry about which tour company you select. (They're all equally bad.)

Tours generally leave Tarifa on the 9:00 ferry and return at 13:00 (15:00 Spanish time), or they depart on the 13:00 ferry and return at 17:00 (19:00 Spanish time).

Those taking the tour have an option to spend the night at a fancy Tangier hotel (about €35 extra, includes dinner). If you stay overnight, the first day is the same as the one-day tour, but rather than catching the boat that afternoon, you take the same boat—on your own—24 hours later.

Independent types can also take the one-day tour (you'll need to stay with your group until you return to the ferry dock) and then just slip back into town thinking, "Freedom!" You're welcome to use your return ferry ticket on any later boat (departures every two hours).

Travel Agencies Offering Tours: Travel agencies throughout southern Spain sell Tangier ferry and ferry/tour tickets. Here are two in Tarifa: Marruecotur (daily in summer 7:40–21:00, across from the TI at Avenida de la Constitución 5, tel. 956-681-242) and Speedlines Tours (Batalla del Salado 10, tel. 956-627-048). Many hotels are happy to book a tour for you (ask when you reserve). If they offer this service and you want a tour, go for it.

You can also just drop by the port in Tarifa and buy your ferry/ tour ticket directly from the ferry company (FRS Maroc at Tarifa's dock, tel. 956-684-847, www.frs.es). FRS also offers a **"VIP tour"** for up to four people. For an additional €15 per person (after buying individual ferry tickets), your group receives a private guide and vehicle, plus lunch. This is actually quite economical if you're traveling as a foursome.

Tangier

Artists, writers, and musicians have always loved Tangier. Matisse was drawn to the evocative light. The Beat generation, led by William S. Burroughs and Jack Kerouac, sought the city's multicultural, otherworldly feel. Paul Bowles found his sheltering sky here. From the 1920s through the 1950s, Tangier was an "international city," too strategic to give to any one nation, and jointly governed by France, Spain, Britain, and Italy. It attracted playboy millionaires, bon vivants, globetrotting scoundrels, con artists, and expat romantics.

Tangier is always defying expectations. Ruled by Spain in the 19th century and France in the 20th, it's a rare place, where signs are in three languages...and English doesn't make the cut. In this Muslim city, you'll find a synagogue, Catholic and Anglican churches, and the town's largest mosque within close proximity.

Because of its "international zone" status, Morocco's previous king neglected the city, denying it national funds for improvements. Neglected Tangier became the armpit of Morocco. But when the new king—Mohammed VI—was crowned in 1999, the first city he visited was Tangier. His vision is to restore Tangier to its former glory.

Thanks to King Mohammed VI, Tangier (with a population of 700,000 and growing) is experiencing a rebirth. Restorations are taking place on a grand scale: The beach has been painstakingly cleaned, pedestrian promenades are popping up everywhere, and gardens bloom with lush new greenery. In the works are a new soccer stadium and a project to move the shipping port beyond the bay where the ferry docks are (which will clear current traffic congestion and make Tangier's ferry terminal much more welcoming). However, the economic downturn has slowed much of the development in the city. Many once-active construction sites are now either empty or at least lethargic, with just a handful of workers and machines in action.

Nevertheless, I'm uplifted by the new Tangier—it's affluent and modern without having abandoned its roots and embraced Western values. A visit here lets a Westerner marinated in anti-Muslim propaganda see what Islam aspires to be, and can be—and realize it is not a threat to the West.

Planning Your Time

If you're on your own, either hire a guide upon arrival (see "Guides," later in this chapter), or stop by the TI first thing to get oriented (you can walk or catch a Petit Taxi from the port to the TI). Exit the TI to the right and continue up to Place de Faro, with its cannons and views back to Spain. Beyond that, at Place de France (at Café du Paris), turn right on Rue de la Liberté, which leads directly into Grand Socco square, the hub of old Tangier. For the quickest visit, first cover the old town (Museum of the Kasbah, Dar el-Makhzen palace, Old American Legation Museum, and Petit Socco). Then catch a taxi to the beach (Plage de Corniche), and sightsee along the beach and then along Avenue Mohammed VI back to the port. You'll rarely see other tourists outside the tour-group circuit.

After Dark: Nighttime is great in Tangier. If spending the night, don't relax in a fancy hotel restaurant. Get out and about in the old town after dark. It's an entirely different experience and a highlight of any visit. (But remember, this isn't Spain—things die down by around 22:00.)

Orientation to Tangier

Like almost every city in Morocco, Tangier is split in two. From the ferry dock, you'll see the old town (medina)—encircled by its

medieval wall—on your right, behind Hotel Continental. The old town has the markets, the Kasbah (with its palace and the mosque of the Kasbah—marked by the higher of the two minarets you see), cheap hotels, homes both decrepit and recently renovated, and 2,000 wannabe guides. The twisty, hilly streets of the old town are caged within a wall accessible by keyhole gates. The larger minaret (on the left) belongs to the modern Mohammed V mosque—the biggest one in town.

The new town, where the TI and fancy hotels reside, sprawls past the industrial port zone to your left. The big square, Grand Socco, is the link between the old and new parts of town.

Because Tangier is the fifth-largest city in Morocco, many assume they'll get lost here. Although the city could use more street signs, it's laid out simply. Nothing listed under "Sights in Tangier" is more than a 15-minute walk from the port. Petit Taxis (described under "Getting Around Tangier," below) are a godsend for the hot and tired tourist. Use them liberally.

Tourist Information

Get a free map and advice at the TI. A little bit of French goes a long way here (Mon–Fri 8:30–16:30, closed Sat–Sun, in new town at Boulevard Pasteur 29, tel. 0539-94-80-50). They try to have a few guides standing by in the morning when boats arrive.

Arrival in Tangier

By Ferry

If you're taking a tour, just follow the leader.

Independent travelers will walk five minutes from the ferry past trucks and warehouses (follow signs to *sortie*), and through the gate at the end of the port. Change money at any little exchange desk (those at the gate are good—they have a straight and fair buy-and-sell rate and are open long hours).

The big Port de Tanger gateway (a few hundred yards from the ferry dock) defines the end of the port area and the start of the city. Leave mental breadcrumbs, so you can find your way back to your boat. Your first glimpse of the city will be a line of decent fish restaurants; restored French colonial buildings; and a fancy palm tree–lined pedestrian boulevard arcing along the beach into the new town. From this delightful square, stairs (on the right) lead up into the old town and the market.

A Petit Taxi is your easiest way into town (described under "Getting Around Tangier"); unfortunately, prices are not regulated from the port. An honest cabbie will charge you 10 dirhams (about $1.25) for a ride from the ferry into town, while less scrupulous drivers will try to charge closer to 100 dirhams. Set your price before hopping in.

By Plane

The Tangier Airport has expanded recently, but it's still quite small. Iberia, Royal Air Maroc, and easyJet fly from here to Madrid (easyJet may also open a route to London as well). To get

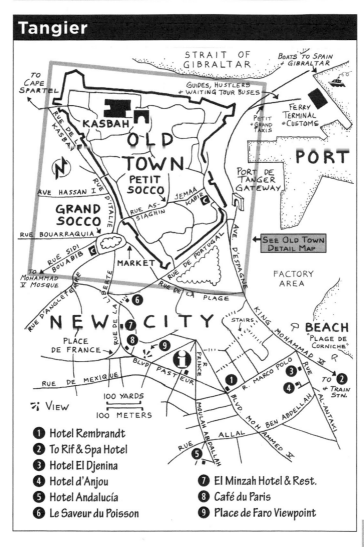

Tangier

- **1** Hotel Rembrandt
- **2** To Rif & Spa Hotel
- **3** Hotel El Djenina
- **4** Hotel d'Anjou
- **5** Hotel Andalucía
- **6** Le Saveur du Poisson
- **7** El Minzah Hotel & Rest.
- **8** Café du Paris
- **9** Place de Faro Viewpoint

into town, taxis should run you about 150 dirhams and take 30–45 minutes.

Getting Around Tangier

There are two types of taxis: Avoid the big, beige Mercedes "Grand Taxis," which are most aggressive and don't use their meters. Look instead for Petit Taxis—blue with a yellow stripe (they fit up to three people). These generally use their meters, are very cheap, and only circulate within the city. However, at the port, Petit Taxis are allowed to charge whatever you'll pay without using the meter, so it's essential to agree on a price up front (see "Arrival in Tangier," earlier).

Helpful Hints

Money: The exchange rate is 8 dirhams = about $1; 12 dirhams = about €1. The most convenient banks with ATMs are opposite the TI along Boulevard Pasteur. There are also several in the Grand Socco. While most businesses happily take euros or dollars, it's classier to use the local currency—and you'll save money. If you're on a tour, they'll rip you off anyway, so just stick with euros. If you're on your own, it's fun to get a pocket full of dirhams. ATMs work as you expect them to. Exchange desks are quick, easy, and fair. (Just understand the buy and sell rates—there should be no other fee. If you change €50 into dirhams and immediately change the dirhams back, you should have about €45.) Look for the official *Bureaux de Change* offices, where you'll get better rates than at the banks. There are some on Rue Pasteur, and a handful between the Grand and Petit Soccos. The first in a row is across from the Mamounia Palace restaurant on Rue As-Siaghin. The official change offices all offer the same rates, so there's no need to shop around.

Convert your dirhams back to euros before catching the ferry—it's cheap and easy to do here (change desks at the port keep long hours), but very difficult once you're back in Spain.

Telephone: To call Tangier from Spain, dial 00 (Europe's international access code), 212 (Morocco's country code), then the local number (dropping the initial zero). To dial Tangier from elsewhere in Morocco, dial the local number in full (keeping the initial zero).

In 2009, Moroccan phone numbers all added a new second digit—either a 5 (for land-line numbers) or a 6 (for mobile numbers). We've listed full numbers here, but in case you see older phone numbers listed elsewhere (on billboards, etc.), keep in mind that all Tangier phone numbers will start with either 0539 (land-line) or 0639 (mobile).

Navigation: Tangier's maps and street signs are frustrating. I ask in French for the landmark: *"oo ay Medina?", "oo ay Kasbah?",* and so on. It's fun to meet people this way. But to avoid getting unwanted company, ask for directions from people who can't leave what they're doing (such as the only clerk in a shop) or from women who aren't near men. There are fewer hustlers in the new (but less interesting) part of town. Be aware that most people don't know the names of the smaller streets (which don't usually have signs), and they tend to navigate by landmarks. In case you get the wrong directions, ask three

Women in Morocco

Most visitors to Tangier expect to see the women completely covered head-to-toe by their kaftan. In fact, only about one-quarter of Moroccan women still adhere strictly to this religious code. Some just cover their head (allowing their face to be seen), while others eliminate the head scarf altogether. Some women wear only Western-style clothing. This change in dress visibly reflects deeper, more fundamental shifts in Moroccan attitudes about women's rights.

Morocco happens to be one of the most progressive Muslim countries around. As in any border country, contact with other cultures fosters the growth of new ideas. Bombarded with Spanish television and visitors like you, change is inevitable. Another proponent of change is King Mohammed VI, who was only 35 years old when he rose to the throne in 1999. For the first time in the country's history, the king personally selected a female adviser to demonstrate his commitment to change. The king also married a commoner for...get this.../love. And even more shocking, she's seen in public. (It's a first—locals don't even know what King Mohammed VI's mother looks like, as she is never in the public view.)

Recent times have brought even more sweeping transformations to Moroccan society. In order to raise literacy levels and understanding between the sexes, schools are now co-ed—something taken for granted in the West for decades. In 2004 the Mudawana, or judiciary family code, was shockingly overhauled. The legal age for women to marry is now 18 (just like men) instead of 15. Other changes make it more difficult to have a second wife. Verbal divorce and abandonment are no longer legal—disgruntled husbands must now take their complaints to court before divorce is granted. And for the first time, women can divorce their husbands. If children are involved, whoever takes care of the kids gets the house. Of course, not everyone has been happy with the changes, and Islamic fundamentalists were blamed for a series of bombings in Casablanca in 2003. But the reforms became law, and Morocco became a trendsetter for women's equality in the Islamic world.

times and go with the consensus. If there's no consensus, it's time to hop into a Petit Taxi.

Mosques: Mosques are not open to non-Muslim visitors in Tangier (unlike mosques in some other Muslim cities).

Guides

If you're on your own, you'll be to street guides what a horse's tail is to flies...all day. In order to have your own translator and a shield from less scrupulous touts who hit up tourists constantly throughout the old town, I recommend hiring a guide. Stress your interest in the people and culture rather than shopping. Guides, hoping to get a huge commission from your purchases, can cleverly turn your Tangier day into the Moroccan equivalent of the Shopping Channel. Truth be told, some of these guides would work for free, considering all the money they make on commissions when you buy stuff.

That said, I've had good luck with the private guides who meet the boat. If you are a decent judge of character, interview guides when you get off the ferry, find one you click with, and negotiate a good price. These hardworking, English-speaking, and licensed guides offer their services for the day for €15.

To avoid the stress of being mobbed by potential guides at the port, book one before you arrive, and arrange for the guide to meet you at the port (through FRS in Tarifa, or through the guides' association—tel. 0539-931-372, dttanger@menara.com). Once in town, the TI (tel. 0539-948-050) can often set you up with a guide.

Aziz Begdouri is a great local guide who will show you the very best of his hometown. He enjoys teaching about Moroccan

society and culture. Aziz can also arrange ferry tickets from Tarifa in advance. He meets you at the boat. If you don't want to do any shopping, make it clear to him (5-hour walking tour-€15 per person, groups limited to 4–5 people; 8-hour grand tour with minibus ride to resorts, the Caves of Hercules, and Cape Spartel-€35 per person; easier to reach him from Spain on his Spanish mobile—tel. 607-897-967—than his Moroccan mobile, tel. 00-212-6-6163-9332 from Spain, aziztour@hotmail.com). Aziz is a friend. Even if you're not hiring him, give him a call if you're in a jam.

Sights in Tangier

▲▲**Grand Socco**—This big, noisy square is a transportation hub, market, and gateway to the medina (old town). Five years ago, it was a pedestrian nightmare and a perpetual traffic jam. Use the map to orient yourself from here, as this is the center of the visitor's Tangier. On the downhill side, a fancy gate leads into the medina. An incredible market is opposite the mosque.

Anglican Church—St. Andrew Anglican Church was built in a Moorish style, but is still Christian. The Lord's Prayer rings the arch in Arabic, as verses of the Quran would in a mosque. The land on which the church sits was a gift from the sultan to the British community in 1881, during Queen Victoria's era. The church was built shortly thereafter. Knock on the door— Mustapha will greet you and give you a "thank you very munch" tour. Leave a donation in the church's alms box.

The Medina and Petit Socco—A maze of winding lanes and tiny alleys weave through the old-town market area. The Petit Socco,

a little square (souk) in the old town, is lined with tea shops. A casual first-time visitor cannot stay oriented. I just wander, knowing that uphill will eventually get me to the Kasbah and downhill will eventually lead me to the port. Expect to get a little lost...going around in circles is part of the fun. Pop in to see artisans working in their shops: mosaic tile-makers, thread spinners, tailors. Many people can't afford private ovens, phones, or running water, so there are economical communal options: phone desks, baths, and bakeries. Notice locals dropping off their ready-to-cook dough at bakeries. Ornate "keyhole" doors lead to neighborhood mosques. Green doors are the color of Islam and symbolize peace. The Petit Socco is a people- (and now tourist-) friendly little square, great for a mint tea and some casual people-watching.

The **Market,** just off the Grand Socco, is a highlight. Wander past piles of fruit, veggies, and olives, countless varieties of bread, and fresh goat cheese wrapped in palm leaves. Phew! Venturing right, you'll eventually come to less perishable (and less aromatic) items—clothing, recordable CDs, and lots of electronics. You'll find everything but pork. The chickens are plucked and hung to show they have been killed according to Islamic guidelines (Halal): Animals are slaughtered with a sharp knife in the name of Allah, head to Mecca, and drained of their blood.

• *When you've soaked in enough old-town atmosphere, make your way*

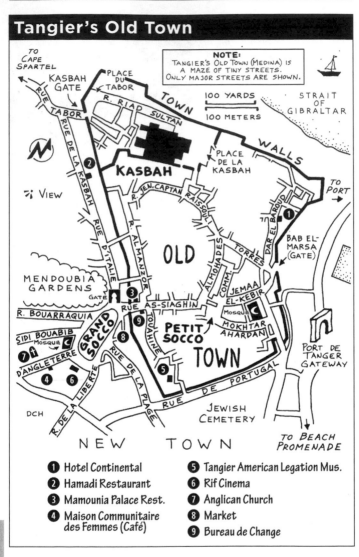

Tangier's Old Town

NOTE:
TANGIER'S OLD TOWN (MEDINA) IS A MAZE OF TINY STREETS. ONLY MAJOR STREETS ARE SHOWN.

1 Hotel Continental
2 Hamadi Restaurant
3 Mamounia Palace Rest.
4 Maison Communitaire des Femmes (Café)
5 Tangier American Legation Mus.
6 Rif Cinema
7 Anglican Church
8 Market
9 Bureau de Change

to the Kasbah (see map). Within the medina, head uphill, or exit the medina gate and go right on Rue de la Kasbah, which follows the old wall uphill to Porte de la Kasbah, a gateway into the Kasbah.

Kasbah—This is the fortress (now a residential area) atop old Tangier. On Place de la Kasbah, you'll find the Dar el-Makhzen, a former sultan's palace that now houses a history museum (10 dirhams, Wed–Mon 9:00–16:00, closed Tue, tel. 0539-932-097, no English, building more interesting than exhibit). You'll also encounter a vivid gauntlet of amusements waiting to ambush parading tour groups: snake charmers, squawky dance troupes, and colorful water vendors. Before descending out of the Kasbah, don't miss the ocean viewpoint. The artist Matisse, who traveled here in 1912, was inspired by his wanderings through this area, picking up themes that show up in much of his art.

Leaving the Kasbah, on your way downhill you'll pass the colorful Kodak-moment hustlers who make their living off the many tour groups passing by daily. (As you're cajoled, remember that the daily minimum wage here for men as skilled as these beggars is $10. That's what the gardeners you'll pass in your walk earn each day. In other words, a €1 tip is an hour's wage for these people.) A few steps past the lowest corner, you come to a musical ambush. If you draft behind a tour group, you won't be the focus of the hustlers. If you take a photo, you must pay.

Tangier American Legation Museum—Morocco was one of the first countries to recognize the newly formed United States as an independent country (in 1777). The original building, given to the United States by the sultan of Morocco, became the fledgling government's first foreign acquisition. This was the US embassy (or consulate) in Morocco from 1821 to 1956, and it's still American property—our only National Historic Landmark overseas. Today this nonprofit museum and research center, housed in a 19th-century mansion, is a strangely peaceful oasis within Tangier's intense old town. It offers a warm welcome and lots of interesting artifacts: a 19th-century safe, a letter with the news of Lincoln's assassination, photos of kings with presidents, and paintings—all well described in English in an evocative building. A visit here is a fun reminder of how long the US and Morocco have had good relations (guided English tour free but donations appreciated, Mon–Thu 10:00–13:00 & 15:00–17:00, Fri 10:00–12:00 & 15:00–17:00, during Ramadan holiday 10:00–15:00, closed Sat–Sun, ring bell, Rue d'Amérique 8, tel. 0539-935-317, www.maroc.net/museums).

Tangier Beach (Plage de Corniche)—Lined with lots of entertaining and fishy eateries, this fine, wide white-sand crescent beach stretches eastward from the port. It's packed with locals doing what people around the world do at the beach—with a few variations. Traditionally clad moms let their kids run wild. Along with lazy camels, you'll see people—young and old—covered in hot sand to combat rheumatism. Early, late, and off-season, the beach becomes a popular venue for soccer teams. The palm-lined pedestrian street along the waterfront was renamed for King Mohammed VI, in appreciation for recent restorations.

Just past the beach on the port side is a zone of nondescript factories. Here local women sew clothing for big, mostly European companies that pay $8 a day. Each morning and evening rush hour, the street is filled with these women commuters...on foot.

Evenings in Tangier—Most important: Be out in the **medina** around 21:00. In the cool of the evening, the atmospheric squares and lanes become even more evocative. Then at about 22:00 things get dark, lonely, and foreboding.

El Minzah Hotel hosts **traditional music** most nights (see "Eating in Tangier"; 85 Rue de la Liberté, tel. 0539-935-885).

The **Rif Cinema** shows movies in French—which the younger generation must learn—and Arabic. The cinema is worth popping into, if only to see the Art Deco interior. As movies cost only 15 dirhams, consider dropping by to see a bit of whatever's on...in Arabic (on the Grand Socco, tel. 0539-934-683).

Sleeping in Tangier

These hotels are centrally located, near the TI, and within walking distance of the market. The first two are three-star hotels and take credit cards; the others are cash-only. To reserve from Europe, dial 00 (Europe's international access code), 212 (Morocco's country code), 539 (Tangier's city code), then the local number. July through mid-September is high season, when rooms may be a bit more expensive and reservations are wise. Most hotels charge an extra tax of 10 dirhams per person per night (included in the prices I've listed here).

$$$ Hotel Rembrandt just feels like the 1940s, with a restaurant, bar, and swimming pool surrounded by a great grassy garden. Its 75 rooms are clean and comfortable, and some come with views (Sb-530–630 dirhams, Db-710–780 dirhams, higher prices are for June–Aug, sea view-100 dirhams extra, includes tax, breakfast-80 dirhams, air-con, elevator, Boulevard Mohammed VI 1, tel. 0539-937-870, fax 0539-930-443, www.hotel-rembrandt.com, hotelrembrandt@menara.ma).

Sleep Code

(8 dirhams = about $1, country code: 212, area code: 539)

S = Single, **D** = Double/Twin, **T** = Triple, **Q** = Quad, **b** = bathroom, **s** = shower only. Unless otherwise noted, credit cards are accepted, English is spoken, and breakfast is included.

To help you easily sort through these listings, I've divided the rooms into three categories, based on the price for a standard double room with bath (during high season):

$$$ Higher Priced—Most rooms 500 dirhams or more.

$$ Moderately Priced—Most rooms between 300–600 dirhams.

$ Lower Priced—Most rooms 300 dirhams or less.

$$$ Rif & Spa Hotel, recently restored to its 1970s glamour, is a worthy splurge. Offering 130 plush, modern rooms, sprawling public spaces, a garden, a pool, and grand views, it feels like an oversized boutique hotel. The great Arabic lounge with harbor view is a momentum-buster (Sb-1,060–1,150 dirhams, Db-1,220–1,460 dirhams, includes tax, see website for specials, breakfast-100 dirhams, air-con, elevator, 3 restaurants, Avenue Mohammed VI 152, tel. 0539-349-300, fax 0539-321-904, www.hotelsatlas.com, riftanger@menara.ma)

$$ Hotel Continental is the Humphrey Bogart option, a grand old place sprawling along the old town. It overlooks the port, with lavish atmospheric and recently renovated public spaces, a chandeliered breakfast room, and 70 spacious bedrooms with rough hardwood floors and new bathrooms. Jimmy, who's always around and runs the shop adjacent to the lobby, says he offers everything but Viagra. When I said, "I'm from Seattle," he said, "206." Test him—he knows your area code (Sb-422 dirhams, Db-552 dirhams, about 100 dirhams more July–Sept, includes tax and breakfast, cash only, Dar Baroud 36, tel. 0539-931-024, fax 0539-931-143, hcontinental@iam.net.ma).

$$ Hotel El Djenina is a local-style business-class hotel—extremely plain, reliable, safe, and well-located. Its 30 rooms are a block off the harbor, midway between the port and the TI. Request a room on the back side to escape the street noise (Sb-292–356 dirhams, Db-356–464 dirhams, higher prices are for mid-May–Aug, cash only, tel. 0539-942-244, fax 0539-942-246, Rue al-Antaki 8, eldjenina@menara.ma).

$ Hotel d'Anjou is a sleepable dive—the best dirt-cheap option I could find—renting 20 safe-feeling rooms on a quiet street two blocks off the harbor (Sb-140–215 dirhams, Db-160–270 dirhams, Tb-220–320 dirhams, higher prices are for summer, breakfast included only in summer, cash only, just off Rue al-Antaki at Rue Ibn Albanna 3, tel. & fax 0539-942-784, Hakim speaks English).

$ Hotel Andalucía is solid, clean, and minimal. It's in the new town, about a 20-minute walk from the Grand Socco. It has 19 rooms, a small reception, and a peaceful lobby (Sb-195–230 dirhams, Db-230–260 dirhams, higher prices are for mid-June–mid-Sept, cash only, Rue Ibn Hazim 14, tel. 0539-941-334, Azdeen speaks a little English).

Eating in Tangier

For the local equivalent of a yacht club restaurant, survey the places along the beach. The first two places I list below are buried in the medina and are disgustingly touristy. As they're designed for groups, the only locals you'll see here are the waiters. Still, they offer travelers a safe, comfortable break. The last three include a seafood paradise hole-in-the-wall; a big, fancy hotel restaurant with live traditional music; and a charity-run refuge that provides a quality, low-stress, and safe lunch.

Tourist Traps: **Hamadi** is as luxurious a restaurant as a tourist can find in Morocco, with good food at reasonable prices (Rue Kasbah 2, tel. 0539-934-514). **Mamounia Palace** is right on the Petit Socco and more in the middle of the action. A meal here will cost you about 100 dirhams for three courses—less if you order from the menu. Both of these places are tour-group hell and make you thankful to be free.

Le Saveur du Poisson is an excellent choice for the more adventurous, featuring one Tiki Hut–type room with a busy kitchen. There are no choices here. Just sit down and let owner Muhammad or his son, Hassan, take care of the rest. You get a rough one-use spoon and fork carved just for you...a fine souvenir. Surrounded by lots of locals and unforgettable food, you'll be treated to a multi-course menu. Savor the delicious fish dishes—Tangier is one of the few spots in Morocco where seafood is a major part of the diet. The fruit punch—a mix of seasonal fruits brewed overnight in a vat—simmers in the back room. Ask for an explanation, or even a look. After trying their dessert, Nuts 'n' Honey will never be the same. The big sink in the room is for locals who prefer to eat with their fingers (150-dirham fixed-price meal, Sat–Thu 12:00–16:00 & 19:00–22:00, closed Fri and during Ramadan; walk down Rue de la Liberté—roughly a block past El Minzah Hotel, take the stairs on the right and go down until you see fish on the grill, Escalier Waller 2, tel. 0539-336-326).

El Minzah Hotel offers a fancier yet still authentic experience. The atmosphere is classy but low-stress. It's where unadventurous tourists and local elites dine. Dress up and choose between a con-tinental (French) dining area or the Moroccan lounge, where you'll be serenaded by live traditional music (music nightly 20:00–23:00, belly-dance show at 21:30 and 22:30, no extra charge for music). Entrées (including *tajines* and couscous) in either restaurant aver-age 180 dirhams. There's also a cozy wine bar here—a rarity in a Muslim country. Light meals and salads are served poolside (daily 13:00–16:00 & 20:00–22:00, Rue de la Liberté 85, tel. 0539-935-885, www.elminzah.com).

Maison Communitaire des Femmes, a community center for women, hides an inexpensive, hearty lunch spot that's open to everyone. A tasty three-course lunch is only 50 dirhams. Profits support the work of the center (Mon–Sat 12:00–16:00, last order at 15:30, also open 9:30–11:30 & 15:30–18:00 for cakes and tea, closed Sun, near slipper market just outside Grand Socco, Place du 9 Avril).

Connections

In Tangier, all train traffic comes and goes from the suburban Gare Tanger Ville train station, one mile from the city center and a short Petit Taxi ride away (10–20 dirhams). If you're traveling inland, check the information booth at the entrance of the train station for schedules (www.oncf.ma).

From Tangier by Train to: Rabat (5/day, 5 hrs), **Casablanca** (station also called **Casa Voyageurs**, 6/day, 5 hrs), **Marrakech** (4/day, 12 hrs), **Fès** (4/day, 4.5 hrs).

From Tangier by Bus to: Ceuta and **Tétouan** (hourly, 1 hr).

From Fès to: Casablanca (9/day, 4.5 hrs), **Marrakech** (7/day, 7 hrs), **Rabat** (9/day, 4 hrs), **Meknès** (10/day, 45 min), **Tangier** (5/day, 5.5 hrs).

From Rabat to: Casablanca (2/hr, 45 min), **Fès** (9/day, 3.5 hrs), **Tétouan** (2 buses/day, 4.5 hrs, 3 trains/day, 6 hrs).

From Casablanca to: Marrakech (9/day, 3.5 hrs).

From Marrakech to: Meknès (7/day, 7 hrs), **Ouarzazate** (4 buses/day, 4 hrs).

By Plane: Flights within Morocco are convenient and reasonable (about $150 one-way from Tangier to Casablanca).

Extended Tour of Morocco

Morocco gets much better as you go deeper into the interior. The country is incredibly rich in cultural thrills, though you'll pay a

price in hassles and headaches—it's a package deal. But if adventure is your business, Morocco is a great option. Invest in a good Morocco guidebook to make this trip. Below are a few tips and insights to get you started.

To get a fair look at Morocco, you must get past the hustlers and con artists of the north coast (Tangier, Tétouan). It takes a minimum of four or five days to make a worthwhile visit—ideally seven or eight. Plan at least two nights in either Fès or Marrakech. A trip over the Atlas Mountains gives you an exciting look at Saharan Morocco. If you need a vacation from your vacation, check into one of the idyllic Atlantic beach resorts on the south coast. Above all, get past the northern day-trip-from-Spain, take-a-snapshot-on-a-camel fringe. (Oops, that's us. Oh, well.)

If you're relying on public transportation for your extended tour, sail to Tangier, blast your way through customs, ignore any hustler who tells you there's no way out until tomorrow, and hop into a Petit Taxi for the Tanger Ville train station one mile away. From there, set your sights on Rabat, a dignified, European-type town with fewer hustlers, and make it your get-acquainted stop in Morocco. Trains go farther south from Rabat.

If you're driving a car, crossing the border can be a bit unnerving, since you'll be forced to jump through several bureaucratic hoops. You'll go through customs at both borders, buy Moroccan insurance for your car (cheap and easy), and feel at the mercy of a bristly bunch of shady-looking people you'd rather not be at the mercy of. Don't pay anyone on the Spanish side. Consider tipping a guy on the Moroccan side if you feel he'll shepherd you through. Relax and let him grease those customs wheels. He's worth it. As soon as possible, hit the road and drive to Chefchaouen, the best first stop for those with their own wheels.

Moroccan Towns

▲▲**Chefchaouen**—Just two hours by bus or car from Tétouan, this is the first pleasant town beyond the north coast. Monday and Thursday are colorful market days. Stay in the classy old Hotel Chaouen on Place el-Makhzen. The Hotel Parador (historic inn, but not the same as the Spanish government–run chain) faces the old town and offers fine meals and a refuge from hustlers. Wander deep into the whitewashed old town from here.

▲▲**Rabat**—Morocco's capital and most European city, Rabat is the most comfortable and least stressful place to start your North African trip. You'll find a colorful market (in the old neighboring town of Salé), bits of Islamic architecture (Mausoleum of Mohammed V), the king's palace, mellow hustlers, and fine hotels.

▲▲▲**Fès**—More than just a funny hat that tipsy Shriners wear, Fès is Morocco's religious and artistic center, bustling with craftspeople, pilgrims, shoppers, and shops. Like most large Moroccan cities, it has a distinct new town from the French colonial period, as well as an exotic (and stressful) old, walled Arabic town (the medina), where you'll find the market.

For 12 centuries, traders have gathered in Fès, founded on a river at the crossroads of two trade routes. Soon there was an irrigation

system, a university, resident craftsmen from Spain, and a diverse population of Muslims, Christians, and Jews. When France claimed Morocco in 1912, they made their capital in Rabat, and Fès fizzled. But the Fès marketplace is still Morocco's best.

▲▲▲**Marrakech**—Morocco's gateway to the south, Marrakech is where the desert, mountain, and coastal regions merge. This market city is a constant folk festival, bustling with Berber tribespeople and a colorful center. The new city has the train station, and the main boulevard (Mohammed V) is lined with banks, airline offices, a post office, a tourist office, and comfortable hotels. The old city features the maze-like market and the huge Djemaa el-Fna, a square seething with people—a 43-ring Moroccan circus.

▲▲▲**Over the Atlas Mountains**—Extend your Moroccan trip several days by heading south over the Atlas Mountains. Take a bus from Marrakech to Ouarzazate (short stop), and then to Tinerhir (great oasis town, comfy hotel, overnight stop). The next day go to Er Rachidia and take the overnight bus to Fès.

By car, drive from Fès south, staying in the small mountain town of Ifrane, and then continue deep into the desert country past Er Rachidia and on to Rissani (market days: Sun, Tue, and Thu). Explore nearby mud-brick towns still living in the Middle Ages. Hire a guide to drive you past where the road stops, and head cross-country to an oasis village (Merzouga), where you can climb a sand dune and watch the sun rise over the vastness of Africa. Only a sea of sand separates you from Timbuktu.

TANGIER

PRACTICALITIES

This section covers just the basics on traveling in Spain (for much more information, see *Rick Steves' Spain 2010*). You can find free advice on specific topics at www.ricksteves.com/tips.

Money

Spain uses the euro currency: 1 euro (€) = about $1.40. To convert prices in euros to dollars, add about 40 percent: €20 = about $28, €50 = about $70. (Check www.oanda.com for the latest exchange rates.)

The standard way for travelers to get euros is to withdraw money from a cash machine (called a *cajero automático*) using a debit or credit card, ideally with a Visa or MasterCard logo. Before departing, call your bank or credit-card company: Confirm that your card will work overseas, ask about international transaction fees, and alert them that you'll be making withdrawals in Europe.

To keep your valuables safe, wear a money belt. But if you do lose your credit or debit card, report the loss immediately to the respective global customer-assistance centers. Call these 24-hour US numbers collect: Visa (410/581-9994), MasterCard (636/722-7111), and American Express (623/492-8427).

Phoning

Smart travelers use the telephone to reserve or reconfirm rooms, reserve restaurants, get directions, research transportation connections, confirm tour times, phone home, and lots more.

To call Spain from the US or Canada: Dial 011-34 and then the local number. (The 011 is our international access code, and 34 is Spain's country code.)

To call Spain from a European country: Dial 00-34 followed by the local number. (The 00 is Europe's international access code.)

To call within Spain: Just dial the local number.

To call from Spain to another country: Dial 00 followed by the country code (for example, 1 for the US or Canada), then the area code and number. If calling European countries whose phone numbers begin with 0, you'll usually have to omit that 0 when you dial.

Tips on Phoning: To make calls in Spain, you can buy two different types of phone cards—international or insertable—sold locally at newsstands. Cheap international phone cards, which work with a scratch-to-reveal PIN code at any phone, allow you to call home to the US for pennies a minute, and also work for domestic calls within Spain. Insertable phone cards, which must be inserted into public pay phones, are reasonable for calls within Spain (and work for international calls as well, but not as cheaply as the international phone cards). Calling from your hotel-room phone is usually expensive, unless you use an international phone card. A mobile phone—whether an American one that works in Spain, or a European one you buy when you arrive—is handy, but can be pricey. For more on phoning, see www.ricksteves.com/phoning.

Emergency Telephone Numbers in Spain: For **police** help, dial 091. To summon an **ambulance**, call 112. For passport problems, call the **US Embassy** (in Madrid, tel. 915-872-240, after-hours emergency tel. 915-872-200) or the **Canadian Embassy** (in Madrid, tel. 914-233-250). For other concerns, get advice from your hotel.

Making Hotel Reservations

To ensure the best value, I recommend reserving rooms in advance, particularly during peak season. Email the hotelier with the following key pieces of information: number and type of rooms; number of nights; date of arrival; date of departure; and any special requests. (For a sample form, see www.ricksteves.com/reservation.) Use the European style for writing dates: day/month/year. For example, for a two-night stay in July, you could request: "1 double room for 2 nights, arrive 16/07/10, depart 18/07/10." Hoteliers typically ask for your credit-card number as a deposit.

In these times of economic uncertainty, some hotels are willing to deal to attract guests—try emailing several to ask their best rate. In general, hotel prices can soften if you do any of the following: offer to pay cash, stay at least three nights, or travel off-season. You can also try asking for a cheaper room (for example, with a bathroom down the hall), or offer to skip breakfast.

Eating

By our standards, Spaniards eat late, having lunch—their biggest meal of the day—around 13:00-16:00, and dinner starting about

21:00. At restaurants, you can dine with tourists at 20:00, or with Spaniards if you wait until later.

For a fun early dinner at a bar, build a light meal out of tapas—small appetizer-sized portions of seafood, salads, meat-filled pastries, deep-fried tasties, and so on. Many of these are displayed behind glass, and you can point to what you want. Tapas typically cost about €2 apiece, but can run up to €10 for seafood. While the smaller "tapa" size (which comes on a saucer-size plate) is handiest for maximum tasting opportunities, many bars sell only larger sizes: the *ración* (full portion, on a dinner plate) and *media-ración* (half-size portion). *Jamón* (hah-MOHN), an air-dried ham similar to prosciutto, is a Spanish staple. Other key terms include *bocadillo* (baguette sandwich), *frito* (fried), *a la plancha* (grilled), *queso* (cheese), *tortilla* (omelet), and *surtido* (assortment).

Many bars have three price tiers, which should be clearly posted: It's cheapest to eat or drink while standing at the bar (*barra),* slightly more to sit at a table inside (*mesa* or *salón*), and most expensive to sit outside *(terraza).* Wherever you are, be assertive or you'll never be served. *Por favor* (please) grabs the attention of the server or bartender. If you're having tapas, don't worry about paying as you go (the bartender keeps track). When you're ready to leave, ask for the bill: *"¿La cuenta?"* To tip for a few tapas, round up to the nearest euro; for a full meal, tip about 5 to 10 percent for good service.

Transportation

By Train and Bus: For train schedules, check www.renfe.es. Since trains can sell out, it's smart to buy your tickets a day in advance at a travel agency (easiest), at the train station (can be crowded; be sure you're in the right line), or online (at www.renfe.es; when asked for your Spanish national ID number, enter your passport number). Futuristic, high-speed trains (such as AVE) can be priced differently according to their time of departure. To see if a railpass could save you money, check www.ricksteves.com/rail.

Buses pick up where the trains don't go, reaching even small villages. But because routes are operated by various competing companies, it can be tricky to pin down schedules (inquire at local bus stations or TIs).

By Plane: Consider covering long distances on a budget flight, which can be cheaper than a train or bus ride. For flights within Spain, check out www.vueling.com, www.iberia.com, or www.spanair.com; to other European cites, try www.easyjet.com and www.ryanair.com; and to compare several airlines, see www.skyscanner.net.

By Car: It's cheaper to arrange most car rentals from the US. For tips on your insurance options, see www.ricksteves.com/cdw. Bring your driver's license. For route planning, try www.viamichelin.com. Freeways come with tolls (about $4/hr), but save lots of time. A car is a worthless headache in cities—park it safely (get tips from your hotel). As break-ins are common, be sure all of your valuables are out of sight and locked in the trunk, or even better, with you or in your hotel room.

Helpful Hints

Theft Alert: Spain has particularly hardworking pickpockets. Assume beggars are pickpockets and any scuffle is simply a distraction by a team of thieves. If you stop for any commotion or show, put your hands in your pockets before someone else does. Better yet, wear a money belt.

Time: Spain uses the 24-hour clock. It's the same through 12:00 noon, then keep going: 13:00, 14:00, and so on. Spain, like most of continental Europe, is six/nine hours ahead of the East/West Coasts of the US.

Siesta and Paseo: Many Spaniards (especially in rural areas) still follow the traditional siesta schedule: From around 13:00 to 16:00, many businesses close as people go home for a big lunch with their family. Then they head back to work (and shops re-open) from about 16:00 to 20:00. (Many bigger stores stay open all day long, especially in cities.) Then, after a late dinner, whole families pour out of their apartments to enjoy the cool of the evening, stroll through the streets, and greet their neighbors—a custom called the paseo. Tourists are welcome to join this people-parade.

Sights: Major attractions can be swamped with visitors; carefully read and follow this book's crowd-beating tips (visit at quieter times of day, or—where possible—reserve ahead). At many churches, a modest dress code is encouraged and sometimes required (no bare shoulders, miniskirts, or shorts).

Holidays and Festivals: Spain celebrates many holidays, which can close sights and attract crowds (book hotel rooms ahead). For more on holidays and festivals, check Spain's website: www.spain.info. For a simple list showing major—though not all—events, see www.ricksteves.com/festivals.

Numbers and Stumblers: What Americans call the second floor of a building is the first floor in Europe. Europeans write dates as day/month/year, so Christmas is 25/12/10. Commas are decimal points and vice versa—a dollar and a half is 1,50, and there are 5.280 feet in a mile. Spain uses the metric system: A kilogram is 2.2 pounds; a liter is about a quart; and a kilometer is six-tenths of a mile.

Resources from Rick Steves

This Snapshot guide is excerpted from *Rick Steves' Spain 2010*, which is one of more than 30 titles in my series of guidebooks

PRACTICALITIES

on European travel. I also produce a public television series, *Rick Steves' Europe,* and a public radio show, *Travel with Rick Steves.* My website, www.ricksteves.com, offers free travel information, free vodcasts and podcasts of my shows, free audio tours of major sights in Europe (for you to download onto an iPod or MP3 player), a Graffiti Wall for travelers' comments, guidebook updates, my travel blog, an online travel store, and information on European railpasses and our tours of Europe.

Additional Resources

Tourist Information: www.spain.info
Passports and Red Tape: www.travel.state.gov
Packing List: www.ricksteves.com/packlist
Cheap Flights: www.skyscanner.net
Airplane Carry-on Restrictions: www.tsa.gov/travelers
Updates for This Book: www.ricksteves.com/update.

How Was Your Trip?

If you'd like to share your tips, concerns, and discoveries after using this book, please fill out the survey at www.ricksteves.com /feedback. Thanks in advance—it helps a lot.

PRACTICALITIES

Spanish Survival Phrases

Spanish has a guttural sound similar to the J in Baja California. In the phonetics, the symbol for this clearing-your-throat sound is the italicized *h*.

English	Spanish	Phonetics
Good day.	**Buenos días.**	**bway**-nohs **dee**-ahs
Do you speak English?	**¿Habla usted inglés?**	ah-blah oo-**stehd** een-**glays**
Yes. / No.	**Sí. / No.**	see / noh
I (don't) understand.	**(No) comprendo.**	(noh) kohm-**prehn**-doh
Please.	**Por favor.**	por fah-**bor**
Thank you.	**Gracias.**	**grah**-thee-ahs
I'm sorry.	**Lo siento.**	loh see-**ehn**-toh
Excuse me.	**Perdóneme.**	pehr-**doh**-nay-may
(No) problem.	**(No) problema.**	(noh) proh-**blay**-mah
Good.	**Bueno.**	**bway**-noh
Goodbye.	**Adiós.**	ah-dee-**ohs**
one / two	**uno / dos**	**oo**-noh / dohs
three / four	**tres / cuatro**	trays / **kwah**-troh
five / six	**cinco / seis**	**theen**-koh / says
seven / eight	**siete / ocho**	see-**eh**-tay / **oh**-choh
nine / ten	**nueve / diez**	**nway**-bay / dee-**ayth**
How much is it?	**¿Cuánto cuesta?**	**kwahn**-toh **kway**-stah
Write it?	**¿Me lo escribe?**	may loh ay-**skree**-bay
Is it free?	**¿Es gratis?**	ays **grah**-tees
Is it included?	**¿Está incluido?**	ay-**stah** een-kloo-**ee**-doh
Where can I buy / find...?	**¿Dónde puedo comprar / encontrar...?**	**dohn**-day **pway**-doh kohm-**prar** / ayn-kohn-**trar**
I'd like / We'd like...	**Quiero / Queremos...**	kee-**ehr**-oh / kehr-**ay**-mohs
...a room.	**...una habitación.**	**oo**-nah ah-bee-tah-thee-**ohn**
...a ticket to ___.	**...un billete para ___.**	oon bee-**yeh**-tay **pah**-rah
Is it possible?	**¿Es posible?**	ays poh-**see**-blay
Where is...?	**¿Dónde está...?**	**dohn**-day ay-**stah**
...the train station	**...la estación de trenes**	lah ay-stah-thee-**ohn** day **tray**-nays
...the bus station	**...la estación de autobuses**	lah ay-stah-thee-**ohn** day ow-toh-**boo**-says
...the tourist information office	**...la oficina de turismo**	lah oh-fee-**thee**-nah day too-**rees**-moh
Where are the toilets?	**¿Dónde están los servicios?**	**dohn**-day ay-**stahn** lohs sehr-**bee**-thee-ohs
men	**hombres, caballeros**	**ohm**-brays, kah-bah-**yay**-rohs
women	**mujeres, damas**	moo-**heh**-rays, **dah**-mahs
left / right	**izquierda / derecha**	eeth-kee-**ehr**-dah / day-**ray**-chah
straight	**derecho**	day-**ray**-choh
When do you open / close?	**¿A qué hora abren / cierran?**	ah kay **oh**-rah **ah**-brehn / thee-**ay**-rahn
At what time?	**¿A qué hora?**	ah kay **oh**-rah
Just a moment.	**Un momento.**	oon moh-**mehn**-toh
now / soon / later	**ahora / pronto / más tarde**	ah-**oh**-rah / **prohn**-toh / mahs **tar**-day
today / tomorrow	**hoy / mañana**	oy / mahn-**yah**-nah

In the Restaurant

I'd like / We'd like...	**Quiero / Queremos...**	kee-**ehr**-oh / kehr-**ay**-mohs
...to reserve...	**...reservar...**	ray-sehr-**bar**
...a table for one / two.	**...una mesa para uno / dos.**	**oo**-nah **may**-sah **pah**-rah **oo**-noh / dohs
Non-smoking.	**No fumadores.**	noh foo-mah-**doh**-rays
Is this table free?	**¿Está esta mesa libre?**	ay-**stah** ay-stah **may**-sah **lee**-bray
The menu (in English), please.	**La carta (en inglés), por favor.**	lah **kar**-tah (ayn een-**glays**) por fah-**bor**
service (not) included	**servicio (no) incluido**	sehr-**bee**-thee-oh (noh) een-kloo-**ee**-doh
cover charge	**precio de entrada**	**pray**-thee-oh day ayn-**trah**-dah
to go	**para llevar**	**pah**-rah yay-**bar**
with / without	**con / sin**	kohn / seen
and / or	**y / o**	ee / oh
menu (of the day)	**menú (del día)**	may-**noo** (dayl **dee**-ah)
specialty of the house	**especialidad de la casa**	ay-spay-thee-ah-lee-**dahd** day lah **kah**-sah
tourist menu	**menú de turista**	meh-**noo** day too-**ree**-stah
combination plate	**plato combinado**	**plah**-toh kohm-bee-**nah**-doh
appetizers	**tapas**	**tah**-pahs
bread	**pan**	pahn
cheese	**queso**	**kay**-soh
sandwich	**bocadillo**	boh-kah-**dee**-yoh
soup	**sopa**	**soh**-pah
salad	**ensalada**	ayn-sah-**lah**-dah
meat	**carne**	**kar**-nay
poultry	**aves**	**ah**-bays
fish	**pescado**	pay-**skah**-doh
seafood	**marisco**	mah-**ree**-skoh
fruit	**fruta**	**froo**-tah
vegetables	**verduras**	behr-**doo**-rahs
dessert	**postres**	**poh**-strays
tap water	**agua del grifo**	**ah**-gwah dayl **gree**-foh
mineral water	**agua mineral**	**ah**-gwah mee-nay-**rahl**
milk	**leche**	**lay**-chay
(orange) juice	**zumo (de naranja)**	**thoo**-moh (day nah-**rahn**-hah)
coffee	**café**	kah-**feh**
tea	**té**	tay
wine	**vino**	**bee**-noh
red / white	**tinto / blanco**	**teen**-toh / **blahn**-koh
glass / bottle	**vaso / botella**	**bah**-soh / boh-**tay**-yah
beer	**cerveza**	thehr-**bay**-thah
Cheers!	**¡Salud!**	sah-**lood**
More. / Another.	**Más. / Otro.**	mahs / **oh**-troh
The same.	**El mismo.**	ehl **mees**-moh
The bill, please.	**La cuenta, por favor.**	lah **kwayn**-tah por fah-**bor**
tip	**propina**	proh-**pee**-nah
Delicious!	**¡Delicioso!**	day-lee-thee-**oh**-soh

For hundreds more pages of survival phrases for your trip to Spain, check out *Rick Steves' Spanish Phrase Book*.

Start your trip a

Free information and great gear

▸ Plan Your Trip

Browse thousands of articles and a wealth of money-saving tips for planning your dream trip. You'll find up-to-date information on Europe's best destinations, packing smart, getting around, finding rooms, staying healthy, avoiding scams and more.

▸ Eurail Passes

Find out, step-by-step, if a rail pas makes sense for your trip—and how to avoid buying more than yo need. Get a bunch of free extras!

▸ Graffiti Wall & Travelers' Helpline

Learn, ask, share—our online community of savvy travelers is a great resource for first-time travelers to Europe, as well as seasoned pros.

Rick Steves' Europe Through the Back Door, Inc

Rick Steves

www.ricksteves.com

TRAVEL SKILLS
Europe Through the Back Door

EUROPE GUIDES
Best of Europe
Eastern Europe
Europe 101
European Christmas
Postcards from Europe

COUNTRY GUIDES
Croatia & Slovenia
England
France
Germany
Great Britain
Ireland
Italy
Portugal
Scandinavia
Spain
Switzerland

CITY & REGIONAL GUIDES
Amsterdam, Bruges & Brussels
Athens & The Peloponnese
Budapest
Florence & Tuscany
Istanbul
London
Paris
Prague & The Czech Republic
Provence & The French Riviera
Rome
Venice
Vienna, Salzburg & Tirol

PHRASE BOOKS & DICTIONARIES
French
French, Italian & German
German
Italian
Portuguese
Spanish

RICK STEVES' EUROPE DVDs
Austria & The Alps
Eastern Europe
England
Europe
France & Benelux
Germany & Scandinavia
Greece, Turkey, Israel & Egypt
Ireland & Scotland
Italy's Cities
Italy's Countryside
Rick Steves' European Christmas
Spain & Portugal
Travel Skills & "The Making Of"

PLANNING MAPS
Britain, Ireland & London
Europe
France & Paris
Germany, Austria & Switzerland
Ireland
Italy
Spain & Portugal

JOURNALS
Rick Steves' Pocket Travel Journal
Rick Steves' Travel Journal

With these apps you can:

► Spin the compass icon to switch views between sights, hotels, and restaurant selections—and get details on cost, hours, address, and phone number.

► Tap any point on the screen to read Rick's detailed information, including history and suggested viewpoints.

► Get a deeper view into Rick's tours with audio and video segments.

Go to iTunes to download the following apps:

Rick Steves' Louvre Tour

Rick Steves' Historic Paris Walk

Rick Steves' Orsay Museum Tour

Rick Steves' Versailles

Rick Steves' Ancient Rome Tour

Rick Steves' St. Peter's Basilica Tour

Once downloaded, these apps are completely self-contained on your iPhone or iPod Touch, so you will not incur pricey roaming charges during use overseas.

Rick Steves books and DVDs are available at bookstores and through online booksellers.
Rick Steves guidebooks are published by Avalon Travel, a member of the Perseus Books Group.
Rick Steves apps are produced by Übermind, a boutique Seattle-based software consultancy firm.

Avalon Travel
a member of the Perseus Books Group
1700 Fourth Street
Berkeley, CA 94710

Text © 2009 by Rick Steves
Maps © 2009 Europe Through the Back Door. All rights reserved.
Printed in the US by Worzalla. First printing September 2009.
Portions of this book originally appeared in Rick Steves' Spain 2010.

For the latest on Rick Steves' lectures, guidebooks, tours, public television series, and public
radio show, contact Europe Through the Back Door, Box 2009, Edmonds, WA 98020, tel.
425/771-8303, fax 425/771-0833, www.ricksteves.com, rick@ricksteves.com.

ISBN (13) 978-1-59880-489-8

Europe Through the Back Door Managing Editor: Risa Laib
ETBD Editors: Cameron Hewitt, Tom Griffin, Gretchen Strauch, Jennifer Madison
    Davis, Cathy Lu, Cathy McDonald, Sarah McCormic
Research Assistance: Amanda Buttinger
Avalon Travel Senior Editor and Series Manager: Madhu Prasher
Avalon Travel Project Editor: Kelly Lydick
Copy Editor: Amy Scott
Proofreader: Jean Butterfield
Production and Typesetting: McGuire Barber Design
Cover Design: Kimberly Glyder Design
Graphic Content Director: Laura VanDeventer
Maps and Graphics: David C. Hoerlein, Lauren Mills, Laura VanDeventer, Barb Geisler,
    Mike Morgenfeld
Cover Photo: Plaza de Espana, Sevilla © istockphoto.com

Photography: David C. Hoerlein, Rick Steves, Cameron Hewitt, Robert Wright, Steve
    Smith, Dominic Bonuccelli, and Cathy McDonald

ABOUT THE AUTHOR

RICK STEVES

 Rick Steves is on a mission: to help make European travel accessible and meaningful for Americans. Rick has spent four months every year since 1973 exploring Europe. He's researched and written more than 30 travel guidebooks, writes and hosts the public television series *Rick Steves' Europe*, and also produces and hosts the weekly public radio show *Travel with Rick Steves.* With the help of his hardworking staff of 70 at Europe Through the Back Door, Rick organizes tours of Europe and offers an information-packed website (www.ricksteves.com). Rick, his wife (and favorite travel partner) Anne, and their two teenage children, Andy and Jackie, call Edmonds, just north of Seattle, home.